THE INEVITABLE CALIPHATE?

'Reza Pankhurst provides a unique and probing examination of modern thinking on the Caliphate. This detailed analysis of the ways in which the Muslim Brotherhood, Hizb ut-Tahrir, and al-Qaeda, as well as smaller groups, reformulate and use the concept today is both judicious and informed. It provides the most reliable guide available to an idea and political symbol that holds attraction for many Sunni Muslims while inciting anxiety, even fear, among others, including many non-Muslims and Shi'a.'

James Piscatori, Professor of International Relations, Durham University

'Until now, no scholar has tried to examine systematically how the Caliphate has animated and inspired Islamic intellectuals and activists, or how alternative conceptions of the Caliphate have been formulated and fought over. Against this backdrop, *The Inevitable Caliphate?* provides a carefully crafted and well documented treatment of the diverse ways in which the Caliphate has figured in the global politics of Islam over the past ninety years. A very illuminating and instructive book.'

John T. Sidel, Sir Patrick Gillam Professor of International and Comparative Politics, London School of Economics and Political Science

'Reza Pankhurst's deftly argued, thought-provoking book addresses the significant yet neglected topic of the Islamic Caliphate, focusing on the attempts of Muslim thinkers and activists to resuscitate the institution following the collapse of the Ottoman Empire in the 1920s. What stands out is the author's ability to situate the contributions of the Muslim Brotherhood, Hizb ut-Tahrir, Al-Qaeda, and other advocates of the Caliphate within the context of normative Islam, rather than weigh them against the yardstick of liberal democracy. This important book, which examines the Caliphate on its own terms, will challenge the way scholars and other observers of political Islam conceive of their subject.'

John Calvert, Associate Professor of History, Creighton University and author of *Sayyid Qutb and the Origins of Radical Islamism*

'In the wake of the Arab Spring and the sustained re-imagination of political possibilities in the Middle East, *The Inevitable Caliphate?* is especially relevant. From Rabat to Riyadh Arabs have re-asserted the right to think about political alternatives, demonstrating the grassroots popularity of Islamic frameworks of legitimacy and laying the groundwork for a renewed and far-reaching conversation about Islamic governance paradigms. Ideas about the Caliphate—as precedent, as social contract, as imagined community—are bound to shape and be shaped by these debates.'

Alia Brahimi, Research Fellow, London School of Economics and Political Science and author of *Jihad and Just War in the War on Terror*

'*The Inevitable Caliphate?* is a timely and much needed contribution to our understanding of the modern Caliphate as a political concept and goal. It is a must-read for scholars, students and anyone who is interested in the post-1924 debate over the restoration of the Caliphate.'

Emmanuel Karagiannis, Assistant Professor of International Relations, Department of Balkan, Slavic and Oriental Studies, University of Macedonia, and author of *Political Islam in Central Asia: The Challenge of Hizb ut-Tahrir*

'An authoritative blend of historical fact married with current Islamic political thought, Pankhurst offers an excellent insight on the institution of the Caliphate in Islam. Gripping, extremely learned, but accessible, this book is a must-read.'

Shahrul Hussain, Lecturer in Islamic Studies, Markfield Institute of Higher Education, Leicestershire

REZA PANKHURST

The Inevitable Caliphate?

*A History of the Struggle for
Global Islamic Union, 1924 to the Present*

HURST & COMPANY, LONDON

First published in the United Kingdom in 2013 by
C. Hurst & Co. (Publishers) Ltd.,
41 Great Russell Street, London, WC1B 3PL
© Reza Pankhurst, 2013
All rights reserved.
Printed in India

The right of Reza Pankhurst to be identified as the author of
this publication is asserted by them in accordance with the
Copyright, Designs and Patents Act, 1988.

A Cataloguing-in-Publication data record for this book is
available from the British Library.

ISBN: 978-1-84904-251-2 *paperback*

www.hurstpublishers.com

This book is printed using paper from registered sustainable
and managed sources.

بسم الله الرحمن الرحيم

In the Name of Allah, the Most Merciful, the Most Beneficent

اللهم انى أسألك حبك وحب من يحبك وحب كل عمل يقربنى الى حبك

O Allah, I ask you for Your love, and the love of whomever loves You, and the love of every action that brings me closer to Your love

CONTENTS

CONTENTS

ACKNOWLEDGEMENTS

اللهم يامقلب القلوب ثبت قلوبنا على دينك

O Allah, the One who changes hearts, keep our hearts firm upon your din (religion/way of life).

To all my family—whose love and support has been constant throughout. To my beautiful wife, Hodan, and my children—the tests and difficulties you faced while I was away for almost four years far outweighed any tests I faced. You kept me company at night through all your letters, and your steadfastness and courage in waging the campaign to build awareness and gain some semblance of justice for us, despite all the obstacles you faced, can never be taken away from you. To my mother, who sacrificed her time and much more to keep us as well fed, read and entertained as possible while inside. As mentioned by a friend in jail, a fifteen year sentence would have been worth it for your prayers, and your remaining constant in them. To my step-father, who has always been and will always simply be "Dad," whom I love greatly and has never treated me as anything less than a son. Your Islam is one of the most precious things to me. To my sister, whom I love and always wish the best for. To my wife's family for all their support, especially while I was away. To all the others in my family, as well as close family friends, near and far, for their support and love.

To my dear friend Ian, who despite temptations and pressures, has remained faithful to Islam and retained his dignity when it would have been easier to compromise and give up. And to his family, who worked hard on the campaign for our freedom despite the difficulties and hardships they faced—they deserve the credit for that.

To my many close companions from the Tora prison, you showed us through your patience and steadfastness the example of those who would not compromise their core beliefs and principles for the sake of material gain, despite the physical and mental pressures upon you, and your status is raised because of it. This book is also written in your memory: a small effort to explain part of the collective struggle of a people seeking the overthrow of oppression and its replacement with a political system built upon their own belief system rather than upon that of others.

Thanks also to those journalists who took an interest in our case and were concerned to report it fairly; our lawyers in Egypt and the UK; and Amnesty International for adopting us as prisoners of conscience.

Returning to the UK in 2006, I found that the Muslim community was the subject of great suspicion and political pressure, and that the vast majority of commentary regarding Islam and its view on social and political issues was inaccurate and ill-founded. This extended to much of the work on and analysis of Muslims, Islam and politics carried out by academics and "experts" in the field. At the same time, the parasitical "counter-terror" and "counter-extremism" industry emerged, which availed itself to the service of governments in a deliberate program intended to divert attention from the central fact that pursuing ill-judged wars and interventions across the "Greater Middle East," as well as engaging in a litany of gross atrocities, whether directly in the jails of Bagram, Abu Ghuraib and Guantanamo Bay, or by rendition, was bound to create more animosity and enmity against the "West" than it was to heal past wounds.

To avoid the charge that a history of regional interference capped by an aggressive foreign policy and the manner in which it was prosecuted were the causes of resistance, there was an immediate need to create another narrative that would shift the blame onto Islamic ideals and the Muslims who believed in them, a requirement eagerly met by a motley cohort of ex-Cold War warriors, self proclaimed "terrorism experts," and kiss-and-tell "ex-extremists" of all hues and color. At the same time, those who combated the crude paradigms brought forward in defense of power, would normally do so while explaining away Islamic motivations and ideals in a manner which accorded with their own world-view

ACKNOWLEDGEMENTS

rather than comprehending how those who carried such ideas understood them.

Finding myself in such an environment led me to believe that there was a duty for different voices to engage in the discussion academically, to present an analysis through an alternative lens that was not grounded in the common analytical paradigm which posits liberal democracy as a universal value that all other political systems and values should be compared to, and would not simply seek to explain the motivations of others through imposed alien constructs. And so began the journey which has eventually led to the publication of this book.

It goes without saying that many thanks for helping this book come to fruition are due to John Chalcraft for all the discussions we had and advice given, John Sidel for the insightful critiques and direction provided, and also to James Piscatori and Fawaz Gerges for their valuable suggestions on how to improve the work for publication.

From my time at university I would like to thank Joanna Lewis who gave me the opportunity at the International History department, and Sue Onslow, Kirsten Schulze and Michael Kerr for their guidance and help. I should also thank the University authorities and the Government department for their support, in particular the head of department at the time, Paul Kelly. Thanks also to my students at the LSE over the time I taught there and to my colleagues in the department for their support and encouragement.

Thanks also to my publisher, Michael Dwyer and the team, for helping to make this book possible.

1

INTERPRETING IDEAS

AN INTRODUCTION

That many governments in Muslim countries are badly in need of reform is not in doubt [...] But why has this sorry state of affairs not led to the emergence of domestic political movements seeking the creation of liberal democracy as we saw, for example, in Eastern Europe? What is different about the Muslim World?

Noah Feldman[1]

Speaking in October 2007, the deputy head of northern Israel's Islamic Movement Kamal Khatib boldly claimed that the world was "on the threshold of a new era." Out with the old and in with a future that "belongs to Islam and Muslims." Israel would soon cease to exist, and the whole country would fall under *shari'a* law as a stage in the reconstruction of a global Islamic caliphate.[2] In the summer of the same year, a crowd of 100,000 people filled Jakarta's Gelora Bung Karno stadium to "push for the creation of a single state across the Muslim World,"[3] the largest in a series of conferences and rallies that spread across diverse locations, from the United Kingdom to Palestine to Ukraine, organized by the Islamic political party Hizb ut-Tahrir (Party of Liberation). Several other groups have also indicated their desire to establish a caliphate, from the secretive Indonesian based group Jemaah Islamiyya, to Moroccan opposition party Justice and Charity. Not to be left out, during a

1

speech aired in mid-2006, al-Qaeda leader Osama bin Laden admonished his "brothers in Jihad" in "Baghdad, the home of the caliphate" that they "must not miss this opportunity to establish the nucleus of the caliphate."[4] Since the Arab uprisings which began at the end of 2010, a number of Islamic personalities from across the countries affected have publicly announced that the resultant changes in the Middle East were a step toward the re-establishment of the caliphate. These calls ranged from the address of prominent opposition leader Sheikh Abdul Majid al-Zindani to crowds of supporters in Yemen[5] and local scholar Sheikh Yusuf al-Eid to demonstrators in the city of Daraa in Syria,[6] to various exhortations on the re-establishment of the caliphate given from pulpits in major mosques in Egypt and broadcast across satellite channels, newly-launched in the more permissive post-uprising atmosphere,[7] to the exuberance of the secretary general of the Tunisia en-Nahda party, Hamadi Jbeli, upon winning his election seat by telling his supporters "we are in the sixth caliphate, God willing."[8]

Notwithstanding the apparent popularity in Islamic nations for the re-establishment of the caliphate, which appears to have some grassroots support as indicated by poll results released in 2007 showing that sixty-five per cent of respondents from across four major Muslim countries wanted to live under a single state,[9] the supposed revival of the idea has not been greeted with universal approval. In particular the administration of George Bush Jr. was consistent in criticizing the concept of a global Islamic caliphate. In 2006 alone, the "caliphate" was mentioned more than fifteen times by Bush, once four times in a single speech.[10] Part of the same administration, Bush's Vice-President Dick Cheney warned that al-Qaeda wanted to "re-create the old caliphate,"[11] and prior to his resignation, Defense Secretary Donald Rumsfeld told Pentagon employees that the goal of extremists was to "establish a caliphate" on the back of the destabilization of "moderate mainstream Muslim regimes"[12] (many of which were in any case subsequently overthrown by revolutions across the region).

"Caliphate" has become a useful phrase on both sides of the Atlantic for politicians seeking to generate public fear to justify foreign excursions and military action, as exemplified by ex-British Chief of General Staff Sir Richard Dannatt's words up to early 2010, explaining the justification for continued military presence in Afghanistan on the grounds that it was the front-line in the battle to prevent the "Islamist's long-term objective" of restoring the "historic Islamic caliphate."[13] This went beyond concern over resistance to military occupation or the advocacy of violence against Western civilians to branding the political aspiration itself as a problem. Leaked Home Office documents outlining the then Labour government's counterterrorism "strategy" showed that Muslims were branded as "extremists" if they "advocate a caliphate," in other words "a pan-Islamic state encompassing many countries," irrespective of the means advocated to achieve such a state.[14]

Since 2011, the issue of the political resolution that would follow the Arab uprisings has also exercised the minds of Western politicians. During the armed uprising that eventually removed Muammar Gaddafi, then Italian Foreign Minister Franco Frattini warned of the "serious threat" that would be posed by the emergence of any "Islamic Arab Emirate on the borders of Europe."[15] In the United States, and upon his return from a trip to his "spiritual homeland," Israel, in August 2011 US Rep. Allen West warned that "this so-called 'Arab Spring' is less about a democratic movement, than it is about the early phase of the restoration of an Islamic caliphate, the last being the Ottoman Empire,"[16] picking up on a theme initially raised by right-wing pundit Glenn Beck[17] (which was widely derided at the time by sections of the media).

It was not just Western interests or the interests of the perceived "moderate mainstream Muslim regimes" which were apparently threatened, with Esfahan's representative to the Iranian Assembly of Experts, Ayatollah Jalaleddin Taheri-Esfahani, stating that "the return of government to a form of caliphate is a great danger that must be avoided."[18] As the notion of a caliphate has been re-introduced into Muslim discourse, other bodies set up in its absence such as the Organisation of Islamic Conferences (OIC)—ostensibly created to represent the collective voice of Muslim States worldwide—have also felt the need to participate in the discussion, with Secretary-General Ekmeleddin Ihsanog stressing in 2010 that the OIC represents the same religious unity and solidarity that existed in the past under the caliphate, therefore fulfilling its function[19] (which, if true, would lead to the logical conclusion that its re-establishment was a redundant issue).

With the rhetoric calling for the re-establishment of a caliphate being introduced more openly into public and political spheres in the Middle East since 2011, it has become a topic of contention between the liberal elements of society and Islamic movements. The leaders of groups that have publicly reconciled themselves to working within pluralistic, civil systems and adhering to a democratic discourse in the political sphere are often asked of their position vis-à-vis the caliphate in the media, generating a variety of responses which usually attempt to highlight their more "pragmatic" approach toward appeasing secular and liberal sentiments. When the head of en-Nahda, Rashid al-Ghannouchi, was asked about his position on re-establishment, he admitted that the caliphate was the hope and desire of all Muslims, though it had no role in his group's political program (at least at this time).[20] The head of the Syrian Muslim Brotherhood, Mohammad Ayad, was much more emphatic in his denial, denying that there were any plans whatsoever for the re-establishment of the caliphate by the movement in the wake of the uprising against the regime of Bashar al-Assad,[21] in an attempt to demarcate the goals of his movement from that of Hizb ut-Tahrir in the region. Meanwhile, the head of the Egyptian Muslim Brotherhood, Dr. Mohammad Badie, stated that the re-establishment of the righteous caliphate and the revival of the Islamic State and *shari'a* were the goals of his party,[22] as stated by Hassan al-Banna, and that they were close to being achieved, perhaps responding to the growing debate within Egyptian Islamic circles regarding the caliphate.

All of these discussions and debates around the caliphate, its relevance for the contemporary era, and how it applies to the political programs of the different movements in the region highlight its relevance today. With the opening of a civil space for more open political discourse in the Middle East as a result of the Arab uprisings, this has only increased.

The last sustained period of global interest in the caliphate occurred more than a century earlier, with Sultan Abdul Hamid II emphasizing his role as the worldwide leader of Muslims to garner international support in an attempt to halt the decline of the Ottoman state during his rule between 1876 and 1909. In India, the Khilafat movement was established in 1919, attracting even non-Muslim leaders such as Mahatma Gandhi to its events, part of their work to support Muslim brethren in Turkey while resisting the colonial British. When Mustafa Kemal formally abolished the caliphate on March 3, 1924, reaction from places as far apart as Egypt, Libya, Syria, Afghanistan and India highlighted the attachment felt to the institution,[23] even though for all intents and purposes it had died years earlier.

The sudden collapse of the caliphate also reverberated around political and religious elites across the Middle East and wider Muslim world, with Sharif Husain of the Hijaz proclaiming himself caliph to the incredulity of the majority of the global Muslim community.[24] A subsequent conference held in Cairo in 1926 was seen as a thinly veiled attempt by Egyptian monarch Ahmed Fu'ad to lay claim to the title himself. The conference had actually been scheduled for 1925, but due to various political complications was postponed. Among the reasons for the delay was the uproar surrounding the publication of a book called *al-Islam wa usul al-hukm* (Islam and the fundamentals of ruling), the main thrust of the text being that the caliphate was in fact an un-Islamic institution and that Islam, contrary to widely-held perceptions of the Islamic community over fourteen centuries, actually had nothing to do with politics. The author, an al-Azhar graduate called Ali Abdul-Raziq, was subsequently stripped of his qualifications and barred from work as a judge by the unanimous decision of a court made up of twenty-four of his peers.[25] However, once the initial indignation and protestation over the ignoble end to a centuries-old symbol of Islamic history had ran its course, by the 1930s the question of the caliphate and any aspirations to it no longer seemed relevant, and the issue appeared to lay dormant in the political sphere.[26]

It is clear that the caliphate represented different things to its various supporters and detractors. In the early twentieth century, the supporters of the institution variously thought it to be a symbol of Islamic unity, a last hope against Western imperialism, a focal point to strengthen communal identity against other new nationalisms, and a useful tool to extend the elite's political influence in the region. Its detractors claimed it was a symbol of a civilization whose time had passed; even anti-modern, totalitarian leaders were afraid it could be used against them in their local political struggles with the various monarchies dotted around the region.

The apparent absence of the caliphate from public consciousness for several decades and its subsequent re-emergence as part of what may be perceived as a broad Islamic revival, as well as the opening of public space for political discussion in the Middle East, raises many interesting questions. These range from what the idea means to those who propagate it, how it is used in the counter-hegemonic discourses of the Islamic thinkers and groups engaged in a struggle to wrest power from entrenched regional ruling elites, and to what extent is it adopted as a symbol of reactionary rejection of modernity and Westernization rather than as a political alternative in its own right. There have been numerous works on different aspects regarding the caliphate, including Sean Oliver Dee's "The Caliphate Question,"[27] Mark Wegner's "Islamic Government,"[28] Soaud Ali's thesis on Ali Abdul-Raziq,[29] and Mona Hassan's "Loss of Caliphate."[30] All of these focus on the period surrounding the abolition of the caliphate, covering Britain's relationship with the Indian Khilafat movement, the debates in Egypt at the time of the abolition, analyzing the work of one of the opponents of the caliphate and comparing the reaction of the abolition of the caliphate in 1924, to the loss of the Abbasid caliphate to the Mongol invasion in 1258 respectively.

The intention of this book is to go beyond that period in time to provide a history of some of the movements making a claim to the call for the re-establishment of the caliphate over the last century, and how those claims fit within the reconstruction of a "Pan-Islam" that James Piscatori has defined as "giving concrete form to the idea of Muslim political unity"—trying to answer how these movements have articulated their belief that the spiritual unity of the Muslim community requires political expression[31] either through the notion of the caliphate or other forms of transnational authority.

It is hoped this will provide a unique contribution toward a greater understanding of the nature and nuances of Islam in politics and the path of Islamic revival across the last century. In so doing, it will examine the waning popularity of the caliphate in Muslim discourse and its subsequent re-emergence, understanding its differing importance to different actors and movements, the importance of symbols and their varying levels of meaning in forming and strengthening political positions against regimes which lack popular legitimacy, and how these ideas are diffused globally across movements and individuals.

As an analysis of Islam and Muslim polity, the use of the liberal democracy as a universal yardstick is avoided and the categorization of Muslims into "Islamists" and others is also rejected, and instead uncovers a normative understanding of Islamic politics that exerts a growing pull upon Muslims today. In place of the artificial paradigms which are unhelpful in understanding the differing trends of Islamic movements, the words of proponents of Islamic governance are placed within the political context they are addressing, while also taking into account their political position and religious understanding. Accordingly, it provides an alternate telling of history, told from within these movements and their surroundings, and encompasses the envisagement of an alternative future opposed to the standard story of progress as a move from the religious to the secular, as well as simply being an interesting story in itself.

Analyzing Islamic Politics Through Imposed Paradigms

Approaches to analyzing the politics of Islamic groups across the Middle East and Muslim world normally fall into two broad camps: Orientalists and their detractors (alternatively named "essentialists" and "contingencists"[32] or "internalists" and "externalists").[33] The common narrative is that Orientalists hold a limited set of conceptual categories derived from the classical texts of Islam that are applied universally in their analysis of political Islam,[34] whereas their opponents view the same approach as reductionist and instead argue that the various social movements and developments should be understood as the product of particular local socioeconomic and political woes.[35] The first approach generally holds the incompatibility of Islam and 'modernity' as the trigger for regional discontent and support for various Islamic movements, whereas the second contends that factors such as the failure of secular nationalist movements to resolve the societal problems of poverty and denial of political representation are the main causes of the backlash. While some Orientalists consider that any calls for democracy by Islamic parties are purely utilitarian in nature,[36] their opponents argue that any reference to Islamic tradition is used instrumentally or simply represents a call for participation and better governance articulated in a more culturally authentic form.[37]

However, for all their differences and arguments, since the end of the Cold War both sides have implicitly made liberal democracy the ultimate reference point in their approach and analysis, such that Michael Salla notes that "the relationship between liberal democracy and political Islam is unidirectional: Political Islam either responds to liberal democratic norms by demonstrating their consistency with the Islamic heritage; or reacts to them as contrary to the Islamic heritage."[38] Accordingly, the two schools of thought could also be categorized into those who believe in the incompatibility of Islam and liberal democracy, and those who argue its compatibility, with both sides implicitly accepting the assumption of the universality of liberal democratic norms, as well as its hegemony.

Since the opinion of the incompatibility school is to stress the oppositional nature of Islam and liberal democracy, any attempt by Islamic parties or groups to participate in local and national elections is seen as merely pragmatic and not grounded in any real belief or conviction in the process. As an example, David Brumberg argues that democracy is used instrumentally by both the current elites and the Islamic opposition as a means of addressing the social and economic crisis of failed regimes,[39] but the goal of the opposition to ultimately establish a unified ethical order based on the *shari'a* by initially embracing liberalism will inevitably lead to conflict between the two.

Though many supporters of these and similar positions hold to the Orientalist view of a single, essential Islam, or perhaps more accurately a single, essential Muslim, another approach has been to dismiss the concept of an "Islamic State" as being a modern invention, an alternative to a world order imposed upon the Middle East by a domineering West. While the notion of a single essential Islam can be rejected, for writers like Bassam Tibi this modern invention is still strong enough to ensure an inevitable clash between the West and Islam. Tibi supports "inclusivist policies," but the "inclusion of Islamists" will not change their worldview since "their goal of establishing an Islamic state cannot be shaken," and any belief that such a state would be compatible with democracy is "naïve and politically dangerous."[40] Even though an essential Islam is rejected, an essential "Islamism" takes its place, with any nuance or differences in thought and method of the various groups and individuals submerged under the general heading of utilitarianism.

The reaction to such essentialisms has been to de-emphasize the concerns of traditional Orientalists of the significance of Islam. This form of "anti-Orientalism" treats Islam as a nominalism, explained as an ethnicity, or as an ideology—in the Marxian mystifying role—or as simply the vocabulary through which legitimacy is represented. Rather than being a monolithic entity, Islam is decentered and dispersed as a collection of "little Islams."[41] As noted by Francois Burgat, "It is easier to study one eternal and intangible Islam than all the thousands of interpretations."[42] In such interpretations, the cause of the instability in the Middle East and the lack of movement towards the full adoption of a culturally acceptable form of liberal democracy are not due to Islam, but rather the failure of national, secular regimes to resolve the political and socioeconomic problems of the post-colonial era. As such, unwarranted

Western interference rather than a rejection of Western political norms is behind the slow development of democratic structures in the Middle East. Rather than the resurgence of Islam in the political sphere being part of a worldwide "revolt against the modern age," as posed by Bruce Lawrence,[43] it is "an effort to find a legitimate basis for the construction of a modern state and a modern economy in the environment of contemporary technologies and sciences."[44]

The underlying idea that Islamic activism is a reaction to a post-colonial vacuum is also evident in much of the work of John Esposito. Monumental events such as the failure of the 1967 war with Israel are seen as triggers for an identity crisis that led to a return to the old tradition of Islamic revivalism. To Esposito, the roots of Islamic reform are not simply a response to the challenge of the West, but rather "are both Islamic (its revivalist tradition) and Western (a response to European colonialism)."[45] The return to Islam is again considered as a return to faith, identity and authenticity, with those promoting secularism (mainly the elites) perceived as indigenous colonialists, and modernizers as apologists. The evidence of several differing groups and programs proves that there is no monolithic version of Islam or political Islam, which is just "a recurrent Western myth that has never been borne out by the reality of Muslim history."[46] Though there may be some specific doctrinal points that do not conform to liberal democratic norms, the revivalists "need to bridge the gap between traditional Islamic beliefs and institutions and the socio-political realities of the contemporary world."[47] Esposito is not interested in the detailed ideas of the varying movements and individuals, but rather how compatible they are with a pluralistic form of governance.

Another proponent of the "authenticity" explanation is Nazih Ayubi. Ayubi dismisses that modernization and a lack of secularization are the reasons for a rise in political Islam. Instead, the rise is linked to the failure of foreign "formulas" of communism and capitalism, while Islam is considered as more indigenous. The rise is explained as a reaction against the alienating policies of local elites in the name of modernization that have engendered a resentment to exclusion, resulting in the quest for a "cultural revolution" which seeks to install what Ayubi calls a "nomocracy," a reign based on the Word of God and the rule of law rather than of any particular elite or theocratic group.[48] This protest against exclusion is merely clothed in Islam, since the development of political Islam is seen as a reaction to the dissolution of the caliphate and loss of independence with no unique or alternative ideas intrinsic to its own framework of thought.

Though Ayubi, Esposito and Burgat lie firmly within the compatibility school by virtue of their assertion that an Islamic form can exist within a pluralistic system based on liberal norms, a different approach, adopted by scholars like Olivier Roy and Fred Halliday, effectively renders Islam as secular and irrelevant; consequently "to ask of Islam the answer to basic questions about politics and society is spurious."[49] Islam is therefore compatible with liberal democratic norms since it actually has nothing to say about them.

In Halliday's view, any analysis of the Middle East should focus on the consequences of post-colonialism, just as in the explanation of any other post-colonial state or region. Islam cannot provide any fundamental ideas or programs, but rather is used as a purely mobilizing force in a utilitarian manner. The universality and supremacy of Western secular political norms is so sure to Halliday that "the issue is not, therefore, one of finding some more liberal, or compatible, interpretation of Islamic thinking, but of removing the discussion of rights from the claims of religion itself."[50] Whereas the Orientalists stress the primacy of Islamic texts in shaping the thoughts of Muslims, Halliday goes to the extreme of effectively denying they exist, since in his view Islam does not "tell us about the circumstances in which the state should be opposed or supported, whether there should be one state or many; whether believers should embrace modernity or tradition." Yet a brief review of traditional Islamic sources provide narrations which mention when a ruler is to be obeyed or fought against, the obligatory nature of unitary rule, and the condemnation of basing actions on anything other than Islamic sources.[51] Though these can be interpreted in varying manners, it is clear that Islam does say something about all these issues, and the real questions concern the interpretation of what it says and whether Muslims pay any attention to it.

This is the view taken by Roy when stating that "the key question is not what the Koran actually says, but what Muslims say the Koran says."[52] However, Roy's own analysis suffers from a number of inaccuracies regarding aspects of Islamic law which are largely agreed upon within orthodox Islamic scholarship, as represented by the major schools of Islamic thought. One example is his claim that those who have considered Jihad to be a *fard 'ayn* (individual duty) rather than *fard kifaya* (collective duty) have introduced an "obvious innovation (*bid'a*)" within Islam,[53] which in fact runs completely contrary to the consensus of classical Islamic opinion which states that Jihad becomes *fard 'ayn* when Muslim land is under attack.[54] He also dismisses those who claim that the re-establishment of the caliphate is a religious obligation as a *bid'a*, on the grounds that "this has never been stated by any classical theologian."[55] Yet Abul Hasan Ali al-Mawardi, Mohammad bin al-Hussain al-Fara Abu Ya'la and Imam al-Haramain Abdul Malik bin Abdullah al-Juwaini, among other noted historical Islamic figures, all state that it is agreed upon by the consensus of scholars that appointing a caliph is an obligation.[56] In any case, Roy holds the opinion that political Islam has failed as a result of its co-optation by the state and has therefore become "normalised,"[57] a thesis that can be safely applied to the most prominent political Islamic movement the Muslim Brotherhood in Egypt. Once he has (re)established the failure of political Islam—he then asserts that its failure "means that politics prevail over religion." He clarifies this by stating that the "Islamization of society has led to the Islamization of secular activities and motivations, which remain secular in essence, business, strategies of social advancement, and entertainment."[58] In such a paradigm, political Islam could never succeed because there is no such thing, since in his view, engagement in politics and government is ultimately a secular activity.

Roy's basic thesis is that "neo-fundamentalism," a new form of religiosity that focuses on the universal *Umma* (community) rather than national and statist dimensions, is borne of the failure of political Islam and the rejection of some of its adherents to normalization within existing political frameworks. In such a narrative, the interest in a global caliphate is a result of the failure of local Islamic movements to sufficiently influence or succeed within the nation-state model. The existence of groups that have worked for global objectives from their inception such as the Khilafat movement in the early and Hizb ut-Tahrir in the late twentieth century raise questions about the validity of the theory, and it can be argued that many groups initially held universal and global objectives, such as the establishment of a pan-Islamic state, but subsequently had to submit to working locally due to the enormity of any universal, transnational project. It is the Algerian experience in the early 1990s in particular that is perhaps the closest to matching his theoretical framework. Another possible example is that of the Egyptian Jihad movement and al-Qaida, which is analyzed in detail by Fawaz Gerges,[59] who relates his thesis specifically to the modern global *jihadi* movement borne out of local groups frustrated at being crushed by state apparatus throughout the last decade of the twentieth century.

For Roy, like Halliday, secular liberal democracy is the benchmark in their analysis as it is for Esposito and Burgat, with the caveat that the word "secular" be removed. In one form or another, either by arguing the complete irrelevancy of Islam or its flexibility and lack of essential nature, the context they are looking at overrides any Islamic textual interpretations. As a result they see no problem with the compatibility of Islam and their own worldview. Those who fall within the incompatibility school focus on the essential nature of Islam, and the belief that any analysis of the politics of the region should primarily be read through interpretation of Islamic texts. While context may influence the reactions of various Islamic movements, in its essential form Islam is incompatible with liberal democracy and therefore there can be no lasting accommodation with Islamic activists.

Both Orientalists and their opponents implicitly accept the universality of liberal democracy and subsequently make it their basis for analysis, failing to consider that the proponents of Islamic government may actually be offering viable alternative paradigms. Neither school strikes the right balance between interpreting discourses while evaluating the influence of context in order to understand the extent to which the ideas produced are merely reactive or derived systematically from alternative worldviews, as well as how symbols are constructed, perceived and used.

This binary approach to analysis also dominates the media, as observed across the news networks during the Arab uprisings in 2011, where the dominant questions asked were how far the clearly popular "Islamist" parties were willing to participate within a pluralistic, liberal democratic framework. No thought or consideration was given to any alternative visions, ironically highlighting the lack of willingness, largely on behalf of the Western media, to accept fundamental political difference, even though the uprisings were targeted against erstwhile Western allies who represented various forms of secular tyranny combined with liberal economic policy and a willingness to largely abdicate their foreign policy for the geo-political concerns of others.

INTERPRETING IDEAS: AN INTRODUCTION

There is some work that takes a critical approach to the methodologies used in interpreting contemporary Islamic movements, including that of Elizabeth Hurd and Michael Salla. Hurd's perceptive and valuable work highlights how even those groups willing to work within the existing frameworks in the Middle East region and Muslim world are commonly misunderstood due to the primacy of a secular epistemological approach to analysis which defines a "normal politics" far out of sync with reality in Muslim majority societies. Islamic-oriented movements are subsequently labeled as an aberration from this "normal politics," and therefore "fundamentalist" and intolerant. Her own understanding is that "Political Islam is a modern language of politics that challenges, sometimes works completely outside of, and (occasionally) overturns fundamental assumptions about religion and politics that are embedded in the forms of Western secularism."[60] But rather than necessarily being an oppositional dialogue, it is more of a discursive tradition. There is an acceptance that the paradigm of secularism, the Western understanding of what is religion as opposed to politics, and their complete independence from one another, cannot be the methodological basis for gaining a real understanding of Muslim politics.

Salla's critique of the implicit assumption of the universality of liberal democracy that underlies much of the analysis of Islam and the Muslim polity has been touched upon earlier. In rejecting this worldview, he states that "it is therefore necessary to expand the debate concerning the study of Political Islam beyond the methodological approaches of the 'essentialist' and 'contingencist' camps, and into the 'ideational' or 'discursive' realms" where "Political Islam should be seen as representing a paradigm that is in direct competition with liberal democracy in terms of the universal appeal and scope of their respective norms."[61] His own proposal is what he calls the "new convergence thesis" where Political Islam is neither a reformist response nor a reaction against liberal democratic norms, but instead is an alternative universality that can be used to critique other epistemological paradigms. His assertion that those who adhere to or promote Political Islam are attempting to articulate a worldview that challenges the epistemological roots of Secularism is valid, and necessitates that one interprets the alternative ideas proposed by the various intellectuals and movements in their own terms to better understand the meaning of their discourse and symbols.

The Caliphate and Normative Islam

At this point it would be fair to ask: why should we focus on the caliphate within the discourse of Islamic movements, and what can this actually tell us? After all it could be argued that two of the major groups that have benefitted from the elections in Tunisia and Egypt, namely the en-Nahda and the Muslim Brotherhood parties, do not appear overly disposed toward talking about it forcefully, and in fact have adopted all the apparent trappings of a discourse rooted in democracy rather than the concept of an Islamic State or caliphate. At times they can appear non-committal to the idea of the caliphate, at least in their immediate political environment, and especially when confronted with the question in the media. This is arguably reflective of the trends highlighted in polls taken on the Arab street—which on the one hand show strong support for the strict application of Islamic law and the unification of Islamic lands under one ruler, while also showing a majority believing that "a democratic political system" was a good thing.[62] The only way to reconcile such apparently contradictory sentiments is to say that the Muslim conception of "democracy" is not that which would be considered representative of liberal democracy as understood in the West, but rather is more likely to be along the lines of what has been noted by the influential Egyptian scholar Yusuf al-Qaradawi when he stated that the call for democracy in the Middle East is a rejection of dictatorship, and not a rejection of the idea that sovereignty belongs to God.[63] In other words, the word democracy is held to be the opposite of the imposed postcolonial collection of monarchies, republics and dictatorships that have dominated the Middle East, and as such represents the ability to choose a leader, but says nothing about the desire (or lack of) for the establishment of an Islamic State or unification of Arab and Muslim lands.

This brings us to why the study of the caliphate, how it is talked about, the role it plays, and how it is understood, is not only important now, but will grow in significance with the further opening up of political discourse across the Middle East. One of the chief reasons behind this is that the uprisings in the Arab world have shown us, without a doubt, that groups which base their legitimacy on Islam have garnered mass grassroots support throughout the region. This trend is reflected in the growing religiosity of the population across the Middle East and beyond, into countries such as Pakistan, Indonesia and elsewhere. Some of the Islamic groups that have historically articulated their position as being from within the Islamic tradition, and representative—at least in terms of their discourse—of non secular frameworks of governance, have emerged as major political players in the region at the expense of liberal or leftist opposition. The success of the Egyptian al-Nour party, the political arm of a loose collection of Islamic leaders who were mostly apolitical (if not supportive of the regime) before (and during) the revolution, is an example of this trend, with the movement representing the second largest political bloc in the Egyptian parliament following elections in 2012. While some of this unexpected result can be attributed to their wide network of grassroots charity activities, their claim to be representative of normative Islam as proponents of the *salafi*[64] trend was also important, especially in differentiating between themselves and the most popular political group in Egypt, the Muslim Brotherhood.

Therefore normative Islam is important within this political context, as to be successful as an Islamic political party necessitates a legitimacy based upon what is seen to be traditional Islamic orthodoxy. What is meant by normative Islam in this context are opinions and views based upon an understanding of the Qur'an and those Prophetic traditions (*sunna*) which are widely held to be authentically traced back to the Prophet, supported by the opinions of historical traditional scholars whom the majority of Muslims would consider as representative of Muslim orthodoxy. Using normative Islam as a framework can help us to better understand political scenarios within Muslim countries, such as the failure of secularization among the largely religious masses across the Middle East, primarily because secularism seemed to them to be an alien concept, contradicting the idea of Islam as a complete *din* or way of life. In turn, an understanding of normative Islam and its importance and significance for the region will indicate why the caliphate is bound to continue impressing itself upon the more open political environment post-2011, because of its central position as the Islamic mode of governance as understood in orthodox Islam.

The results of research mentioned earlier, which found that an average of 71 per cent of those interviewed across four Muslim countries (Egypt, Morocco, Indonesia and Pakistan) agreed with the goal of requiring "strict application of *Sharia* law in every Islamic country," with 39 per cent agreeing strongly, while also finding that sixty-five per cent agreed with the goal of unifying "all Islamic countries into a single state or caliphate," should not be surprising. These opinions are in line with the classic orthodox Islamic position, which holds that there is an indisputable consensus that there should be a single ruler for the Muslim community, and that this ruler is charged with ruling by the law of God. The basis for this kind of unequivocal consensus is the abundance of clear evidence that can be found in the primary sources of Islam, the Qur'an and the Prophetic narrations, which make these two points explicitly clear.

There are numerous verses from the Qur'an which indicate that revelation is the basis of legislation, and that it is the law as ordained by God that should be used to judge between men. Included amongst them are the words "And whosoever does not judge by what Allah has revealed, such are the Disbelievers," "And so judge among them by what Allah has revealed and follow not their vain desires," "But no, by your Lord, they can have no Faith, until they make you (O Muhammad) judge in all disputes between them," "O you who believe! Obey Allah and obey the Messenger," "And in whatsoever you differ, the decision thereof is with Allah"[65] amongst numerous others, which have led to the consensus of understanding that in Islamic law the legislator is God, meaning that His revelation, as represented in the Qur'an and the words of His Prophet, form the basis for legislation. For this reason, in the traditional books of the Islamic jurists who authored the science of jurisprudence (*usul al-fiqh*) there is agreement that God is the legislator (*al-Hakim*) and that legislation is for God alone.[66] The difference between a system that adopts this legislation as its basis and what would be termed a theocracy in the Western sense, is that in normative Islam it is the role of scholars and rulers to discern the law from the sources of revelation, and to implement it. However, no individual after the Prophet is considered divinely guided[67] and is therefore both susceptible to mistakes (and must be corrected by the people), and bound by the law they interpret and implement.

There are also numerous texts found amongst the Prophetic narrations in the books considered the most authentic in traditional Islam (the two most authentic collections considered to be *Sahih al-Bukhari* and *Sahih Muslim*) which articulate that the role of the ruler is to rule by Islam. Amongst them is the famous long narration that "There will be Prophethood for as long as Allah wills it to be, then He will remove it when He wills, then there will be caliphate on the Prophetic method and it will be for as long as Allah wills, then He will remove it when He wills, then there will be biting Kingship for as long as Allah wills, then He will remove it when He wills, then there will be oppressive kingship for as long as Allah wills, then he will remove it when He wills, and then there will be caliphate (once again) upon the Prophetic method."[68] Another is the shorter narration "If the pledge of allegiance is given to two caliphs kill the latter of them,"[69] one of the most common evidences used as a basis for unitary leadership being obligatory.

These examples, along with several others, have been used to establish a consensus of orthodox opinion that the Muslim nation must have a single ruler who is responsible for the running of their affairs in accordance with Islamic law, which is articulated in detail in books specifically on Islamic governance that had emerged by the eleventh century. Islamic international relations were based upon a dichotomous "*dar*" paradigm, with the concept of *dar al-Islam* (abode of Islam) referring to the fundamental idea that any territory that came under the authority of Islamic law was part of the *dar*. *Dar* was, therefore, a territorial entity, with the rule of law applying over the territory that fell under the authority of the central executive, in effect an early formation of a territorial State. As mentioned by Mohammad Shaybani, "a *dar* becomes the *dar* of the Muslims through the application of the laws of the Muslims, and so the Imam makes it *dar al-Islam*."[70] The most famous exposition of the Islamic theory of State was by Abul-Hasan al-Mawardi, who claimed that the establishment of the caliphate was an Islamic obligation agreed upon by the scholars.[71] His treatise, *al-Ahkam al-Sultaniyya* (The Rules of Governance), remains one of the major classical references for Islamic political theory.

These ideas were not articulated by al-Mawardi alone. His claim of a consensus upon the obligation of the caliphate is mirrored by everyone else who wrote on the subject in the period and beyond, including prominent authorities well known within Islamic scholarly tradition such as Mohammad bin al-Hussain al-Fara Abu Ya'la,[72] Abdul Qadir al-Baghdadi,[73] Ali bin Ahmad bin Said bin Hazm al-Dhahari,[74] Abdul Rahman bin Ahmed al-Egee[75] and Abu Abdullah Al-Qurtubi,[76] amongst others. So while some modern academics such as Asma Asfaruddin claim that there was a "diversity" of opinions on the matter of the obligatory nature of the caliphate within Islamic scholarship prior to the post-Mawardi period,[77] the reality is somewhat different, and their conclusions are largely down to inaccurate readings of the texts. As an example, Asfaruddin takes her view from the statement of the eleventh century *Mu'tazila*[78] scholar Abul Hasan Abdul Jabbar, who wrote that there were three opinions regarding the caliphate—the first being that it was not obligatory. However, a further reading of Abdul Jabbar informs us that those who held the opinion that the caliphate was not obligatory were in fact part of the heretical sect known as the *Khawarij*,[79] and therefore their rejection should not be taken into consideration. The phrase he uses is that there is a "consensus on [the caliphate] being obligatory" and "any opposition against this consensus is rejected" since "the *khawarij* and those upon their methodology are not taken into consideration."[80] Furthermore, with respect to the issue of the obligation of appointing a single leader, Abdul Jabbar is equally emphatic, noting that while there is no deduction based purely on ration which would prohibit the appointment of two leaders of a state, it has been prohibited by the revelation, as well as being confirmed by the "consensus of the companions and those after them that it is not permitted to be contracted except to one" and that "once they are confirmed it is not permitted to contract a second."[81] A second common claim is that the famous thirteenth century scholar Taqiudeen ibn Taymiyya, a polarizing figure today held in high esteem by the modern *salafi* movement, did not consider the caliphate to be an obligation, which is an unfounded assertion as has since been explained.[82]

As has been mentioned, this point of Islamic law is confirmed in practically every single book written on Islamic governance up until the twentieth century, all of which narrate an agreement on the obligation to establish the caliphate which goes beyond that even of orthodox scholarship, and also includes practically all of the minority sects, as summarized by al-Dhahari, who stated "all of *ahl al-Sunna*, all of the *murji'a*, all of the Shia, and all of the *Khawarij*[83] have agreed on the obligation of *Imama* [another term used for the caliphate], and that the *Umma* is obliged to appoint an Imam who will apply the rules of Allah and look after their affairs with the rules of the *Shari'a* which the Messenger of Allah brought, except for some of the *Khawarij* [who did not agree upon the obligation of the caliphate]."[84] In more recent scholarship, Abdulrahman al-Juzayri has stated that there is agreement that the appointment of an Imam is obligatory and that it is "not permitted for the Muslims to have two leaders within the whole of the Earth at one time, whether they were in agreement or discordance."[85] In conclusion, there is such an overwhelming consensus on the issue of the obligation of a single leadership who is responsible to rule by the law of God that any opposition has historically been rejected as an anomaly and in contradiction to normative Islam and traditional scholarship.

Due to the position and importance of the caliphate as the Islamic method of ruling and leadership within traditional Islam, it is not surprising that most Islamic groups, whether involved in politics or not, will have discussed it at some point, if not made it their proclaimed goal. Given its central importance, understanding what has been said about the caliphate and the role it plays within the methods and goals of the various Islamic political movements will inform us about the role of normative Islam, how it is interpreted within contemporary political circumstances and used in political programs and discourses, and the relevant importance and adherence of these movements to it.

Studying the Caliphate and its Callers

As expected given its central position in Islamic orthodoxy, historically the Islamic caliphate has been one of the most enduring and important political symbols for Muslims worldwide, significant enough for several dynasties and ruling elites to lay claim to it,[86] considered to represent the lofty ideals of Islamic unity and solidarity[87] as well as being viewed as a sanctified institution that had to exist[88] (even if not in an ideal or relevant form). In 1924, Thomas Arnold wrote a treatise specifically on what he considered to be the origins, underlying theory and historical usage of the term. He argued that the caliph was a political rather than spiritual functionary, but remained an Islamic formulation since he considered that there was no separation between "church" and "state" in Islam, an obvious point since there is no Church in Sunni Islam. Penning his thoughts after the abolition of the caliphate under Mustafa Kemal, Arnold concluded that "there seems no immediate prospect of a political community being established in the Muhammadan world under the headship of one Khalifah, such as Muslim doctrine requires." However, he felt that "the ideal is still cherished, and is likely to survive as a hope in the hearts of Muslim peoples for many generations to come" since "every Muslim regards himself as the citizen of the ideal state [...] this state knits together all his brethren in the faith, under obedience to the Imam-Khalifah."[89]

Arnold's study makes interesting reading, despite his somewhat pedantic Orientalist concern with tracing the origin of the Arabic root of the word and finding its usage within the Qur'an, as though this could decisively prove or disprove the authenticity of the idea behind the word. In this case, such scrutiny is particularly unwarranted since the word *khalifa* is only one of many words used to designate the same concept, with other choices including *al-amir, amir al-mu'minin, al-Imama al-kubra*, and so on. Whatever the root of the word, Arnold stated that irrespective of how religious a particular "Mohammadan" may be, "they are still attracted by the glamour of a distinctly Muslim culture and long to break the chains of an alien civilization" imposed by the European colonialists. While guilty of Orientalist essentialism, generalization and stereotyping, there is ample evidence that the idea of a caliphate did retain some of its resonance and importance for numerous individuals across the colonized territories, even if it was not as widespread or uniformly understood as Arnold would have his readers believe. With such a key role foreseen for the symbol of the caliphate in any counter-hegemonic Muslim program by Orientalists such as Arnold, one would expect to see significant consideration given to its study. The re-emergence of the caliphate in public discourse internationally indicates that Arnold may not have been inaccurate in his belief of the lasting power of the political ideal.

Academic studies of the history of the discourse which has surrounded the caliphate since the era of its abolition by the Turkish government have normally focused either on specific time periods or specific individuals and movements, sometimes as a stand-alone study or as a small part of a wider historical work. Most of this work has focused around the debates of 1923 to 1926 between the relevant supporters and opponents of the caliphate at the time of its destruction, often focusing on the heated debate surrounding the publication of Ali Abdul-Raziq's *al-Islam wa usul al-hukm*, such as work by Mohammad 'Amara,[90] Mohammad al-Rayyis,[91] Mark Wegner,[92] Armando Salvatore[93] and Eli Kedourie.[94] Mona Hassan's more recent work on this area compares the reaction in the region to the loss of the caliphate in 1924 with that of the fall of the Abbasid caliphate in 1258.[95] Others, such as Azmi Ozcan,[96] have focused on the earlier phase of an increased push to try to utilize pan-Islamism in the final days of the caliphate, particularly under the leadership of Sultan Abdul Hamid II. Some of this work is valuable in helping to understand what the institution represented to the various protagonists involved, such as 'Amara's analysis that those opposed to the concept of the caliphate, including Raziq and his supporters, were actually engaged in a struggle against King Fu'ad's totalitarian designs as well as English imperialism, while Rayyis takes the opposite stance, that those who were against the caliphate were actually supporting the British by helping them to destroy any potential form of pan-Islamism previously represented by the Ottomans. These analyses are a useful resource, particularly those regarding the debate around the period of the formal dissolution of the caliphate, having uncovered several primary sources which inform the empirical basis for any wider analysis.

The studies of the various individuals and movements closely associated with support for the caliphate cover a more extensive period when taken in totality. One of the most valuable contributions is Gail Minault's work on the Khilafat movement, which analyzes the different meanings of the caliphate in the Indian context. Minault considers that the symbol "may have been romantic in some of its manifestations," but it was still "grounded in the pillars of the faith" as well as making "good political sense in the Indian context"[97] since it could be used as a basis for solidarity among Indian Muslims to counterbalance their minority status vis-à-vis the Hindu majority. Since the movement was composed of various 'ulama' (Islamic scholars), politicians and activists, the caliphate held different meanings for its members, including the rule of Islamic law, the principle of religious freedom and self-determination, or simply the faith of Islam itself. While historically rich in detail and critically perceptive in highlighting the various instrumental uses of the caliphate as a symbol by politicians, if there is any shortcoming in Minault's work it is the lack of any real investigation into the fundamental ideas carried by the founders of the movement. The caliphate is just assumed to be a religious obligation of some sort, accepted by the people as a symbol for the religion, without any details as to why or how this was the case from an ideational point of view.

Suha Taji-Farouki's book *A Fundamental Quest* covers Hizb ut-Tahrir,[98] a group established in Palestine that describes itself as a political party whose ideology is Islam with the goal of reviving the Muslim *Umma* through the re-establishment of the caliphate. The study contains a single chapter detailing a history of the party from its origins in the 1950s and subsequent development up to the 1990s. Along with a detailed review of the internal structure, organization, administration, and international strategy of Hizb ut-Tahrir, Farouki also analyzes the ideas of the group's founder, Palestinian judge Taqiudeen al-Nabahani. In her view, his formulations were "the response of an Islamic scholar and talented intellectual to the break-up of the Ottoman empire, the fragmentation of its territories into nation-states, the creation of Israel and the impotence of Muslim societies in the face of neo-colonialism."[99] These axiomatic events led al-Nabahani to establish Hizb ut-Tahrir in order to realize his vision of establishing the caliphate, which in Farouki's analysis meant "a divinely prescribed, complete and definitively detailed system, broadly identifiable in its institutions and forms with those of the Abbasid period."[100] The book presents an in-depth study of the group, explored primarily through its literature as well as the context in which it emerged and operated, and while it suggests that al-Nabahani was influenced by what the author considers as modern (and therefore by implication un-Islamic or alien) concepts such as rationality, she sees his thought as being somewhat independent because of his comprehensive rejection of Western value-orientation and ideological constructs. Other notable and more recent contributions to the work on Hizb ut-Tahrir include that by Emmanuel Karagiannis, who focuses on the presence of the movement in Central Asia and argues that the group has been the sole persistent and systematic advocate for a worldwide Muslim State.[101]

The argued rigidity of al-Nabahani's thought stands in contrast to the image of Rashid Rida painted by Mahmoud Haddad, the most famous and active individual promoter of the caliphate in Egypt during the final Ottoman years. To Haddad, Rida's primary concern was to maintain the political independence of Islam in any way possible. Rida was "clearly a pragmatist," who was "willing to sacrifice theoretical considerations about the caliphate for the arrangement most likely to guarantee Islam's political independence."[102] In this analysis, the caliphate has become to Rida an instrumental symbol for the unity and sovereignty of the Muslims rather than a theoretical or theological concept that has to be strictly adhered to. Haddad's research positions Rida and his writings in the historical context of the Ottoman decline, and traces the development of his thought regarding the caliphate through four distinct phases.[103] In each phase the caliphate takes on a different meaning and usage as Rida adapts his concepts according to pragmatic considerations, deemed necessary to prevent the collapse of Muslim unity and the complete loss of any independence from colonial rule. Though Haddad's final reading of Rida's ideas is open to debate, the method employed in arriving at his conclusions strikes a meritorious balance between context and text over a period of time.

Minault, Farouki and Haddad's respective works are all excellent studies into some of the different individuals and movements who have formulated, adopted or used theories of the caliphate. All provide a strong analysis that can be tapped in trying to explain the history of the idea of the caliphate and its use from the First World War to the present. Comparative analysis between movements and thinkers has been undertaken by a number of academics in studies covering various aspects of the Islamic movement. The most promising approaches consider the ideas studied as political theories in their own right rather than as a result of socio-economic conditions, as argued by contingencists, or simply different articulations of a monolithic essence, as proposed by the essentialists.

Religious Epistemology and Ijtihad

With respect to explanations of the emergence of the idea of "Pan-Islam" since the nineteenth century—particularly when expressed explicitly in terms of the caliphate—there are a number of common arguments that can be discerned from the literature. The first account of the utilization of the caliphate by thinkers and leaders in their discourse focuses on state-led interests with purely political intentions. Examples include figures such as Sultan Abdul Hamid II, who utilized Pan-Islam as a tool to hold the Ottoman State together in the face of Western encroachments and internal divisions borne of emerging nationalisms;[104] Rida, who tried to maintain the political independence of Islam; and state elites for the sake of legitimizing their rule and leadership in the immediate post-caliphate era.[105]

A second approach views the development of "Pan-Islam" as built upon the culture, ideas and sympathies that lay latent within Muslim societies, held throughout the Muslim world, and coming to the fore as the result of a combination of the emergence of newspapers and the growth of literacy. This was coupled with a perceived need to link weakened and subjugated Muslim populations to a central Muslim power, possessing military strength, in an effort to resist colonialism and encroachment by foreign powers, India being a prominent example. In such analyses, Indian attachment to the Ottoman caliphate was indigenous rather than created and controlled by the Ottoman State.[106] Another strand of analysis, broadly within the same approach, considers the development of pan-Islam from within the Ottoman State, and that its adoption was based upon existing emotions and rose partly as a result of the failure of the Eurocentric international system which in turn led to the creation of other region-based associations in a sort of defensive reaction. This sees the rise of pan-Islam as akin to other unity-based movements such as pan-Asian ideology, part of a wider attempt to form alternative blocs to the West, each based upon their own cultural ties.[107] In the contemporary context, such ideas and sympathies remain a potent force, but have no state support and therefore remain confined to the ideational realm.

A third explanation is that recourse to a more general global Islamic unity was due to the failure of political Islam at the national level, whether at the ballot boxes or through the use of armed struggle, leading to either a "neo-fundamentalist" recourse to the worldwide *Umma* and utopian ideas of a global caliphate while rejecting nationalist or statist dimensions, or possibly, in its most extreme variant, a war against the "far enemy."[108]

None of the above explanations can satisfactorily explain the varying attraction of the caliphate as an idea to thinkers, movements and elements of the wider population in their construction and articulation of transnational political authority, reflecting the claimed spiritual unity of Muslims. Consequently, an alternative approach is warranted, adopting elements of these analyses but also introducing greater concern with and study of the content of what is being said. One of the initial questions surrounding what kind of approach is best suited to the analysis of Islam and the idea of a global Muslim polity revolves around the issue of how to analyze this phenomenon through a balanced use of both contextual and textual analysis. This is of particular importance given that both essentialists and contingencists are ultimately arguing that the discourse of proponents of the different strands of political Islam is unimportant, since the first argues that any analysis of the movements and individuals of political Islam should be explored through the prism of a limited set of conceptual categories universally applied, while the other asserts that these movements are simply the product of circumstance. In both paradigms, what is said by the object of study is of secondary importance and only useful when validating the initial hypothesis of the analyst. As has already been discussed, an understanding of the role normative Islam plays should be adopted within any analysis in order for it to accurately reflect the subject studied.

Bobby Sayyid identifies five other common themes that are often quoted to explain the general rise of the call for Islam in the political sphere. These are the failure of national secular elites, the lack of opportunity for political participation, a crisis of the petit bourgeoisie, petrodollars and uneven economic development, or being a nativist response to inclusion in a Western led global system. As such, the cause given is always some external factor or response to a structural crisis. As Sayyid notes, these explanations can be recognized as a set of empirical descriptions to what is happening to the current political order, but do not explain why particular political formations based upon Islam emerge as opposed to the various alternatives, for example liberalism.[109] He suggests that Islam should be seen as a "discursive construct," with Islam becoming the "master signifier" or the "unifying point of the discursive production of Islamists."[110] Consequently, any analysis of the rise of political Islam needs to take an interpretive approach focusing upon the discourse of the various movements involved in order to understand the development and rise of the call to the idea of the caliphate and what it means.

Though it is clear that some kind of socio-economic deterministic approach to explaining the phenomenon of the rise of the call for an Islamic form of polity generally, and the call for the caliphate across the Muslim world in particular, is deeply unsatisfying, it is also clear that any approach that relies solely upon a reading of the various discourses produced by the different groups and activists outside of their context and without an appropriate interpretive framework would also be erroneous. Rather, an analysis of the discourse produced over time and read in light of the different contextual conditions would help in arriving at a clearer understanding of the motives and intentions of the various authors. It is not enough to recognize that various individuals and groups call for the re-establishment of a caliphate, but it is important to understand what is meant by the caliphate, whether the call for it is consistent and if not then why is it adopted at particular times.

The approach intended here is to tread a path that traces a history of ideas, where the importance of the context in which ideas are generated and expressed is not neglected, but equally is not elevated as an all-encompassing explanation.[111] Quentin Skinner debates the strength of approaches that rely upon contextual explanations for the emergence of ideas as opposed to more textual analysis. Skinner notes that although social context may help in the explaining of a text, he denies that the ideas of any given text should be understood only in terms of that context. As such, a study solely of contextual conditions is neither a sufficient nor an appropriate methodology for the understanding of the statements made.[112] Conversely, a methodology which relies purely on the supremacy of the text rests on a presumption of the universality of ideas and accepts the timeless element of the text. Consequently, any contradictions between texts of the same author are to be rationalized, explained away and accounted for rather than, for example, indicating a development or change in the thought of the intellectual in question.[113] He also contends that any analysis of the text is lacking unless an appreciation of the motives and intentions involved can somehow be ascertained.

However, even with such an approach, the question of the paradigm in which analysis of the various discourses should be undertaken remains, with the possibility of falling into the trap of evaluating the Islamic phenomenon though an inappropriate "Western" model, such as one that might take Western Christianity as a model against which other religions may be judged, one that views that the development of human society as linear, or one that classifies history as ancient, medieval and modern. All of the previous examples are borne out of an assumed universality of the Western experience, under which it is the only model that other societies ought to emulate. If Islam is the "master signifier" or unifying point for the various discourses of political Islam, as argued by Sayyid, and they are informed by an understanding of its primary sources, it is therefore necessary to recognize the different epistemological bases adopted by those responsible for producing this discourse. Herein again is an indication of the importance of understanding the role Islam plays in determining the actions of the advocates of Islamic government.

Consequently, in adopting an interpretive approach which considers the views of the various proponents of the caliphate in their own terms, the process of derivation of rules and laws from Islamic doctrine should be taken into account. This suggests an approach that tries to trace the thought processes which led to the articulation of differing solutions, all claimed to be Islamic, within the various texts utilizing the classical Islamic science of *usul al-fiqh*, or the basis of jurisprudence, defined as the rules and comprehensive evidences which are used to derive jurisprudence.[114] Within *usul al-fiqh* is the process of *ijtihad*—the comprehensive exertion of a jurist to derive an Islamic ruling by the method of extraction from Islamic sources.[115] Though the debate over what qualifies as an Islamic source and discussion of the detailed rules for extraction clearly fall outside the realm of this study, it is sufficient for our purposes to consider the Qur'an, the Prophetic traditions (*Sunna*), consensus (*ijma'*) and analogy (*qiyas*) as the widely agreed upon Islamic sources. It is also adequate to note that although the general and detailed rules of how to extract a ruling from the sources are many, any process of *ijtihad* would require an articulation of how the reality for which a verdict is sought is understood, a search within the sources for evidences, and a verdict on the reality derived from the evidences.

This process is important and relevant since the moral and intellectual leadership offered by the various movements and theorists depends in part upon how they relate their aims and methodology to Islamic authoritative sources while appearing relevant and practical, especially true for any proponents of an alternative political system that is claimed to be Islamic. In other words, since these individuals and movements seek legitimacy on the basis of Islam, it is important to trace exactly how they claim such Islamic validity, both in relation to orthodoxy and normative Islam. Even the most convincing *ijtihad* may not be sufficient in winning mass support or acceptance. However, should an *ijtihad* fail to prove its Islamic legitimacy and position within a framework of understanding that is true to normative Islam, it can result in the denial or withdrawal of support, particularly where there exists competition between Islamic groups. An example of this occurred during the Egyptian elections at the end of 2011 where the Islamic credentials of the Muslim Brotherhood were questioned by the newly formed al-Nour party, who based their own legitimacy on a more strict, or in their opinion, valid understanding of Islam within the personal and social sphere. This is arguably also what has happened to groups such as al-Qaida, whose view on the legitimacy of killing civilians lost them support given that it is not considered an *ijtihad* with strong evidence or precedence.

This type of hermeneutic approach requires an understanding of the circumstances surrounding the origins of any idea or movement, why and on what basis particular fundamental ideas were adopted, how those ideas were used, altered and added to over time, and the context in which changes occurred, in order to help analyze what a particular symbol or idea means. In other words, when looking at the individuals and groups that have adopted a call for the caliphate, any analysis would need to identify the origin of the group, its original ideas and whether the caliphate was a part of those initial fundamental goals. If this is the case, upon what basis or justification was the goal adopted, and if not, then at what point, under what circumstances and as a result of what reasoning was the call for a caliphate adopted. Once the call for a caliphate has been identified within the core literature or statements of a group, tracing its use over time and consistency according to the varying circumstances in their arena of work would also provide indications of the motivations and intentions behind such a call.

In adopting this approach it is necessary to undertake a series of case studies which will form the basis for an analysis of how and why the call for a caliphate has been used or neglected in projects seeking the construction of a global political expression representative of the Muslim *Umma*. These studies should encompass the major events relating to this call and the major movements that have used or adopted it. The choice of case studies should also reflect some of the major genealogical thought strands such as those movements that propose gradualism or "bottom-up" change as opposed to wholesale revolution, peaceful as opposed to violent, and national (or even transnational) as opposed to international or globalist movements. This would provide insight into the different conceptions, meanings and uses of the caliphate within the various discourses of these groups, according to their opposing methodologies, and highlight the varied ways powerful symbols can be used in political discourse.

The initial starting point for us here is the struggle which occurred before and around the official abolition of the caliphate in 1924, and in particular the heated debates which took place in Egypt between Ali Abdul-Raziq and his family's party, the Liberal Constitutionalists, and the mainstream Muslim *'ulama'* of the time. Though I will not embark on a major study of the Khilafat movement in India given the fact that its main activities were before the caliphate was abolished (as well as the existence of ample resources regarding the movement, its roots and potent symbolism), reference will be made to the fundamental ideas and writings of some of the movement's intellectual leaders. The importance of this debate lies in its role in highlighting the symbolism of the caliphate from both a political and doctrinal angle, and will help further clarify the misconceptions already identified by scholars such as Roy over the lack of any doctrinal justification for the obligatory nature of the existence of a caliphate within Islam. It will also highlight just how far the caliphate had fallen from practical consideration as a viable political alternative, despite maintaining a central position in the minds of many academics.

Since its abolition in 1924, three different movements have laid claim to the call to re-establish the caliphate: the Muslim Brotherhood, Hizb ut-Tahrir and al-Qaeda. These movements and their leaders will be examined, looking at how their call relates to their efforts to reconstruct a global or transnational religious and political authority. Each group represents a separate strand of thought in terms of their approach: the Muslim Brotherhood has adopted a gradualist line, operating within national confines but arguably with a transnational outlook; Hizb ut-Tahrir are an international political party largely operating outside of national political systems; and al-Qaeda are a global, violent reactionary movement. Despite their differences, each has been widely influential in affecting currents of thought around Islam and politics. Finally, the use of the caliphate within the discourse of movements which were founded outside of the Arab Middle East will be considered, primarily focusing upon the sub-continent based Tanzeem-e-Islami, the diaspora movement Jama'ah-tul-Muslimeen and the convert-founded Murabitun—thus covering a significant variety of groups. Other movements and thinkers representing minority sects such as the Shia are not considered as although the wide spectrum of Islamic belief agrees upon the obligatory nature of the caliphate—or Imamate—from a theological perspective, the fundamental cause for the differences between the two major Islamic schools in existence today is that mainstream Shia belief holds that the leader has been divinely appointed and therefore the responsibility of the Muslims is to await the return of said appointed leader (the "Mehdi") to take political control, whereas the Sunni belief holds that it is a matter of choice and consent. Considerations of how the Shia, under the leadership of Ayatollah Khomeini, felt compelled to articulate the theory of *walayat-e-faqih* (guardianship of the Islamic jurists) in the absence of the Mehdi and any other Islamic based ruling under the secular leadership of the Shah of Iran, fall outside of the scope considered here.

The sources used in this study consist of a wide range of the primary materials produced by the groups in question and their respective leaderships, including published and unpublished books, leaflets, press releases, internal communications and online multimedia materials. Where possible, biographical accounts written by internal sources have also been utilized, and archival sources are also used where relevant. Given the range of groups covered, interviews were not conducted for the research presented and are not considered of primary importance due to numerous factors including but not limited to the chief objectives of this work and the wealth of information immediately available to the author.

In conclusion, this study contends that those political leaders, thinkers and movements that advocate Islamic governance and utilize the call for the re-establishment of the caliphate do so in various ways according to their differing interpretations of the root causes behind the political malaise in which they exist and which they were established to resolve, and which methods ought to be adopted to remedy this political situation. In other words, the alternative solutions adopted and subsequently developed as a result of their *ijtihad* dictate what role the caliphate plays in their discourse, ranging from a minimal and actively downplayed role, to the use of the caliphate as a call for a radical alternative form of government, to promoting the imagery of the caliphate as a uniting symbol in the face of aggression from foreign, non-Muslim powers. As movements struggle to re-establish a polity which expresses the unity of the *Umma* and presents a recognized religious authority, the caliphate has often been ignored, had its significance minimized or denied, reclaimed and promoted as a theory and symbol in different ways, in both the regional and international struggle over the future of the "Greater Middle East."

2

THE END OF AN ERA

THE CALIPHATE BETWEEN REJECTION, REFORM
AND REVIVAL

To unite different nations under one common name, to give these different elements equal rights, subject them to the same conditions and thus to found a mighty State is a brilliant and attractive political ideal; but it is a misleading one. It is an unrealisable aim to attempt to unite in one tribe the various races existing on the earth, thereby abolishing all boundaries.[1]

Mustafa Kemal

While narrating the political intrigues and manoeuvres he had undertaken as head of the Ottoman state after the First World War, Mustafa Kemal recollected that in his telegram communication with Colonel Refet Basha on 16 March, 1920, he claimed that the liberation of Istanbul from occupation would win "the applause of mankind" and pave "the road to liberation which the Islamic world is yearning for" by delivering "the seat of the caliphate from foreign influence" and defending it "with religious fidelity in a manner worthy of our glory," as well as realizing "the independence of the nation."[2] By 1922, Kemal was a man of much greater influence after stirring military victories prior to the Lausanne conference, and was able to dictate to Refet Basha that "we shall separate the caliphate from the Sultanate and abolish the latter,"[3] thus separating the institution from any vestige of temporal power, expecting but not receiving any resistance from the erstwhile supporter of the "Sublime Porte." While addressing the Turkish Assembly on 1 November of the same year, Kemal justified the separation of the caliphate from the Sultanate with the claim that "the issue of the caliphate is actually the greatest Islamic affair," since it was a "leadership that binds together all the people of Islam," but this leadership was not to be political since it "was completely natural for the position of the caliphate to exist side by side with the authority of the people."[4]

Though sensitivity to popular opinion and general religious attachment to the caliphate may have previously constrained his actions, by the beginning of March, 1924 the situation had changed, giving him the opportunity he required to consolidate his position in the face of strong Islamic opposition. Ironically, this was thanks in part to letters sent from India by Agha Khan and Amir Ali championing the cause of the caliphate which caused uproar amongst Turkish politicians, largely due to the fact that the authors were widely seen as tools of the British government,[5] working against the nascent republic. Kemal was therefore in a sufficiently secure position to stand in the Assembly and state that "in order to secure the revival of the Islamic faith" it was necessary "to disengage it from the condition of being a political instrument" thereby foiling foreign intervention. The final act in the abolition of the caliphate was completed two days later, on 3 March, with the words "the caliph is declared disposed, and the dignity abolished."[6] Dignity was indeed formally abolished for the incumbent caliph, Abdul Majed, forced to leave his palatial residency and sent into exile, while the "Pan-Islamic" policy based around the institution of the caliphate, pursued energetically in particular by Sultan Abdul Hamid II but also subsequently by the Ottoman State during the First World War, lay in tatters, buried beneath the secular and nationalist Kemalist revolution.

To Kemal, and those from amongst his supporters who adopted his ideology, the caliphate was an unrealistic utopian concept, "a brilliant and attractive political idea" but at the same time "a misleading one" since it was pursuant to the "unrealizable aim to attempt to unite in one tribe the various races existing on the earth." Moreover, he felt that "there is nothing in history to show how the policy of Pan-Islamism could have succeeded," and instead thought that the "clear and fully realizable" political system would be based around "national policy."[7]

However, this feeling was clearly not universally agreed upon, with various emotional, political and religious attachments to the caliphate existing both nationally and internationally, as evidenced by Kemal's own reticence in openly expressing his convictions in the period between 1920 and his speech before the Grand Assembly in 1927. Even though he clearly held Islam and those who called for adherence to the religion in disdain, he felt compelled to justify the abolition of the caliphate with the claim that it was necessary for the revival of the faith.

The loss of territories at the end of the First World War, the fear of what may happen to the caliphate at the hands of the Allies, and the subsequent actions of the Turkish Assembly all contributed to the struggle over the position, relevance and meaning of the caliphate within the Muslim polity during this intense period. This monumental upheaval, which altered the map of the region in both a literal sense and in terms of self-perception, incited discussion of the caliphate and how it was understood by different intellectuals and politicians from a variety of backgrounds and regions. Given the amount of material on the historical events and political intrigues of this period, there is no need to go over well trodden ground, but a pinpoint study of the discourse regarding the caliphate in this period is warranted, highlighting how the institution was perceived around and after the time of its abolition by its opponents and proponents and how limits within Islamic discourse were drawn and enforced even though Islam was being marginalized politically, as well as serving as the background for the remainder of this book.

The struggle around and over the caliphate in Muslim discourse in this period can be divided into three distinct phases, with reference to the precluding history dating back to the Ottoman claim to the caliphate and the effects of the policies linked to "Pan-Islam" up until the end of First World War. The first of the three phases was that immediately prior to the separation of the caliphate and the Sultanate, or its temporal powers; the second phase the subsequent discussion over the relevancy of the institution; and the final phase being after the formal abolition of the caliphate. Throughout these three distinct phases a number of different groups engaged in the political discourse at different times and with differing levels of interest, amongst them Islamic activists and revivalists who were engaged in anti-colonial struggles for independence and sovereignty alongside a revival of Islam, the secularists who supported the separation of the institution of the caliphate from political authority and were convinced that future prosperity lay in adopting European thought, models of governance and values, and the religious scholars, or *'ulama'*, who were concerned with upholding the Islamic law, or *shari'a*.

By tracing the evolution of the debate surrounding the caliphate through these three periods, it will be shown that the caliphate was either seen as a symbol of the independence of Islam and proof of the political power of Muslims, as an institution misappropriated and misinterpreted to oppress the masses in the same manner as the Church in medieval Europe, or as an aspect of the religion, or *din*, whose contracted existence was deemed obligatory by the rites of Islam. In doing so, my argument is complemented by the previously mentioned work of both Mark Wegner and Mona Hassan, who cover some of the debates and reactions to the loss of the caliphate at the time, concluding that the caliphate symbolized the common Islamic identity of the global *Umma*. Both authors' explorations refuse to examine the theological debates and shared reactions to the abolition of the caliphate in isolation, but rather situate them within a wider discourse covering the period after, in order to position the discussion within the framework of subsequent efforts at its reconstruction. Interestingly, most of the protagonists in this struggle, including some of the secularists, made reference to *ijtihad* (juristic reasoning) as evidence for the righteousness or suitability of their solutions, indicating that conflict within the discourse was as much a struggle over the identity of Islam as it was over the future of the caliphate. This struggle included whether *ijtihad* was to be restricted to generally accepted sources of Islamic law, or whether there was to be an Islamic-style reformation that would see *ijtihad* redefined to simply mean an open-ended interpretation without restriction. The evolution of the claims to the caliphate begin as a struggle over its political meaning and relevance and end when the caliphate became a symbol not of contemporary political strength but merely a title for the spiritual head of Islam struggled over by elites for the sake of prestige and reputation, a reflection of the apparently final sidelining of Islam as a political force, relegated to the spiritual realm.

The Caliph—Politician or Pope?

Though the importance of the caliphate as a political institution throughout history has been questioned, it is generally considered to have existed up until 1924 in one form or another. Indeed, it was relevant enough for several dynasties to lay claim to it,[8] including the Ottomans. Some scholars, Mahmoud Haddad for example, express the view that the Ottoman Sultanate did not make a claim to the universal caliphate until the late eighteenth century,[9] but Azmi Özcan provides convincing evidence of earlier acceptance of and deference to their claim by other Islamic dynasties such as the Mughals, indicating the presence of an Ottoman claim earlier in history. He goes further, to assert that the pan-Islamism of Abdul Hamid was not a late development but rather "the practical formulation of already existent political tendencies and feelings in the Muslim world developed through centuries."[10] As an example, in the Indian context Özcan writes that the "one most important factor that made the pro-Ottoman Indo-Muslim feeling in India so widely felt and so common was the development of native newspapers,"[11] through which Muslims became aware of the situation of their brethren and responded as best they could. In other words, print capitalism was not only responsible for the spread of nationalism and the development of national identities, but was also used to further pan-Islamic ideals and sentiments.

The first recognition of the Ottoman caliph in international agreements occurred between the Russians and Ottomans after the Crimean War in 1774. In the treaty the Ottoman sultan was recognized as being the "Supreme Muhammedan Caliph," with the prescription that the Muslims in the Crimea were "to conduct themselves towards him as is prescribed in the rules of their religion, without, however, compromising their political and civil independence."[12] As noted by Haddad, the striking aspect of this and other similar international treaties between the Ottomans and non-Muslim states is that the notion of division between the spiritual and temporal is implicitly recognized, with the caliph being officially recognized by other states as a spiritual figurehead for Muslims who were not living in the domains under his authority.[13] This did not indicate a change in doctrine, but rather served to help the Ottomans retain influence within the territories they had been forced to cede militarily. This tradition within the Ottoman era of what Özcan calls "Pan-Islam" dates back to at least the seventeenth century, when the

Muslims from the areas of Aceh and India called upon the Ottoman caliph to provide military support against European incursions, and early correspondence between the Persians and Ottomans indicates that Ottoman efforts to achieve recognition as the universal caliph for all Muslims pre-dated the treaty with the Russia.[14]

Irrespective of the terms used within these treaties and what they may have implied, some of the Muslims outside the borders of the Ottoman state continued to claim that their primary loyalties lay with the caliphate, especially given that it was the strongest independent Muslim power which appeared capable of maintaining its independence. This was in part the legacy of Abdul Hamid, who had adopted a strong pan-Islamic policy to maintain the integrity of the Ottoman State, utilizing several Sufi scholars from Syria to Morocco to build stronger ties with the common people across the Arab world in order to deliver his message of representing the supreme universal caliphate to them.[15] In particular, the Khilafat movement of India proved to be a thorn in the side of the British, who looked at Pan-Islamism with a wary eye due to fears of the unrest it could cause in their dominions from Cairo to Bombay. In reality, since the deposition of Abdul Hamid and his replacement by Muhammad Rashad in 1909 by the Committee for Unity and Progress, the caliph had once again become a purely nominal figure, but the institution was still able to wield influence abroad up until and during the First World War, and was the target of considerable machinations and plots by the British and their allies in the Arabian peninsula.

The defeat of the Ottomans at the end of the First World War led to fears of the destruction of the last major independent Muslim power. The designs of the British and French in Eastern territories were well known after various secret documents, including the Sykes-Picot agreement, which detailed concessions and imperial control, were leaked into the public sphere by the Bolsheviks in 1917. It was these fears, along with any local, particular consequences that might arise if they were realized, that led to different parties reasserting the political salience of the caliphate. In India, the All-India Muslim Conference held in September 1919 declared that "the spiritual power of the sultan of Turkey was bound to his temporal power," and so the proposed division of the Ottoman Empire was considered "an assault" upon Islam.[16] In a memorandum written after the dismemberment of the Ottoman state addressed to the British Prime Minister Lloyd George, who had previously promised that Britain would respect the sanctity of Muslim holy places, the Egyptian based scholar and activist-reformer Rashid Rida claimed that "Muslims were not concerned that their holy places would be demolished or that access to them be denied" but rather "their real concern was for Islamic (political) sovereignty without which Islam itself and its mosques could not be safe." The preservation of this sovereignty was considered of great importance, and explained why "Muslims in the world passionately cling to the Turkish state and consider it representative of the caliphate although it lacks all the caliphate conditions except power and independence."[17] During the same period, the Turks also used religious language and symbolism to garner moral support both internationally and within their own borders, though the true intentions of the Kemalist movement became more transparent soon afterwards, to the dismay of some of their supporters.

Amongst the foremost supporters of the caliphate were the Indian Khilafat movement, founded in 1919 by a group of prominent Muslim figures to lobby the British government for the protection and integrity of the Ottoman caliphate in any post-First World War settlement, and continuing its activities until 1924. The participants ranged from religious scholars and political figures to activists, with the caliphate holding a variety of meanings for them, ranging from the rule of Islamic law to the principles of religious freedom and self-determination, and even simply the faith itself.[18] Gail Minault, a researcher of the movement, stresses its national character and posits it as part of an independence struggle built around Muslim solidarity. It formed an alliance with the Indian National Congress, participated in the non-cooperation movement in 1920, and some of its leaders had a close relationship with Mahatma Gandhi. According to the opinion of one of the major figures in the movement, Abul-Kalam Azad, a journalist brought up in a household of *'ulama'*, the Khilafat grievances had only arisen because they were under foreign rule, meaning Indian Muslims could neither follow Islam nor the caliphate properly as they were not free.[19] In other words, the core aim of the Khilafat movement to Azad was Indian freedom, with the caliphate providing a symbol of Muslim solidarity built upon widespread pro-Ottoman feelings.

This type of thinking does not seem to have been limited to the Indian Muslims, with a District-Governor in occupied Palestine remarking that "in Moslem countries that have lost their independence, there still remains an attachment to the caliph" derived from "an instinct which impels them to recognize some central universal religious authority other than the secular power which dominates them." This "instinct" was often "inspired by dislike of the occupying power" and subsequently "employed as a manifestation of discontent" which would vary "in inverse proportion to the good relations between the protector and protected."[20] The views of the British Consulate in Syria seemed to concur, with the analysis that "the recognition of the caliph by Sunni communities in Syria is, as elsewhere in the East, based largely upon political grounds" since "the existence of a strong independent Islamic State is regarded as a restraint on European encroachment on Muslim lands."[21]

In such paradigms, the caliphate became a symbol around which Muslim unity could be built and was used as the central focus for independent Muslim authority to help in the struggle for independence by anti-colonial activists. It should be noted that such views rely on an understanding of the caliph and the caliphate as encompassing temporal power, rather than as purely spiritual entities. Though it is argued that activists both inside and outside of India were able to gather local and international support for the caliphate, their remains a question over what exactly the caliphate signified, as perceived and articulated by its proponents, that provided it with this potent symbolism.

To explain the concept, Azad authored a booklet after the end of the First World War named "The Islamic Caliphate" in Urdu which was subsequently translated into Arabic and serialized by Rida in his periodical publication *al-Manar* at the beginning of 1922. In it, the author explains that the word is used to mean "the leadership of the religion, the general government, and the complete authority on the Earth." After explaining the linguistic meaning intended, he goes on to explain that "the goal of this caliphate, is to establish an *Umma* (nation) on the Earth" which would "unfurl the flag of divine justice, and erase oppression, injustice and misguidance."[22]

Writing at a time when the caliphate was still officially in existence and was not yet thought to be on the verge of total erasure at the hands of fellow Muslims, Azad did not concentrate on extrapolating all the various Islamic evidences to prove its necessity from a religious perspective, since this kind of *ijtihad* would have been of little practical value. Instead, he was intent on explaining particular issues that were pertinent given the political situation of the day, namely the intrigues surrounding the fate of the Ottoman state, the defense of the integrity of the caliphate in the face of the challenges posed by nascent Arab nationalism as represented by Sharif Hussain, who was rumored to covet the position for himself, and the continuing attempts to present a unified Muslim voice within India. As such, the thrust of his writing was to detail the various evidences that explained the doctrinal importance of unity based upon obedience to the ruler, with that ruler in Islam being the caliph. He therefore argued that Hussain's claim to the caliphate, based upon his family lineage, was invalid, and that unity was paramount, clarifying the intrinsically political nature of the caliph as a response to the fears of a European intervention demarcate the importance of the caliphate as having more than a purely spiritual function.

To Azad, the verse in the twenty-fourth chapter of the Qur'an which mentions that "Allah has promised those among you who believe and do righteous deeds, that He will certainly grant them succession in the land" and "that He will grant them the authority to practice their religion which He has chosen for them,"[23] contained the Qur'anic meaning of *al-khilafa*, or succession, which was "succession upon Earth, or government and sovereignty in it." Therefore, it was concluded that "it is imperative that the Islamic caliphate is entrusted with the coercive power to enforce order and prohibitions, and complete government," because "he is not like the Christian Pope, or their Patriarchs" since "their authority was spiritual."[24] Rather, the caliph's authority was temporal since "he is the ruler and sovereign on the earth alone," to the extent that "he does not possess the least amount of heavenly sovereignty." This would also contradict the idea of the caliphate being a form of theocracy as nor "does he hold any legislative power" so "he is unable to change anything from the *shari'a*, and he can neither add to it nor remove from it"[25]—in other words, "he does not have the right of legislation at all."[26] To fully delineate the difference with the religious hierarchy of Christianity and the theocratic justifications which were often used to legitimize various monarchical rulers, as seen in Europe, Azad keenly stressed that it was "incumbent upon the Muslims collectively to appoint him" and that in any disputes between the Muslims and their ruler "it is mandatory upon him and upon them collectively to refer back to the Book and the *Sunna* (tradition) of the Prophet" so he could argue that "in this circumstance there is no sovereignty for the caliph, rather the sovereignty is for Allah and His Messenger."[27]

In this expression, the caliphate is a temporal authority constricted by the *shari'a*, and a focal point for the resolution of disputes in society. Azad proposed that it was "necessary for the social life (society) to have a center," so "Allah made a center for it, and made the *Umma* encompass it like a sphere" and "the Muslims named this societal center 'the caliphate.'" The relationship between the center and the sphere was such that "if the center calls, it obeys, and if it moves then it moves, and if it stops then it stops." Unity was demanded since disobedience to the center was equivalent to "*jahiliyya* (the time of pre-Islamic ignorance) from which there is no return except through obedience to it."[28] The issue of Quraishi descent, which was commonly cited as a condition for the caliph within classical texts on the subject, was circumvented by Azad through his appeal to the universal nature of Islam, in what was most likely an attempt to help foster unity by buttressing the Ottoman claims to the title while simultaneously undermining British support for the separatist Sharif Hussain.

Though the Khilafat movement had opposed any European attempts to separate the spiritual and temporal powers of the caliph, the Turkish leadership under Kemal took the decision themselves towards the end of 1922. Kemal wanted to sideline the Sultanate as a political entity, but was cautious to do so without risking the ire of the Muslim population both within and outside of Turkey. Although he ultimately ended up abolishing the caliphate completely, at that stage he was still looking for a less drastic solution, as suggested by the claim that he offered the title of caliph to the Libyan resistance fighter and Sufi leader Sheikh Ahmad al-Sanussi—an offer the Sheikh refused at the time due to his belief that it was his duty to remain loyal to the incumbent sultan.[29]

With the Khilafat movement isolated in India and with no choice or tangible influence over Kemal, the Turkish decision to abolish the caliphate was rationalized away by prominent members such as Dr. Ansari, who declared that the spiritual and temporal powers had not really been separated, but that the sultan had been made into a constitutional monarch. Kemal was also to be applauded for re-establishing the correct practice of electing the caliph.[30] Though this type of explanation may seem as imaginative as any modern political spin, like much of the general public, many of the Islamic scholars of the time were in awe of Mustafa Kemal and his military exploits, and were therefore willing to overlook the action taken to remove the then caliph, Wahidudeen, who was widely seen as a pawn under the control of the British. Support was expressed by the Egyptian scholar Mohammad Shaker who wrote an article published in the al-Ahram newspaper claiming that the victory of the Kemalists was a glorification of Islam,[31] and even went on to ask "what is the point of the caliphate after this change?" on the grounds that "after this is it not appropriate for the Muslims to be thinking about overthrowing this ancient system[…] in order to rescue Islam and the Muslims from these disasters."[32] A British memorandum noting the atmosphere in al-Azhar university at the time mentions that "it was early reported that anger and consternation were felt by the students, while a manifesto was anticipated from the higher authorities of the University," but it appeared that "the feeling was by no means unanimous." In fact, "an 'advanced party' were working against any immediate action, and had succeeded in blocking the projected Manifesto,"[33] Some newspapers even condemned those who raised the discussion of the caliphate of furthering British interests by inciting hatred against the Kemalists, seen across Muslim lands as heroic due to their successful fight to maintain independence.

Progressive Politics or Impractical Fallacy

For all the talk of the caliphate by Indian Muslims, there was a consensus against the caliph Wahidudeen in Turkey and across the Middle East due to his collusion with the allies under occupation, and it is clear that independence and the ability to withstand foreign aggression were paramount in the minds of many Muslims. Among them was Rashid Rida, an enigmatic reformer and student of the prominent modernist Mohammad 'Abdu, whose politics seemed to oscillate between pragmatism and orthodoxy. He initially followed his teacher's footsteps in believing that successful reform could only come through co-operation with the British, but this hope was dashed by agreements made by the Allies during the First World War such as Sykes-Picot. Education reform had been the center of 'Abdu's program with little involvement in the caliphate, but Rida had been eager to engage in the politics of his time, and maintaining political independence for Islam took priority after the onset and subsequent aftermath of the First World War. In his discourse, he stressed the necessity of religious unity and the caliphate from both a religious and practical position, while criticizing the Kemalists for their irreligiousness, with education reform still present on his agenda, but now intrinsically linked to the political position of the caliph.

Writing in his journal, *al-Manar*, at the end of 1922, Rida opined that the Muslim peoples supported the Turks "for the sake of their military power," which forced the Europeans to accept Turkey's right to independence. Such support was "not for the sake the caliph or the caliphate." Rather, "if the Muslim Turkish people lost this extraordinary military power" then the Muslims would cease to care about their issues irrespective of whether "the caliph was established with them or not."[34] Rida did not agree with the decision taken by the Turks since he held that "in Islam there is no spiritual authority in the meaning [...] known to the Christians," and rather that "the authority of the caliph according to Islam is purely governmental." In other words, like Azad he held that the caliph was a temporal position: the political leader responsible for governing the *Umma* in accordance with the *shari'a* rather than a sanctified spiritual figure who held privileged such as the infallible interpretation of Islamic texts, enjoying a spiritual authority over Muslims without any temporal powers. However, he felt that "the most important political benefits for the Muslims at this time would be to support the Kemalist Turks in their situation in front of the European nations hungry to steal what remains with the Muslims in terms of territory and leadership," and that the they "should not make their [the Turks] mistake with respect to the issue of the caliphate as a reason to weaken them while in this position." In other words, though the caliphate had been stripped from the Sultanate, the primary issue of the time remained unity in front of a common European imperial enemy. Instead, once their independence was finally guaranteed, it could be explained to them that the caliph was "the representative of the authority of the *Umma* and its unity" with the temporal powers required by this role.[35]

Though many of the *'ulama'* had either tacitly accepted the new caliph or remained largely apathetic or in shock, as an activist and reformist, Rida's concern with the caliphate went beyond simply ensuring that some form of institution existed, which at least superficially fulfilled a juristic requirement. Calculating that the decision enforced by the Kemalists was an indication of their intention to halt any attempts at reform based upon Islam, and to pursue a purely national policy, Rida collected his work on the caliphate and Islamic reform and published it in his book simply entitled *al-Khilafa 'aw al-Imama al-'uthma*, (The

Caliphate or the Great Leadership), which he also released as a series of articles in his journal. While Azad's work was written with one eye focused on the perceived intention of the European powers to secularize Islam in a manner similar to the separation of Church and State, Rida was primarily addressing the Muslims of Turkey after the formal separation of religion and state had taken place. This was in order to convince them of the political relevance and role of Islam, its compatibility with modern science and its superiority to Western models of government.

His book was intended as a "gift" for the Turkish people, which would explain the reality of the caliphate and its details, and would "explain all of mankind's need for it" while exposing "the criminality of the Muslims upon themselves," the result of "treating it in a bad manner" and "removing it from its position." Writing soon after the First World War, having heard of the astonishing scale of destruction and loss of life across Europe, Rida opined that "Islam is the most powerful moral force on Earth" which could "revive the Eastern civilisation" and "save the Western civilisation." This was because "civilisation does not last without morality," and "morality cannot be achieved except with religion," yet there was no religion "that is compatible with science and civilisation except Islam." Noting the conflicts that occurred in Europe between science and the teachings of the Church, he felt that the loss of belief over time led to a loss of balance that religion would have provided. As such "the need of humanity for spiritual and civilisation reform with fixed principles has greatly increased," reform which would then "wipe away the genocide of the weak by the powerful," as well as "the humiliation of the poor by the rich," and conversely "the danger of Bolshevism on the rich," but that this could not occur "except with the government of Islam." The Turkish people, being the most capable of fulfilling this hope, should "rise up to renew government of the Islamic caliphate" in order to "combine the guidance of the *din* and civilisation to serve humanity,"[36] which would not be threatening to Western states.

In appealing to the Turks, Rida first paints his picture of what he sees as the true meaning of caliphate. He then proceeds to pragmatically discuss the various available candidates for its reconstitution, while also detailing the underlying causes that led to the decline of Muslim influence in world affairs, and his proposed remedies. While doing so, three groups of intellectuals are identified: the first are those who blindly follow the West; the second are the dogmatic section of the *'ulama'* who blindly follow the Islamic books of jurisprudence; and finally, the third are the party of reform, who combined the independence of thought and *ijtihad* in understanding the Islamic jurisprudence and *shari'a* while also adopting the best of European civilization.

Those who were enamored with Western thought were unable to differentiate between the good and bad aspects of Western civilization, and instead idealized it wholesale. For them, Islam was incompatible "with politics, science and civilisation" and they considered that "it is imperative to separate the position of the Islamic caliphate from the state." Depending on their religiosity, the caliphate was either considered as undesirable in the first instance, or as unrealizable in the age of the civil state. Whatever the case, their conclusion would either be that the caliph "should be kept within the Turkish State as a title as it had been during the Ottoman State," in order to benefit from its symbolism while also "protecting against the evil of eradicating the caliph," thereby "leaving the government to be freed from the constraints of adhering to the *shari'a*," which was considered impractical, or to "be completely without need of it,"[37] and move to discard it completely.

The majority of the religious *'ulama'* were also to blame for the malaise at the time, with Rida scorning them as "incapable of making military, financial, and political laws, relying upon imitation of previous legislation," and their refusal "to accept comprehensive *ijtihad* in all the worldly transactions" to the point that "if the revival of the issue of governance was left to them they would most definitely be incapable." It was the "the falling short of the *'ulama'* in explaining the reality of Islam" and being able to defend "what is required from the situation of the present era" that was the "largest reason for the apostasy from Islam of most of those who had been Westernised." Since they were the ones who had been incapable of "managing the issues of the state" and "clarifying the capability of the *shari'a*"[38] in dealing with contemporary issues, the blame fell upon their shoulders for the decline of the Ottoman caliphate to the point that the caliph became merely a political tool in the hands of others.

In the end, Rida apportioned the blame between the two groups, while the solution would require "the reform party to unite the stance of the Muslims by attracting most of the people of influence." This would be achieved by "transforming the *'ulama'* from amongst them away from dogmatic imitation" and for them to expose "the doubts cast upon the *din* and the *shariʻa* by those who had been Europeanised". At the same time it was necessary to explain "the danger in nationalism" and convey to the disparate leaders in Arabia the necessity of unity while "helping them in the necessary preparation of power and infrastructure." With the knowledge that most of the leaders and rulers across the Muslim world at that time thought "that the position of the caliph, and other issues from the rules of Islam are the reason for the weakness of Muslims," it would also be necessary to "explain the structure of the government of the Highest Islamic caliphate with a system that is suitable for this era," which "would be unique from the system of the other eras." Then they would have to work to convince "those influential people in the Islamic lands to implement it," "to prefer it in place of all the other types of government found in the world" and to be made aware of "the practicality of its implementation."[39]

This would entail "bringing the *din* and *shariʻa* to life," which could only occur through independent knowledge or "comprehensive *ijtihad*,"[40] since it would "not be possible for the Muslims to merge the guidance of Islam and its culture from the angle that it is a *din* of sovereignty and authority except through undertaking *ijtihad* in the issues related to legislation."[41] Though the basis of legislation would be Islam, there were areas of legislation left open for man to derive such as the "system of administration and judges [...] tax collection and planning warfare." Consequently, legislation and the extraction of such legislation through *ijtihad* was "one of the necessities of human society", with the caliph's role as the "source of the [derived] legislation,"[42] or *ijtihad*, while remaining bound in other areas by that which had been clearly defined by Islamic sources. In other words, where there were multiple interpretations of Islamic law or areas linked to administrative issues, as the highest political authority in the state the caliph's decision would be considered as the final arbitration, binding so long as it was not contrary to the *shariʻa*, making the text itself theoretically paramount. As long as it was based upon its true foundations, the caliphate would be central to any program of revival derived from *ijtihad*. Given Rida's long history of work in educational reform, it is unsurprising that his most practical recommendation was the establishment of an Islamic seminary to train future candidates for the position of caliph in the necessary aspects of the Arabic language and juristic sciences that would equip them with the capability to undertake *ijtihad* so that future rulers could fulfill the necessary prerequisites.

The revivalist goals that Rida was seeking through the creation of a corrected caliphate were the "establishment of a consultative Islamic government" and "return of the Islamic civilisation with sciences, arts and industry around which power and infrastructure revolves [...] that combines the blessings of the material world with the morality of the spiritual religion."[43] The aspect of consultation (*shura*), which featured heavily, claimed to be the original philosophical basis of Islamic rule which had been corrupted by "foreigners", such as the Persians and Turks, who had elevated the position of caliph to one of spiritual authority "until they had opened the door of despotism for them" as an unquestionable figure. Rather, the ruler was to be chosen by election and was "nothing other than the head of a restricted government" with "no control or supervision over peoples' spirits." Instead, he was only "the implementer of the law," with "obedience to him restricted to what was related to obeying the law, and not the individual." The Shia were particularly singled out because the Arabs had been "distanced from the original consensus based (or democratic) Islam" as a result of their perception of their leaders as theocrats,[44] which led them to elevate the opinion of the Ayatollah so that it was equal to the Qur'an and *Sunna* (Prophetic narrations) within their doctrine of infallibility. It should be noted, given Rida's view at the beginning of the century, that if the Iranian government was to establish a consultative body it would mean that "there would not exist on Earth a true Islamic government except for the Persians."[45] It seems his opinion of Islamic governance was not based on sectarianism as much as the type and form of governance itself.

Independence, accountability and consultation as the principles of governance ran contrary to the contemporary experience of the Ottoman caliphate at the time. The institution was seen as superficial and had been supported by the British with a policy described by Rida as neither allowing the state to live or die, while being exploited primarily as a bulwark against Russian imperialism. However, the most prominent alternative, Sharif Hussain, was unacceptable for a number of reasons, including the fact that he was supported by an un-Islamic power, considered an "enemy of knowledge and science," and that his form of governance was unrestricted personal rule.[46] In other words, he was neither independent nor accountable. Additionally, his poor Arabic meant that he was unlikely to become caliph.

Instead, Rida argued that success depended on unity between the Arabs and Turks, with "the independence of each of them in respect to the administration of their lands and sovereignty" and "the connection between [...] the two [...] by the position of the caliph."[47] In this it seems that there was another clash between pragmatic considerations and the caliphate theory as espoused by Rida, with the caliph supposedly to receive comprehensive temporal powers restricted by the sovereignty of independent states beneath him.

Unfortunately for Rida, he felt that the Turks would be unresponsive to his call as a result of their lack of knowledge of Islam and weakness in Arabic,[48] restricting their ability to undertake *ijtihad* and closing off any understanding of how Islamic jurisprudence could be applicable in modern times. They believed that "there was no way to contain [the caliphs'] despotism and prevent their oppression except by imitating the European forms of government." Instead, they saw the caliph as a "temporary illusion" with no executive powers, and held that "the caliphate was nothing except an official title" that could be exploited to gain outside sympathy and support. It was therefore unsurprising that Rida ignored the incumbent Abdul Majed, and instead called for "free and fair" elections to decide the government, while leaving the issue of the caliphate to be decided by all Muslims with its proposed seat in Turkey.[49] As noted by Haddad, Rida was obviously "willing to sacrifice theoretical considerations about the caliphate for the arrangement most likely to guarantee Islam's political independence."[50]

The Turkish government responded with their own book, translated as *The Caliphate and the Sovereignty of the People*, in which Rida's view of the caliphate was confirmed in so far as he was "the leader of a group of Muslims" without the "general sovereignty of the Pope," which was spiritual in nature and extended over Catholics wherever they may reside. In its correct formation with all prescribed conditions fulfilled, "one could not picture in the world a government better than it for mankind,"[51] echoing Kemal's assertion that "the issue of the caliphate is actually the greatest Islamic affair."[52] However, if a caliphate was similar in form but lacked the stipulated juristic conditions, "in reality it is not a caliphate, but a Monarchy or Sultanate."[53] In this case all the caliphs who, for example, did not fulfill the condition of Quraishi descent or had not been chosen by a valid method, were nothing but kings or sultans and their state could only be classified as a "superficial caliphate."

So while it would not be correct or acceptable to restrict the role and powers of a legitimate caliphate as practiced by the first generation of Muslims, it was possible to separate the current (false) caliphate from its temporal powers as an application of the juristic principle that allows actions to be taken to avoid harm and distress. By example of precedence, the book argued that throughout the history of the caliphate the caliph was often nothing more than a figurehead with no real political authority or influence.

While the author admitted that it was an obligation incumbent upon Muslims to appoint a leader who had to be obeyed, they developed the argument that "what is obligatory and necessary is the establishment of a government" rather than a specific individual in the role of caliph. What would be prohibited was therefore not the removal of the caliph from his position as head of government, but rather the "absence of government" thereby "leaving the *Umma* in a state of confusion and anarchy."[54] Recognizing that this was not the preferred option for Rida and those within the Turkish republic who continued to support and advocate the caliphate and a return to its idealized form, the issue was dismissed as being outside of the current government's responsibility since the position had been corrupted for over a thousand years.

Rida was dismissive of this counter-argument, holding that there was no distinction between real and superficial caliphates, but rather there were caliphs elected by choice who were qualified for the position, and caliphs who imposed themselves and were obeyed to ensure unity, even if they did not fulfill all the necessary conditions, echoing the arguments commonly found within the later books of classical Sunni Islamic scholarship. As for the argument that the caliphate was not prescribed for its own sake but rather to establish rule and remove anarchy, and could therefore be replaced by any other form of government, he wrote that the correct opinion would be to state that the caliphate was "the leadership of the Islamic government which would establish justice, protect the *din* and ensure the independence of Islamic lands." It was certainly "not permissible to abolish it or replace it with another form of government." The harshest criticism was, somewhat naturally, reserved for the argument of historical precedent, since "in history there are [precedents of] much misguidance [...] oppression and disbelief."[55]

For both the activists and the scholars drafted in to support the position of the Turkish government, the real model of caliphate was that of the first generation alone, with acknowledgement that what came afterwards was far from the prescribed ideal. Rida reconstructed the caliphate through reference to the Qur'an and Prophetic precedence, with a nod to trends in European governance since "whatever they have in terms of truth and justice our *shari'a* already confirmed,"[56] offering it as "the best government with which the situation of the Muslims would be reformed" with the potential of also correcting "the situation of the rest of mankind."[57] The Kemalists preferred to draw upon their own understanding of history, bemoaning the "centuries" for which the "nation was guided under the influence of these erroneous ideas." It was time to "put an end to the catastrophes into which the people had been dragged" as a result of self-deception and misjudging their "real rank and position in the world,"[58] with the caliphate historically representing dynastic despotism, misjudged dreams and the backwardness of so-called Islamic governance.

The End of "Empire", and the Orthodoxy Strikes Back

In October 1923, the Grand National Assembly declared that Turkey had become a republic, with the temporal powers previously vested in the caliphate officially handed over to Kemal as President and Ismet Pasha as Prime Minister. The monarchy had been abolished, and as Kemal himself opined, "after the abolition of the monarchy, the caliphate, being only an authority of a similar description under another name, was also abolished."[59] All that remained was an opportune moment to complete the final deed, provided by Agha Khan, an Ismaili Shia (considered heretical by the orthodox Muslims of Turkey and the Middle East, as well as by many other Shia sects), who had not had any interest or involvement in the Khilafat movement of his home country. In a letter widely distributed amongst Turkish officials and subsequently printed in *The Times* of London on 14 December, 1923, he claimed that "Islam, as a great moral and cohesive force, is losing among large sections of the Sunni population, owing to the diminution in the caliph's dignity and prestige, its weight and influence." In his unlikely role as self-appointed spokesman for Sunni Islam, Khan argued that the loss of temporal powers was irrelevant since Kings and chieftains could simply obtain from the caliph "investiture in order to validate their title to rule and to lead at prayers, the usual concomitant of secular authority." He also advised that if "Islam is to maintain its place in the world as a great moral force, the caliph's position and dignity should not, in any event, be less than that of the Pontiff of the Church of Rome."[60]

Kemal and his supporters moved quickly to claim that this intervention by "heretics", who were also branded as British agents (the greater accusation of the two), was an attempt to undermine the newly formed Republic and that the abolition of the caliphate was necessary "to disengage it from the condition of being a political instrument."[61] Though the previous "secularization" of the position did not cause widespread backlash from across the Muslim *Umma*, especially given that there were few noticeable practical implications to the move, the removal of this symbol of unity on 3 March, 1924 not only upset the supporters of the institution within Turkey, but also evoked an international response alternating between disbelief and fury from those who had previously given the benefit of the doubt to the Kemalists.

Within Turkey popular uprisings took place in Istanbul, Northwestern, Southern, and Southeastern Anatolia against the caliphate's abolition, even though any protests were punishable by death according to the modified Law of High Treason.[62] In the same period, the Kurdish population who had responded positively to the call to Jihad by the Ottoman caliph in the First World War, and were known to have held the caliphate in high esteem,[63] rebelled under the leadership of religious scholar Sheikh Said. Though there are debates over the exact nature of the rebellion, and how far religious rather than nationalist motivations played their part, there is no doubt that the loss of the caliphate played a distinctive role, with the head of the military tribunal held against the leaders in 1925 noting that some of them "invoked the defence of the caliphate" as a pretext for their actions.[64] The decision also evoked anger and disappointment, expressed vocally from Albania to Libya. Foreign Office dispatches record Albanian papers lamenting the move, which had driven the "religious centre" of Muslims' lives out of Turkey.[65] In Jeddah, the population was reported as being upset at the abolition of the caliphate, which they had previously hoped would eventually liberate them from the "nightmare" rule of Sharif Hussain. The *'ulama'* of Tripoli in Libya wrote an open letter to Mustafa Kemal expressing their deep offence, describing the caliphate as the "life-giving essence" of Islam, and therefore to the Islamic religion what the soul was to the body. From the pulpit of the Umayyad Mosque in Damascus, Sheikh

Abdul-Qadir al-Muzaffar gave a rousing sermon lionizing the Ottoman caliphate as the global defender of Muslim honor, and the hope of Muslim prayers for liberation.[66]

In a message sent to the Turkish republic published in the *Pioneer Mail* on 14 March, 1924, the Khilafat committee urged Mustafa Kemal to "uphold the Khilafat and Islam" and warned that "this sudden abolition is an act against the religion of Islam." Mohammad Ali of the Aligarh University stated that the caliphate was the essence of Islam, and Muslims were "the enemy of those who would destroy the Khilafat, be they English or Turks." The reply from Kemal made it clear that the caliph had been deposed and since the caliphate was contained in the sense and meaning of the Government and the Republic, the office was no longer necessary. He also pointed out that the existence of a separate caliphate office within the Turkish Republic proved to be disturbing to the foreign and internal political union of Turkey.[67] The author of a piece in *Aman-i-Afghani* disagreed, claiming the caliphate was "considered by the generality of Moslems and Islamic thinkers to be one of the essential Islamic institutions, and to be an excellent means for securing the unity of Islam and a most important instrument for the conclusion of political alliances." He lamented the view of Kemal that "Islamic unity […] is an unreal figment of the imagination which has never existed and will never be found to exist" and argued that "in the opinion of the generality of Moslems, this view of Mustapha Kemal Pasha […] is mistaken and arises from an extreme fondness for imitating Europeans."[68]

In Egypt, home of the bastion of Islamic orthodoxy al-Azhar University, the move seemed to arouse Islamic sentiment and emotions across society since the presence of the caliphate was considered a uniting factor for Muslims and a proof of the continuity of their history.[69] Those newspapers that were previously supportive of the separation of the powers of the caliph from that of the state were now in dismay, asking questions of the unity and solidarity of Muslims.[70] Attacks were launched by previously supportive people such as Muhammad Shaker, who wrote in the Egyptian *al-Muqattam* desperately asking "what is this violent hurricane?" He lamented the "crazy" decision, (that he had suggested himself less than two years earlier), and argued that given that "the caliphate was never a national system, even for a day," the "leaders of the Turkish republic had no right to decide to abolish it."[71] There were numerous calls for the caliphate to be re-established in Egypt, such as that from Sheikh Muhammad Husnayain who claimed in *al-Ahram* that "in it (Egypt) are great numbers of scholars of the *din*, students of knowledge and al-Azhar." Most other newspapers at this time carried similar opinions, such as *Masr* and *al-Siyassa*, but undoubtedly some of these imagined the future Egyptian caliph as one based upon the post-1922 secular model.[72]

It became clear this was not the idea of the *'ulama'*, who after a council meeting in al-Azhar on 25 March, 1924, released a notice in which they restated the orthodox view that the caliphate was the "general leadership in the *din* and worldly affairs," representative of the Prophet in "the protection of the *din* and the implementation of its laws." In fact, they claimed that "the caliphate of the leader Abdul Majed was not a legitimate caliphate," since "the *din* of Islam does not recognize the caliph by this meaning that it was restricted to" after the separation of its powers, as well as the fact that the oath of allegiance, or *bay'a*, was not given to him by the Muslims in a way that the *shari'a* recognized.[73] This, of course, raises the question of what the al-Azhar *'ulama'* had been doing since November 1922 as that would have been when the caliphate actually ceased being according to this understanding. However, this new ruling meant that no regard had to be paid to the deposed caliph, and in fact the Muslim *Umma* could commence the business of filling the position, to be discussed during a proposed conference to be held in Cairo, attended by representatives from across the Islamic world.

The various rulers of the time, including King Fu'ad, Sharif Hussain and ibn Saud, all feigned initial disinterestedness, though Hussain did claim to occupy the position for a short period after taking fealty from a number of supporters, but his "premature" pretensions were not taken seriously by those in his immediate vicinity, let alone the wider Muslim community.[74] In the words of one of the Egyptian contemporaries, Ahmed Shafiq, "it was agreed upon in Egypt that there was a necessity for the caliphate to exist in one form or another, and it was also agreed upon that Husain bin Ali would not be the caliph."[75] Some people held the opinion that the hands of the palace lay behind the al-Azhar *'ulama'*, with it "being said that the English wanted Fu'ad to become the caliph"[76] as a smear by his political opponents, namely the party of Liberal Constitutionalists, a highly ironic position given that the family who founded the party was acknowledged to be supportive of the English in

Egypt and was known to have a close relationship with the British Consul in Egypt, Lord Allenby.[77] The conflict between the King and Allenby's party was a constitutional and legal struggle that had little to do with al-Azhar, but the uproar that occurred following the publication of a book entitled "Islam and the Fundamentals of Ruling," which challenged the orthodox concept of caliphate, was used by both sides to undermine the other.[78]

The author of the book, Ali Abdul-Raziq, was an al-Azhar graduate from a political family who founded the Liberal Constitutionalist party. Due to family influence and affluence he was able to study in Oxford University before the outbreak of the First World War, but returned to Egypt to work as a judge in the *shari'a* courts. In the midst of the general mourning over the fate of the caliphate, and the aforementioned agreement in Egypt that the caliphate should be re-established in some form, Raziq's book flew in the face of Islamic orthodoxy and challenged the prevailing sentiments of the time. The caliphate, to Raziq, "has nothing to do with the *din*, and neither does the judiciary nor anything else from the governmental positions and centers of the state," which were "purely political issues," since the *din* "neither acknowledges it nor denies it, and has no commandments regarding it nor any prohibitions," but rather has only left it for us, to refer back to the rules of reason, the experiences of nations, and the fundamentals of politics."[79]

According to Raziq, the classical views of leadership were that the caliph either took his authority from God directly or from the *Umma*, and he compared this to the respective arguments of Hobbes and Locke.[80] In discussing some of the numerous Prophetic narrations relating to laws, the caliphate and the *bay'a*, he referred to the Bible and the words, attributed to Jesus, to "render to God what belongs to God, and render to Caesar what belongs to Caesar," explaining that "everything which is found in these narrations of the Prophet mentioning the leadership and the caliphate and the *bay'a* do not indicate anything more than what Jesus was indicating when he mentioned some rules of legislation about Caesar's government."[81] He also rejected several of the other proofs generally used to validate the orthodox position on the obligation of the caliphate, in particular by rejecting the concept of consensus wholesale.

Historically, the state at the time of the Prophet "was an Islamic unity and not a political unity," with "the leadership of the Messenger between them a religious leadership," and "their subservience to him was one of belief, not subservience to government and authority."[82] The rule of those who came after the death of the Prophet, including the first generation of Muslims, "was not connected to the Message and was not established upon the *din*," and rather than being an Islamic state it was in fact an imperial Arab entity.[83] The caliphate, according to Raziq, "was only ever, and still remains, a calamity upon Islam and Muslims."[84] He finished by urging that "nothing in the *din* prohibits the Muslims from competing with other nations," and that it was incumbent on Muslims to "destroy that obsolete system which they debase and submit themselves to," while building "the fundamentals of their leadership, and the system of government, upon the most modern of what has been produced by human minds."[85]

In conclusion, the book which Raziq claimed he had been working on for up to nine years was an attempt to sever any link between Muslims and the caliphate, and to reconstruct Islam in the image of European Christianity, but in this case without the pope. According to Mohammad 'Amara, up until that point secularism had been seen as a purely European solution to a European problem, and one that was rarely propagated in the Middle East except by a small section of the community known to blindly imitate Western culture and political trends. On the other hand, Raziq's position was one of a critic in "Islamic clothing," who saw Islam like Christianity, and the caliphate like the rule of the Church, and so for him secularism became "an Islamic solution to an Islamic problem."[86]

Naturally, Rida was amongst the first to denounce the book in *al-Manar* as "a devilish innovation" that "had never been said before by anyone who claimed to be within Islam, whether honest or not." In fact, the "Islamic caliphate is the best system known to man," and far from what was being claimed, "the Muslims were the greatest nation when they established it," and their decline had only come about as a result of leaving it.[87] He then encouraged the other *'ulama'* to denounce Raziq, since he had "denied the caliphate, and yet it was an Islamic institute which was obligated by the *shari'a*."[88]

Raziq was summoned in front of the Council of Grand Scholars in order for his book to be judged by twenty-four of his peers. On 12 November, 1925, a ruling was published with the unanimous decision to censure Raziq and expel him from the circle of scholars. The claims, such as that Islam was a purely spiritual religion, that the system of rule in Islam was unclear, or that the rule applied by the early generations of Muslim leaders were not based upon the *din*, were all considered heretical, and the council ruled that "it is enough that his innovation puts him in the ranks of the *khawarij* and not in the ranks of the masses of the Muslims,"[89] forcefully echoing the normative understanding regarding the caliphate and politics in traditional Islam.

Raziq countered that he had simply created "a new school of thought in the issue,"[90] and his family and friends from the Liberal Constitutionalists and newspapers such as the party mouthpiece *al-Siyassa* rallied against the ruling, claiming that the issue at stake was one of freedom of speech. He was feted by his supporters as the "Egyptian Luther," and his view was presented as a call for sovereignty to be returned to the *Umma*[91] which struck against the machinations of the Palace. Other major Egyptian politicians had very different opinions, such as Sa'ad Zaghloul, who said in private that he was "amazed first of all by how could a scholar of Islam write in this manner on this issue," and even though he had "read a lot from Orientalists and those similar to them," he "never came across anyone from them who attacked Islam with such an anger." In the end Zaghloul felt that Raziq was "ignorant of the fundamentals of the *din*," since "if not, then how could he claim that Islam is not a civilisation, and that it does not have a system suitable for rule?"[92] Whatever the demerits of the book, in reality the confrontation between the Liberal party and the government was largely based on other issues and it was simply used as a cause célèbre for political expediency.

Such was the level of sustained anger against the book that several refutations were written by scholars inside and outside of Egypt. From within Egypt the blind Azhari scholar Sheikh Yusuf al-Dijwi wrote a refutation of Raziq which was printed in the Egyptian paper *Al-Akhbar*, only to be subsequently ridiculed by Raziq's supporters, further increasing tensions. The Tunisian Mohammad ibn 'Ashur criticized the claim that there was a school of thought in Islam that the caliph takes his power from Allah, and disputed the analogy drawn with European thinkers Hobbes and Locke since no such dichotomy existed in Islamic thought.[93] Rather, "Islam is supported by the State" and "its state is part of it because of the mixing of *din* with the state *(dowla)*."[94] In its true meaning, the caliphate was "a religious pillar," or rather it was "the protector for all of the pillars of the *din*," and as for Raziq's accusation that it was a purely political creation, this was contradicted by the fact that the *bay'a* from the time of the first generation of Muslims onwards was always "pledged upon the Book of Allah and the traditions of the Prophet."[95]

The two most comprehensive and dynamic refutations came from Muhammad al-Khidr Hussein, a Tunisian scholar who had spent time in Syrian jails for agitating against the French, and Muhammad Bakhit, the then head of al-Azhar University. Bakhit rejected Raziq's claims from the angle that there was no Islamic evidence to back them up, reminding the reader that "it is not permitted to delve into these issues with reason alone" since *ijtihad* in Islamic jurisprudence was "to rely upon text from the Qur'an, or the *Sunna*, or consensus, or analogy."[96] He also decried Raziq's claim that the caliphate had only ever been a "calamity," and, contrary to Raziq's clear admiration for Europeans, thought it was the Muslims after the death of the Prophet who were "the first to practice that the *Umma* is the source of all authority, and that she chooses who rules her,"[97] and that this was laid down by the *shari'a*. Bakhit's book reads as a devastating critique, with almost one hundred pages dedicated to detailing out several political aspects of the state under the leadership of the Prophet, from dispute resolution to propaganda and diplomatic correspondence, with clear disdain for his target in evidence.

Al-Khidr Hussain, a close friend of Raziq, set aside personal feelings in his *Refutation of the Book "Islam and the Fundamentals of Ruling,"* which addressed the original arguments line by line with attention to detail. In his opinion, "the power authorised to the caliph is no greater than the power which any head of a constitutional government holds," with his election "only for a fixed period," which would be as long as he "establishes the rule of consultation as it should be" as well as "the spending of his efforts in protecting the rights of the *Umma* and the absence of his standing in the path of their freedom."[98] He, like Ibn 'Ashur, also rejected the comparison with European philosophers and schools of thought, specifically addressing the thought of Hobbes.

According to al-Khidr's understanding, Hobbes believed that every individual should submit to the authority of the King, whereas the scholars of Islam stated that the ruler is not to be obeyed unless he orders with the truth. Where Hobbes claimed that for the ruler to submit to an individual from his people contradicts the necessary nature of hierarchy, the scholars of Islam say that it is upon the ruler to submit to the lowest of the people in stature if that person orders him by the good and forbids him from the wrong. Additionally, Hobbes made religion submit to the King, whereas the scholars of Islam say that it is imperative that the rulers submit to the rule of Islam, meaning that which is specified in the Islamic sources or that which is derived from them by *ijtihad*.[99] Far from being an oppressive system, "Islam waged war against despotism from all sides,"[100] with the caliphate having "opened many lands and allowed them to taste the sweetness of justice after they had drunk the torment of oppression and despotism."[101]

Just like Bakhit, the process of what would constitute a valid *ijtihad* was emphasized by al-Khidr, with "the proofs of the *shari'a*" being "restricted to the Book, the *sunna*, consensus and analogy,"[102] as well as certain specific rules derived from these sources also being considered as acceptable evidence for any rulings. So if the Qur'an does not contain clear evidence pertaining to the obligatory nature of the caliphate, the proof can be derived definitively from the other sources that have been agreed upon. Any judgment or opinion based upon anything other than these sources was not considered an *ijtihad*, and far from being considered a "new school of thought," Raziq's opinions were roundly denounced as being derived from an un-Islamic *ijtihad*, and lost any religious credibility.

The limits of Islamic discourse and *ijtihad* were firmly upheld, and since the book fell outside the bounds of orthodoxy it was left to be feted by the secularists among his contemporaries, including Taha Hussain and Mohammad Husain Haikal, who generally argued that the Islamic caliphate had been a perversion of the religion, with the caliph acting as a despot, and that the Qur'an was a historical document which had to be read in context rather than a revelation upon which *ijtihad* could be based. The author himself retracted his views later in life, refusing several requests years later to allow the book to be reprinted, and according to his family he had been working upon a personal refutation at the time of his death.[103] While Souad Ali's thesis concludes that Raziq's book was and remains a significant contribution to the role of Islam within politics, the reality is that, from a normative perspective, Raziq's ideas were roundly derided at the time, and though the book played a role in the political melee that was Egypt in the 1920s, it remains recognized as a study that falls well outside the boundaries of accepted orthodoxy. However, Ali is correct in the sense that Raziq's thesis is the original source of those who contest that the caliphate is not an Islamic obligation, and is the genealogical root of such claims after the *khawarij*.

However, irrespective of the victory for the *'ulama'*, the damage to the proposed caliphate conference at the time had already been done. In addition to a one-year delay, it was ill-attended due to the widely held belief that its intention was to crown King Fu'ad as caliph, largely the result of the propaganda spread by other candidates and the controversy surrounding the publication of the book, which was promoted in the opposition papers as a conflict between al-Azhar, acting on behalf of the King's caliphal aspirations, against the ideas of Raziq. A rival conference in Mecca encouraged by Fu'ad's main competitor, Sharif Hussain, was also ineffective, and no decision of any merit was taken in either conference, nor in any that took place subsequently. Though Raziq's book had been soundly beaten in the academic field by the orthodoxy, it was utilized at the time to political advantage by some of the opponents of the monarchy in thwarting Fu'ad's supposed ambitions.

The Caliphate Debates Reviewed

Apart from the short-lived Kurdish rebellion and vocal denouncements of the abolition of the caliphate from across the Muslim world, there was no real program to respond to the fait accompli of Mustafa Kemal other than the push for conferences and congresses to resolve the question by electing a caliph, a response which had its roots in the beginning of the twentieth century, when various congresses had been either suggested or attempted, often with British backing.[104] For all their claims of disinterestedness, the British also continued to be exercised by the matter, with a dispatch from Cairo advising that in any election "British Islam" (in other words the Indian Muslims) would hold the decisive vote, pushing for the election of a caliph that would be "friendly to His Majesty's Government."[105] Such ideas were not new by any means and had been mooted earlier as the British strategy changed towards the last quarter of the nineteenth century from maintaining the integrity of the Ottoman State to ensuring that they were in the best position to inherit it. This was reflected in the thoughts of Robert Bulwer-Lytton who at one time held the position of Viceroy of India when he wrote in correspondence to Lord Salisbury in 1877 that the British strategy should not be to "share" in the "Russian spoilation of Turkey," but rather to look to inherit it completely, "keeping the destinies of the Sultan" under their control while "imperfectly reducing him to the level of the Pope."[106] Others had pushed for an Arab caliphate, with a series of letters in *The Times* from the same year arguing that the Ottoman caliphate was a "usurpation" and that the position should be transferred to a "more pliant hand" such as the Sharif of Mecca at the time.[107]

In sum, the original congresses being held at the turn of the century were generally intended as a pitch for either an Arab caliph or a more spiritual role for the caliphate. The conferences held after the abolition of the caliphate were to look for a re-establishment of the position, an entirely different proposition since the original aim was to either reform or sideline the institution, something unnecessary now it had been abolished. However, various meetings went ahead and a congress was convened in 1924 as far away from the seat of the last caliphate as Indonesia, where the Indonesian *'ulama'* gathered to call for the re-establishment of the caliphate while proposing that Mustafa Kemal be elected caliph,[108] a position he consistently refused to consider. From one perspective, Kemal was the pragmatic choice for those who wanted to see the caliphate tied to political power and independence.

However, there were at least thirteen different candidates mentioned for the vacant post, ranging from political rulers and monarchs to resistance fighters and Ottoman officials.[109] One notable (re)entry was Sheikh Ahmad al-Sanussi, who began to actively seek the position of caliph from the end of 1924. His secretary claimed that his image of the position was that of becoming a new pope with the caliphate the equivalent of the Vatican.[110] Others were looking to cement their own position as monarchs and solidify their regional prestige and influence, such as the Kings of Morocco and Egypt and Sharif Hussain of Mecca. As mentioned previously, the main competition was between Fu'ad and Hussain, with Hussain's subsequent expulsion from Saudi Arabia ending his challenge. Fu'ad, on the other hand, had many domestic opponents, from both liberal and religious backgrounds. A prominent dissenting voice was that of al-Dijwi, who refused to accept Fu'ad as caliph unless he intended to implement *shari'a* law,[111] which was never seriously considered by the Egyptian palace. In reality, there were no serious contenders for the position of caliph as intended by someone like al-Dijwi, who saw it as an active and powerful role representing Islam's political unity. The position competed over was one devoid of any meaning beyond that of a spiritual leadership (if it even reached that extent), and fast becoming a title rather than a role. In other words, the various congresses and suggestions were not aimed at re-establishing a caliphate, but merely electing a caliph. Their failure was encapsulated in the comment of one of the attendees to the Cairo conference, who exclaimed that "if there is one thing that can be said about this congress it is that it demonstrated to the entire world the absolute collapse of the caliphate."[112]

In a book printed in Paris in 1924 simply entitled *Caliphate*, the Indian Mohammad Baraka called for the election of a spiritual caliph drawn from outside the rulers of the day. Amongst the reasons given was that "public opinion and feeling in the non-Muslim nations stands clearly against the political unity of the Islamic world," since "the word Islamic Unity in these days is a symbol that scares the European world."[113] Though Baraka's reasoning that the selection of a pope-like figure may have been more palatable to the imperialists was most likely correct, this would also mean a caliph that would have been of little use to all those interested. The caliphate that was needed was one that could unite and liberate, and possessed the ability and vision to enact reforms. In other words, one that fulfilled the original conditions and the ideal theory, and if not then it was simply seen as a burden by those who carried it. By the end of the 1920s, the issue of electing a caliph had lost all momentum, and though prominent ex-Khilafat activists such as Showkat Ali tried to keep it on the agenda it was ultimately left sidelined and off the agenda by the time of the 1931 General Islamic Congress in Palestine.

To the Kemalists the caliphate was a sign of backwardness, a reminder of an Islamic civilization that had no place in the modern scientific world. The ideas of Pan-Islamism were "erroneous" and utopian, and Kemal exclaimed that "neither Turkey nor the handful of men she possesses could be placed at the disposal of the caliph so that he might fulfill the mission attributed to him, namely, to found a State comprising the whole of Islam." To put an end to the caliphate was to "put an end to the catastrophes into which the people had been dragged by following those who deceive themselves and misjudge our real rank and position in the world."[114] Turkey would have its independence, and its freedom from carrying the responsibility of the rest of the *Umma* on its shoulders.

With the Ottoman caliph no longer available as a uniting symbol, the Indian Khilafat movement soon fizzled out. The caliphate had represented Islam and Islamic unity, and could be used to forge a distinct alternative center of allegiance to the colonialist administration. Azad even tried to replace the caliphate symbol with the Turkish one and wrote a series of articles in April 1924 entitled "The Khilafat Problem and the Turkish Republic," in which he claimed that the act of the Kemalists had merely rectified the previous unsatisfactory division of spiritual and temporal powers of the caliph, and that the most powerful independent Islamic government automatically has the caliphate vested in it. Though the president of Turkey had not been formally recognized as the caliph, the caliphate nevertheless continued to reside with the Turkish government.[115] Over time, Azad adopted Indian nationalism directly, embraced the leadership of Gandhi, rejected the idea of a separate homeland for Muslims and instead advocated a secular united India based upon socialist principles. However, it should be noted that other more orthodox members of the Khilafat movement did not follow Azad in his re-imagining of the caliphate or embracing of secularism within a united India, though it is true that many were not in favor of separatism.

Rida's prime concern was not nationalistic, but rather with maintaining some form of temporal Islamic power, with his caliphate, one of reform and *ijtihad*, providing a model based upon a return to the original sources and philosophy of Islamic government in order to reverse the decline of the Islamic nations. As it became clear that there was to be no renewed caliph, and that there was no real support for his proposed seminary to train future candidates for the position, he gave his backing to the nascent state run by Ibn Saud, and printed literature for the budding Wahabi movement through *al-Manar*, believing it to be the most independent and reform-minded regime at the time. Ever concerned with the loss of independence, after failing to unite and reform around a new caliphate, Rida addressed what he considered to be the next most pressing issue of his time, Palestine and the Zionist movement.

Most of the *'ulama'* that had risen up with him against "Islam and the Fundamentals of Ruling" faded back into the confines of al-Azhar, but without the author amongst their ranks. For them, the caliphate was a representative of Islam and the proof of the existence of the *shari'a*, and its presence, in whatever guise, was enough to satisfy them that the *din* was intact. Once it was abolished, the limit of their meaningful engagement was through academic refutations. Though they defined the limits of discourse around Islamic orthodoxy, they were unable to provide any *ijtihad* within those parameters that would reverse the situation. The more dynamic characters amongst them, such as Sheikh al-Khidr Hussain, remained committed to the public defense of Islam in the face of secular intrusions, writing refutations of other prominent thinkers of the time such as Taha Hussain.

For both the proponents and opponents of the caliphate, theoretically the political authority lay with the *Umma*. While the activists and other *'ulama'* believed that this authority was represented in their theories of a reconstructed caliphate based upon the original Islamic sources, the secularists and those with them equated the caliph with Kingship and the caliphate with theological obscurity no longer relevant or useful at the beginning of the twentieth Century, if it ever had been. With power in the Muslim world generally held by those in the second camp, whose philosophy was mainly derived from imported thought and alien paradigms, Mark Wegner's conclusion, that "the failure to salvage the caliphate robbed the Middle East of a culturally authentic framework within which to construct a genuinely modern political order,"[116] rings true from one perspective, while at the same time it can be argued the caliphate had basically lost its appeal and relevancy for a significant constituency as a result of the events of the era.

The abolition of the caliphate and the failure to revive it reduced the potency of the caliphate as a political symbol, and the caliph who was once seen to represent the last independent Muslim power was relegated to an irrelevancy as the secular Turkish state established by Kemal strode energetically to take its place amongst newly formed nations, its final image being that of an impotent tool used by the imperial powers. While nationalism, the nation-state and secularism stood tall as symbols of independence and modernity, the caliphate was at best a symbol of the past, at worst an image of the impotency of Islamic politics in the modern era, easily manipulated by foreign agendas in the way previous caliphs were manipulated domestically. However, the failure to revive or re-establish the caliphate did not remove the issue from Muslim discourse eternally, since as Bakhit mentioned, "the claim of the extinction of the caliphate in Islam is not correct, and rather the only thing that has become extinct is the presence of the caliph, and as for the caliphate it still remains obligatory upon the *Umma*."[117]

3

GLOBAL UNITY THROUGH A NATION STATE

BANNA, THE MUSLIM BROTHERHOOD
AND AUTHORITY UNDER OCCUPATION

Dear Brothers, you are neither a welfare organisation, nor a political party, nor a local association with strictly limited aims. Rather you are a new spirit making its way into the heart of this nation—reviving it with the Qur'an; a new light dawning, dispelling the darkness of materialism through the knowledge of Allah.

Hassan al-Banna[1]

A few years after the formal abolition of the Ottoman caliphate and the failure of subsequent caliphate conferences, a young man sat listening to the Azhari Sheikh Yusuf al-Dijwi commenting on the "appearance of poison" in Muslim societies, and the weakness of the "Islamic forces in front of those who would conspire against them." The Sheikh lamented how despite his own prominent efforts in refuting the work of Ali Abdul-Raziq in the Egyptian press in 1925, as well as the efforts of the other *'ulama'* of Azhar university, they had been unable to stem the tide of the un-Islamic currents, and he had since gathered around him a group of scholars under the banner of "The Revival of Islam," participating in various conferences and writing letters and booklets to support this aim, all to no avail. There was no benefit in these efforts, and "it would suffice a person to work for himself and thereby save himself

63

from these testing times."[2] As was mentioned in the Qur'anic meaning "Allah does not burden a soul more than it can bear."[3]

The words agitated the young man into a passionate reply, proclaiming complete disagreement with the sheikh, stating his belief that "the issue should not mean that we are simply weak, and remain inactive, running away from difficulties." Rather than seclusion and separation from society, the situation called for a greater effort and attempt to gather the people around Islamic teachings, something which was attainable "since they are a Muslim people [...] overflowing with belief."[4] The junior protagonist was called Hassan al-Banna, who went on to form the Muslim Brotherhood in 1928, with a small number of companions, upon a pledge with God that they would "be soldiers in the *da'wa* (call) to Islam," believing that was the path to achieve "the life for the country and the honour for the *Umma*."[5] Though more than one hundred Islamic groups were established in Egypt and elsewhere between 1927 and 1945, the majority with the aim of combating Westernization and reviving the *shari'a*,[6] it is this group that remains as one of the largest Islamic movements today with analysis of its aims and methods an issue of contention from the time of its founding until the present.

Established in the Egyptian port town of Ismailia as a result of the implorations made to him by six men motivated by his charisma, al-Banna would subsequently state that his group had "made the idea of caliphate and the work for its return at the head of its method."[7] Due to statements such as this, writers such as Tariq al-Bishry have accused the Brotherhood of putting their own aims ahead of the national goal of liberation. Since the caliph was previously claimed to be a tool in the hands of European powers, al-Banna was actually aiding colonial interests and was being used to buttress King Fu'ad against nationalists such as the Wafd party.[8] This view is debated by Dr. Zakaria Buyumi, believing that the British were more concerned with preventing the return of any caliphate, as highlighted in an official Foreign Office telegraph expressing displeasure at Fu'ad's attempts to adopt the mantle of the caliph since it was held to be "xenophobic."[9] Rather, since the position of the caliphate in orthodox Islam was well established, it was obvious that any Islamic thinkers would be compelled to formulate some form of response to the abolition of the Ottoman Sultanate.[10]

There is disagreement over how seriously the intent of al-Banna's statement should be taken. Musa Husaini claims that the Brotherhood had put the caliphate at the head of their reform program, but recognized that it would need to be preceded by a number of steps.[11] This opinion is basically taking the words of al-Banna verbatim, something that Richard Mitchell, the first Western academic to study the group, rejects, since in his view the main goal of the Brotherhood was to create an "Islamic system," and they were therefore indifferent to the caliphate or any kind of Islamic state. The creation of a moral order and the implementation of the *shari'a* were the real concerns, irrespective of the political order through which this was achieved,[12] with other issues considered as empty rhetoric. Mitchell's opinion seems at odds with the wealth of comments by al-Banna regarding an Islamic state, and though his argument that the Brotherhood was pragmatic in terms of their view on the structure of government has merit, the accusation of indifference is too strong. More likely is the view of Ahmad Moussali that the caliphate represented the Muslim unity that the Brotherhood were aspiring to, and was a sign of their commitment to Islam, but due to the perceived difficulty in its establishment, it would be more practical to first establish an Islamic state, a political entity that would implement the *shari'a* working within the nation state.[13] It is for that reason that Anwar al-Jundi claims that the caliphate was not articulated as the focus in their discourse, but instead a general call to Islam and Islamic unity was more prevalent.[14] According to Hamid Enayat, the idea of an Islamic state was an alternative to the caliphate as a reaction to the secularization of Turkey and a need to resolve the conflict between the concept of a universal Islamic government and a modern nation state,[15] another view which essentially places al-Banna as someone willing to work within the political constructs and constraints he faced.

All of these opinions contain varying elements of truth, with belief, aspirations, a sense of practicality, pragmatism and a weighing of priorities all playing their part in how the ideas and discourse of the Muslim Brotherhood were formed. Though the re-establishment caliphate was stated as the ultimate aim of the group, it played a minor role in the public discourse of their leader. This is not surprising given the environment in which the Brotherhood was established, al-Banna's chosen philosophy of not working against the established national polity while they remained under occupation and his *ijtihad* that the root of the problem was individual corruption and the moral decline of society. His group was emerging in the midst of a series of failed initiatives that sought to elect a caliph, which came to be seen as a title devoid of its legalistic meaning or even its power as a symbol of unity. Though the abolition of the caliphate affected al-Banna deeply, the route to Islamic revival was clearly not to be found in the attempts to reinstitute a caliph in the manner suggested by those seeking to either anoint an existing monarch or by establishing a spiritual pope-like figure with no temporal power. By looking at Banna's words in the political context of his time, it will be seen that the role of the caliphate in the discourse of the leaders of the Brotherhood was never more than a utopian symbol, a figurehead rather than an alternative system, representing a unity unachievable as long as the country remained under the political and social restrictions imposed by colonialism.

While the attempts at a nominal caliphate remained considered as an irrelevancy to revival and therefore largely absent from the discourse of the time, the Brotherhood instead sought to posit and re-articulate the idea of a universal Islamic polity within the emerging nation-state framework, working within post-First World War paradigms rather than seeking a radical rupture to the past. However, this was born of pragmatic considerations, with the goal of Muslim unity under a single Islamic polity remaining as part of al-Banna's orthodoxy, but peripheral to his discourse, as he sought to insert Islam into a political medium that considered it to be largely irrelevant.

The Brotherhood—Its beginning and aims

To understand the early Muslim Brotherhood is to understand the personality of Hassan al-Banna, its founding leader and dominating personality up until his assassination in 1949. Born in 1906 and raised in a household with strong Islamic sentiments, under a father who was an Imam as well as an author of Islamic work, al-Banna not only memorized the Qur'an during his youth but was also a regular attendee at the various study circles held by different *'ulama'* (religious scholars) in his community. He was also influenced by the spiritual traditions of Sufism, to the extent that he was a member of a local Sufi order, the Hassafiyya, that was to leave a lasting impression on him. At the same time, he did not exclude himself from supporting various demonstrations against the British rule in Egypt.[16]

The Muslim Brotherhood was formed in a period that saw the decline of the caliphate from the public consciousness across the Muslim world.

Though the academic struggle primarily within the Islamic and journalistic circles between those upholding the orthodox Islamic view of the necessity of the caliphate, such as Rashid Rida and Muhammad al-Khidr Hussain, and those opposing it, specifically Ali Abdul-Raziq, had resulted in the expulsion of the latter from al-Azhar and the rejection of his ideas, this proved to be a pyrrhic victory. The majority of the Muslim masses, whether in India, Morocco or Egypt, had not risen up together in sustained outcry against the abolition of the caliphate or to demand its reinstatement, nor were any practical moves made for its re-establishment other than the cynical jockeying for prestige and position between King Fu'ad and Sharif Hussain by way of their respective caliphate conferences. Even though the theory of the caliphate had been reasserted as an integral part of orthodox Islam, it made little difference if society was not concerned with following Islam as a community, orthodox or otherwise. Indeed, the rise in prominence of not only Raziq, but writers promoting European-style secularism and culture, such as Taha Hussain, and women's liberation, such as Salama Musa, or even articles which questioned the fundamental tenets of the Islamic belief like Amil Zaydan's "Freedom of Thought," published in 1924,[17] were all seen by people like al-Banna as contributing to the moral decline and general trend away from Islam in Arab society generally and Egyptian society specifically.

The issue of the caliphate may have also appeared of little consequence while many of the Muslim lands remained without real independence from the colonial powers, with Egypt, still under the occupation of Imperial Britain, being a prominent example. The struggle for the independence of Muslim lands had been the issue of importance for thinkers such as Rida before the caliphate was abolished, as exemplified previously by his comments that Muslim peoples supported the Turks "for the sake of their military power," which forced the Europeans to accept their rights of independence, irrespective of whether the caliphate was invested within them or not.[18] However, while the caliphate was in existence, there was the possibility of its reformation, which would ideally aid an Islamic revival, and the hope that a reinvigorated Islamic power could lead the liberation of occupied lands. With its abolition, this possibility was removed from consideration. In fact, its removal made it seem to those who remained committed to it either an impossibility or at the very least a distant goal, with liberation from occupation an immediate concern, meaning that no political aims regarding the structure of government could be practically realized without its achievement. The failed conferences and manoeuvres to claim the title for either personal glorification or a sense of spiritual fulfillment also cemented its irrelevancy in the minds of Islamically-minded political reformers and activists at the time.

Accordingly, al-Banna did not mention the issue of the collapse of the caliphate as the central or singular cause that stimulated his thinking about the need to achieve reform, but rather his awareness of immoral behavior and bad manners in the Egyptian capital pushed him to think about how the situation could be improved. In adopting the opinion that moral decay was the cause of societal and political decline, al-Banna was also following some of the ideas previously articulated by Rida. Though there were a few Islamic groups at the time focused on the improvement and perfection of morals, they seemed insufficient in the face of the movement to liberalize society, which he believed was gathering pace in the wake of the abolition of the caliphate and the "separation of the state from the religion,"[19] or in other words the secularization of society.

In the face of this apparent decline in public morality and the exclusion of Islam from the political arena, al-Banna felt that talks held within the mosques were not a sufficient method to engage the wider society, especially considering mosque attendance was generally poor and limited to certain sections of society. As al-Jundi mentions, even if the fall of the caliphate was considered as the first challenge obstructing the road of the caller to Islam, it was no longer considered sufficient for the revivalist movement to be limited to words and articles, but rather there was a need for a new stage—that of culturing and education.[20] After his discussion with Sheikh al-Dijwi, whose ultimately failed activism for the sake of the caliphate institution along with that of Rida must have been well known to al-Banna, who was close to both of them, al-Banna started his own magazine called *al-Fath* or "The Opening"[21] as an attempt to address wider society as well as participating with other movements such as The Muslim Youth, who used sport as a method to gather youth with the intention to educate them about Islam. However, within a short time taking part in the sport itself became the main focus rather than concern over the religion,[22] making the group an inappropriate vehicle for any reform-minded activism. As an alternative, al-Banna and a group of his friends formed the Hassafi Welfare Society, a reform organization named after the Sufi order that they had pledged their allegiance to, with the aim of building the moral character of people while also trying to check certain missionary activities taking place at the time.[23] It was this group that was the precursor to the Muslim Brotherhood.

Interrupting his life at this point, in 1927 al-Banna was assigned as a teacher in a primary school in the port town of Ismailia. Taking up this post entailed separation from his group of peers in Cairo, as well as becoming estranged from the circle of influential religious figures that he had grown accustomed to frequenting while in the capital. Ismailia at the time appeared completely dominated by British rule and culture, with attendance at mosques limited to the elderly. As had been his practice in Cairo, al-Banna took to the cafes to preach to the general public, giving short talks and reminding people of their religious obligations and lost moral character.[24] He continued doing this until he had attracted a number of youth to his call, and in March of 1928 six of them came to his house complaining to him about the state of the Muslims, who were seen to have no honor or position, and whose wealth was being exploited by the colonialist foreigner. They called upon him to be a leader over them, imploring him that "we cannot comprehend the path as you are able to comprehend it, or know the way to serve the country and *din* (religion) and the *Umma* as you know."[25]

And so the Muslim Brotherhood was born, not so much out of design but more out of the zeal of a group of youth touched by the preaching of a charismatic young leader who was trying his best to reconnect Islamic teachings with wider society and the younger generation specifically. The group was founded upon the idea of the helplessness of the Muslims in Egypt who remained under the colonial influence of Britain, the decline of public morality and the removal of religious influence from the public space. It cannot be said that in such a situation al-Banna founded the Brotherhood with a clearly considered and deliberate goal in mind, but rather the pledge he and his followers founded the organization on was that they would "be soldiers in the call to Islam, and in that is the life for the country and the honour for the *Umma*." As subsequently explained, it was a pledge to "revive brotherhood" and to "work for Islam and Jihad in its path."[26] With such a vague statement of intent at the moment of birth, it was perhaps unsurprising al-Banna was complaining years later that their "revival remains unclear, no styles, no goals, no methods and no program."[27]

In fact, al-Banna later declared that the work of the Brotherhood would proceed through three stages to achieve change. The first stage was to be "defining the call which specifies its idea and clarifies its goal," which confirms that the establishment of the Brotherhood was more a reactive decision based upon the awareness of problems in society rather than a deliberate development based upon a critical analysis of reality and how the issues of the day should have been confronted. The second stage was that of recruitment and mass mobilization, or "the formation of rows in which the believers can join together," with the final stage being that of "implementation," the natural progress to the establishment of an Islamic state. Each stage would take approximately ten years, with the first taking place roughly between 1928 and 1938.[28]

With such an undefined structuring and political basis, it is natural that the Brotherhood's development was carried by the ideas of their leader as they developed, rather than any collectively agreed political program. It is apparent that from the beginning al-Banna believed in Islam as a comprehensive system, an "all embracing concept regulating every aspect of life," detailing "a solid and rigorous order"[29] for its adherents whose neglect had led to the decline of the Muslim nations, perhaps explaining his preference for the use of the word *nahda* (revival) more than "reform", "modernising" or "civilising."[30] One of the consistent messages held by the Muslim Brotherhood from their inception has been the emphasis that "the right of the Qur'an" entailed that it was "to be made the basis for the laws governing the life."[31] This went beyond individual reform since Islam had "made the government a pillar from amongst its foundations," and was a "rule and implementation" and a "legislation and teaching" as well as being "a law and judgement" with each couplet considered inseparable.[32]

The public call of the Brotherhood developed to encompass two central goals—the first being independence from the colonialists, or "freeing the Islamic homeland from all foreign authority" since freedom was "a natural right belonging to every human being which only the unjust oppressor would deny." Once the homeland had been liberated, the second goal would be "the establishment of an Islamic state within this homeland," which would "apply its social regulations, advocate its sound principles and carry its mission to the whole of mankind." Without the establishment of this state, every Muslim would be living in sin and "responsible before Allah for the failure and slackness in establishing it."[33]

However, regardless of the stated aims, al-Banna was essentially individualistic in his approach, which focused mainly on personal and social reform rather than large political programs or any schemes for revolution. The first recorded speech given by al-Banna was addressing a Muslim youth institute, where he identified the most important areas to be utilized in helping education, upbringing and culturing as the home, the school, and the (public) environment.[34] Al-Banna believed that there could be "no revival for a nation without manners," and that "the pillar of revival is culturing" such that "culturing of the *Umma* must take priority" until "she understands her rights completely."[35] In other words, the corruption of society had become rooted in individual corruption, and the way to revive the nation was for the masses to return to the morals of the past. This entailed that occupation of the land by the colonialists, poor governance, economic decay and intellectual decline were all secondary, or at least could not be reversed until the individual character of the people was reformed, and this reformed individual could then undertake the work for liberation and subsequent revival of the nation.

The Ijtihad of Al-Banna—Unity, the Islamic State and the Caliphate

As mentioned in the introduction, any process of *ijtihad* carried out would be an attempt to find a solution from the Islamic evidences to deal with a particular reality confronting the *mujtahid*, or person carrying out the *ijtihad*. In other words, trying to work out a solution to a problem while remaining true to the authenticity of the religion. Therefore a *mujtahid's* understanding of the reality in front of them is central to seeing the progression of their thought process.

The establishment of the Brotherhood fell in the period directly following the abolition of the Ottoman caliphate, with an Egyptian government ostensibly independent, but in reality still in the control of the British High Commissioner, backed by the remaining military forces. Formal independence had been granted in 1922 at the end of the three year Egyptian revolution which had broken out after national leaders like Sa'ad Zaghloul had been exiled by the British to the often used detention island of Malta (the twentieth century equivalent of Guantanamo Bay where the leaders of the Indian Khilafat movement were also being kindly hosted), but even this official declaration was limited by four British-imposed conditions: the security of imperial communications, defense of Egypt against aggression, protection of foreign interests and minorities, and continued British administration of the Sudan. In 1923, a new constitution, modeled on Western parliamentary systems with constitutional monarchies, was introduced into the Egyptian political landscape. The power to dissolve parliament was placed in the hands of the King (formally known as the Sultan), and hence the stage was set for internal competition between the various existing and newly formed political entities and the monarchy all under the watchful eye of the (ostensibly former) colonial power.

In this manner the energies of independence movements, such as the Wafd party led by Zaghloul, became embroiled in competition within the "democratic" system, focused internally on political rivalry rather than on the question of the full liberation of the nation. This political disunity and unrest is reflected in the numerous times the parliament was either suspended or dissolved, such as directly after the Wafd's overwhelming victory in the first parliamentary elections held in 1924, as well as the replacement of the constitution with another in 1930 for a period of five years. It is quite logical that the partisanship which engulfed the political classes in this period was often observed as being to the detriment of the interests of the country as a whole.[36]

The question of political unity occupied al-Banna greatly, with division seen as one of the critical reasons for the dissolution of the Islamic state previously. These factors included "political differences, partisanship, and the struggle for supremacy and prestige," even though there was a "strict prohibition against this in Islam," alongside differences in "schools of thought" also contributing to internal weakness.[37] Disunity at a time of occupation, with the "division of the nation into parties which engage in mutual throat-cutting" and other forms of party-based politics, led to the paralyzation of the nation and an inability to move forward coherently. Divisions were seen to be ultimately shaped "by their personal motives and goals" in accordance with "selfish interests" which would allow "the enemy to take advantage of this," with the continued British influence seen as "encouraging this fire to blaze all the more fiercely."[38] For these reasons al-Banna declared opposition to the multi-party system, believing it to be detrimental to the real cause, as he perceived it.

Though against the party politics that dominated the political arena in the post-1923 constitution era, the Muslim Brotherhood sought to unite with as many factions as possible, all pursuant to the ultimate goal of liberation. The monarchy as a symbol of Egyptian pride was part of this, with al-Banna ordering workers in Ismailia to explicitly go out to greet King Fu'ad during his visit to the town in order that the "foreigners," or British, could know the respect and love they had for their leader.[39] During the first ten years of the work of the Brotherhood, where much of the focus was on challenging the various missionary activities taking place in Egypt, the Consultative Council of the group wrote to Fu'ad mentioning that on behalf of the Brotherhood they were raising the "signs of loyalty and sincerity to the throne" while encouraging him to defend Islam by monitoring the missionary schools and removing permissions from any hospital or school proven to be engaging in missionary activities.[40]

This relationship continued initially with Fu'ad's successor, Farouk, who became King in 1936, seen by al-Banna as an opportunity to achieve results quickly if he could be convinced of the call of the Brotherhood. Arrangements were made for a meeting to take place in Alexandria of the same year, where the two would shake hands after a Friday prayer.[41] Events like these and the gathering of the Brotherhood at the gates of the royal palace after Farouk's inauguration to congratulate and demonstrate loyalty to the King while simultaneously calling out "God is Great" and "the Qur'an is the constitution of the World"[42] is what led analysts like al-Bishry to claim that the organization was simply a tool to protect the monarchy and entrenched interests. However, as Lia has discussed, the relationship between the two was not so straightforward, and in fact the attempts to imbue the King with an Islamic image as the "Righteous King" and the adoption of the title "*Amir al-Mominin*," or "Leader of the Believers," was rejected by the Brotherhood.[43] This view, however, does not discount that the Brotherhood was utilized by the monarchy and subsequent governments throughout their history, due to a combination of their political naivety and their pragmatic approach, which generally results in a perpetuation of the status quo.

Farouk had supposedly begun to pursue his own claim to the caliphate by 1938. According to Foreign Office dispatches regarding the possibility that he may seek the title there was a rumor that the foundation for his claim was by virtue of the "Right to the Sword", meaning he had been bequeathed the title at the request of the exiled last caliph,

Wahidudeen.[44] Oddly enough, when the Turkish government were made aware of his possible claim, they simply suggested that the power of the caliph was purely civil and not spiritual, a reverse of their position between 1922 and 1924, thereby avoiding any claims to owe allegiance to the potential future title-holder. In any case, the British were not keen on the symbolism being revived and tried to dissuade any further developments, and public apathy to the suggestion at the time meant that the issue did not develop further. Al-Banna addressed the issue indirectly at the time during the fifth annual conference that the group convened, claiming that although they had made the idea of the caliphate their main goal, they believed that "it requires many preparatory issues which are necessary to have" and that "the direct step to bring back the caliphate requires many steps beforehand,"[45] an implicit rejection of the call of Farouk to be anointed as the caliph. The relationship between the monarchy and the Brotherhood would subsequently sour to the point of open animosity in the years prior to al-Banna's assassination.

The reality is that al-Banna viewed unity between Muslims in the face of the British or other colonial powers as an issue of utmost priority. This entailed working with the current system as far as possible to achieve the objective of liberation. Though the Brotherhood was against some aspects of the political arena, such as the multiplicity of political parties, al-Banna was not fundamentally against the system. Since the Egyptian constitution explicitly mentioned that Islam was the official religion of the country, he felt that this entailed that legislation should be based upon the Qur'an and other Islamic sources. In fact, al-Banna even argued that the constitutional system was "derived from the Islamic system" since it agreed with the principles of "individual freedom, *shura* (consultation), the people being the source of authority and the responsibility of the ruler in front of the people." For this reason, "the system of constitutional rule is the closest system of rule in the world at the moment to Islam,"[46] with the claim that "the key principles that the Egyptian constitution are based upon do not contradict with the principles of Islam."[47]

Though the constitution was not necessarily in direct contradiction with Islam, it was left ambiguous enough to draw criticism from al-Banna. It was this lack of clarity which allowed the laws which governed the society to run contrary to certain explicit Islamic imperatives and prohibitions. In an article written in 1936, al-Banna complains that although Islam was the official religion of the state, "almost everything about general life in Egypt contradicts Islam" with the social system ostensibly "officially Islamic" and yet in reality "far from the situation that Islam prescribed it to mould the personality of the people,"[48] with the drinking of alcohol, gambling and relations outside of marriage all left permissible.

With all of the various shortcomings of the system, the Brotherhood considered that it was essentially Islamic, with the problem lying in the implementation rather than in the principles, so they would often take the position of advisor to those in power rather than as direct opponents. For this reason al-Banna counseled that the denigration or mocking of any government from amongst the Islamic governments or institutions (Egypt amongst them) would be a "big mistake", since he considered that their position was either "working by Islam for Islam within the limits of their circumstances and ability" or "they are constrained by Islam, gathering around it" perhaps due to the pressure of groups like the Brotherhood.[49] As noted previously, this naïve approach to the political classes of the time along with their non-confrontational stance opened them up to the criticism of effectively maintaining rather than challenging the status quo. On the other hand, al-Banna viewed the primary conflict at the time as one with colonialism rather than the nominally independent governments. That he didn't recognize these governments as tools of the colonizers could be taken as further evidence of the view that considers the Brotherhood at best as lacking political awareness.

This sort of critical advice is exemplified by al-Banna's letter to the Prime Minister of the time, al-Nahhas Basha, in June of 1936, criticizing al-Nahhas's praise of the "genius" of Mustafa Kemal, which went beyond military plaudits to credit the way he had built the modern Turkish state. Al-Banna exclaimed that the position of the Turks "with respect to Islam, its laws, teachings and legislation" was well known, that they had turned the caliphate into a republic and removed the Islamic laws in entirety, something blameworthy since it is mentioned in the Qur'an that "whoever does not rule by whatever Allah has revealed then they are the disbelievers."[50] On top of that they openly claimed in their constitution that they were "a government without a *din*," and subsequently freely introduced a host of legislation opposite to Islamic teachings.[51]

Another important conflict between the Brotherhood and the government was at the time of the Anglo-Egyptian agreement of 1936, which allowed the continued presence of British troops in the Suez canal region. This fundamentally contradicted one of the central goals of the Brotherhood—liberation from foreign influence and occupation whether military or otherwise. In response, al-Banna wrote a specific treatise entitled "Towards the Light" which was sent to several leaders across the Muslim world, and is particularly illuminating with respect to the *ijtihad* that he was following.

Al-Banna clearly laid out the priorities ahead of the leaders and their nations, the first step being "to liberate the nation from its political bonds" in order that it may "regain its lost independence and sovereignty." Once liberation had been achieved, the second goal would be the reconstruction of the nation so that it could "follow its own path among other nations" competing with them "in its progress towards social perfection."[52] The issue of liberation again is highlighted as the primary problem, with development only being possible once the nation had achieved its independence and opportunity to develop in a manner which matched their culture and history.

However, the political currents of the time, particularly amongst the elites, were more inclined towards foreign, specifically Western, modes of politics, a natural consequence of colonialism. Hence when al-Banna offered possible solutions, he emphasized his belief was that "the way of Islam, its principles and rules, is the only way which ought to be followed." Internal political divisions meant that the countries "political foundations" were "being destroyed by dictatorships," while "strange ideologies and widespread revolutions are undermining its social foundations,"[53] a double swipe at both the monarchies established as the primary vessels for ruling and the spread of Western influences, such as secularism and liberalism, championed by some of the political parties.

Al-Banna's view of religion and state echoed that of the Azhari scholars in their debates with Raziq. He criticized "the study of the Western Renaissance" by some of the Arab leaders, and the Western conviction that it had only been achieved "by overthrowing religion, destroying the churches and freeing themselves from papal authority." Though he concedes that this may be true in the case of the European situation, he argued that "it could never be the case for the Islamic nations, since the nature of Islamic teachings" is "unlike that of any other religion" with the jurisdiction of the religious authorities being "defined and limited" and "powerless to alter (Islam's) statutes or to subvert its institutions."[54]

In conclusion, what happened in the West in terms of secularization and the separation of religion and state could not be applied to Islam and the Islamic nations.

A further factor which meant that the Islamic nations could not simply follow the trajectory of the European Renaissance and the separation of the religious clergy from political affairs is that, though terms such as "religious authority" had "crept into" the Arabic vernacular "by way of imitation", the usage in terms of the meaning behind the word "clergy" was "peculiar to the West." According to Islamic understanding, the "religious authority" would include all Muslims "from the least to the most outstanding of them," with none having a right over the other in terms of access to religious interpretation and *ijtihad*.[55]

Though secularism was a construct alien to the Islamic nations, and incompatible with al-Banna's view of revival based upon Islamic principles, the question of nationalism and its role at the time presented an interesting dilemma. As confirmed, the primary goal for the Brotherhood was the liberation of the people from colonialism, and then subsequently the reconstruction and revival of the Muslim nations. Liberation came first since without independence there could be no political progress upon an independent path free from foreign influence. The main idea propagated as the foundation of the liberation struggles during the era of colonialism was that of nationalism, of both secular and religious varieties. The concept of the caliphate should naturally conflict with the concept of the nation state, irrespective of its ideological foundation, given that the first is a universal state whose citizenship is not based upon language or ethnicity within a geographical location whereas the second is normally defined according to those very characteristics.

This clash between the idea of a united Muslim *Umma* and separate independent nations meant that the political factions within the society who felt threatened by the Brotherhood and were very much against their views on party politics could accuse them of putting other interests before that of the "nation." This quandary clearly affected al-Banna, who on the one hand denigrated the divisions of the Muslims and claimed that the Brotherhood "do not accept these political divisions," since he believed that they had "torn the Islamic nation into small and weak mini-states that can easily be swallowed by their aggressors."[56] However, at the same time he believed that "each nation demanding its right to freedom as an independent entity" was something positive, though it was alongside the rising tide of "concepts of localised nationalism" which meant that the idea of unity between the future liberated states was "purposely ignored," but somehow he still concluded that "the outcome of these steps will result in the consolidation and return of the Islamic empire as a unified state embracing the Muslims that have been scattered around the world."[57]

Yet a belief in the Islamic concepts of unity, and the political unity of Islam and the state under a universal caliphate, should surely have compelled the Brotherhood to take a stance against the Arab nationalism being promoted in the same era. Ibrahim Ghanim notes that after reading more than a thousand articles and numerous booklets penned by al-Banna there was not a single direct criticism of it, even though it was fundamentally based upon secularism and nationalism. Ghanim's analysis is that al-Banna was more concerned with the ongoing occupation, the Palestinian issue (which was also raging throughout the time), and so was concerned with broadening his call for the sake of unity.[58] This may explain the open praise displayed when al-Banna claimed that "Arabism [...] has a special place in our invitation," qualified by the Arabs being "the Islamic nation" and the "chosen community." Accordingly, the work for Arabism was "in reality working for the welfare of Islam and the World."

However, al-Banna also seemed to back Egyptian nationalism, claiming that it also "has a definite place in our call," given that the Brotherhood were Egyptians, and therefore it was "a right that should be defended."[59] In fact, the method employed by the Brotherhood to reach a unity which "does not recognize geographical borders and does not consider national differences" seemed to be based upon concurring with a foundation that explicitly did both. Therefore, at the same time the Brotherhood believed that their first priority was to contribute to their own land, Egypt, and then to contribute to "Arab unity" since it was considered to be the "second link in revival" with the final stage being for the "Islamic league."[60] Similar considerations were mentioned to the leaders when al-Banna urged them to work towards "strengthening the ties between all Islamic countries, especially the Arab countries, to pave the way for a practical and serious consideration concerning the departed caliphate."[61] In other words nationalism could be viewed positively as long as it was used against colonialism, and the unity of the nation would be the first step towards the unity of the *Umma*. The caliphate would only then be a realistic consideration, as the final seal to an already established bond between national polities.

This simply confirms that al-Banna was willing to work within the Egyptian political order, believing the government and its system to ultimately be in accordance with Islam, but simply constrained by the circumstances of occupation. In the stages of culturing and recruitment (which would take approximately twenty years by al-Banna's reckoning), it was his opinion that the optimum way forward would be to win the leaders over rather than direct and open conflict. Indeed, the issue was not the structure of the state but rather those who practiced power within it, so the Brotherhood would seek to "purify the executive power from the hands of those who do not practice the rules of Islam."[62] His constant hope of convincing those in positions of influence to adopt the Islamic ideals as he perceived them led him in 1939 to call upon then Prime Minister, Ali Maher, to openly announce that the Egyptian government was in fact an Islamic government in order to undermine the British position in their colonies with substantial Muslim populations, in a manner similar to the relationship between the Ottoman caliphate and the Khilafat movement which had caused consternation just subsequent to the First World War.[63]

Confrontation—Morality, Jihad and Liberation

Given that al-Banna's call to liberation would naturally lead to a confrontation between the Brotherhood and the British at some point, there would come a stage where they would also have to confront any political entities that were entrenched within the status quo. The Palestinian uprising in 1936 was adopted by the Brotherhood, who began to attack the British directly in their publications, as well as the Jewish emigration and activities there, with the publishing of a book exposing pictures of torture entitled "The Fire and Destruction in Palestine" being rapidly distributed, leading to al-Banna's arrest under the charge of spreading literature that would "provoke the people against a friendly and allied nation."[64] As well as organizing boycotts and releasing propaganda, various Brotherhood members also participated in the armed conflict,[65] which they would also do in the 1948 "Arab-Israeli" war.

The beginning of a more confrontational phase between al-Banna and the government caused casualties within the Brotherhood, who were by then deep into their second phase of "mass mobilisation." Some of the members felt that they were not forceful enough against the ruling elite, referring to the Qur'anic verse "And whosoever does not rule by whatever Allah has revealed, then they are the disbelievers"[66] to claim that those engaged in the Egyptian political system were actually aligned with the British and should be treated in the same manner. Led by a senior member called Ahmed Rafat, the group also believed that the time for physical action had already come upon them and that they should be more involved in the physical struggle in Palestine.[67] The malcontents were eventually removed from the Brotherhood in 1940 by al-Banna, which, along with the decision to present candidates to the 1942 parliamentary elections, was in the estimation of some analysts a final proof that they intended to reform the government from within rather than through revolution against it.[68]

This understanding, though correct, lacks the consideration of al-Banna's first milestone to achieving an Islamic state, namely the complete liberation from occupation which was shackling the Egyptian government at the time (in his view). The reform of the government itself, as has already been stressed, was a secondary consideration up until this time, as was the liberation of neighboring Palestine. When justifying their position in a 1944 article entitled "Why Did the Brotherhood Take Part in the Elections for the Members Assembly?" the parliament is described as a "pulpit to raise the call to Islam."[69] There is no doubt that they had adopted a gradualist approach, and the growth of the movement coupled with the weakness of the colonial nations as a result of the Second World War meant that the confrontation between the Brotherhood and the British was sure to increase, with the former hoping to garner the support of society and government alike.

It is for these and similar reasons that al-Banna established the infamous "Secret Apparatus" around 1940, described by one member as "an Islamic army" to defend the call of the Brotherhood, especially since there were no independent Arab armies worth their name in existence.[70] This move was not surprising since as the Brotherhood were actively seeking to reform education, fighting poverty, disease and crime, and working "to create an exemplary society deserving to be associated with the Islamic *shari'a*,"[71] it was in effect becoming a state within a state through providing grass-roots support and services. In the same way, a military force within that state was required, especially since al-Banna believed that the only way to achieve independence was through Jihad.[72] This is why within one year of the inception of the Muslim Brotherhood he completed a short treatise written specifically about Jihad in Islam, where he opines that "degradation and dishonour are the results of the love of this world and the fear of death,"[73] preparing society for the conflict that lay ahead in their struggle for freedom. It was a result of his pragmatism and gradualism that the first material steps to fulfill his treatise's aims came more than a full decade later.

To prepare the people to undertake that struggle required a "period of rebuilding", with the humiliation of the Muslim nations being linked directly to the comment of the Prophet Muhammad that "the love of life and the fear of death" would enter into the hearts of the believers. According to al-Banna's *ijtihad*, the reason for the humiliation and weakness of the people was "the feebleness of their spirit, the weakness of their minds, and the emptiness of their hearts devoid of any morality." Though the colonized nations were lacking in material strength to fight off the colonialists, the more important resource was the "spiritual strength consisting of great moral character,"[74] such that he questioned whether there is "a true crisis in our national situation other than the spiritual crisis and the *wahn*[75] of the hearts."[76]

The stage of "rebuilding" could not be left completely open-ended, as evidenced by the tensions that erupted within the Brotherhood over the time and place of confrontation and how that confrontation should participate in the rebuilding. This is why al-Banna's rhetoric in 1940 included the threat to "use practical power" when other doors are shut, but only when he was sure that they had "perfected the Belief and Unity." He was careful to claim that they were not thinking about revolution, but warned that "if the government does not reform and seek to cure the societal illnesses, then that will definitely lead to revolution" from others apart from them.[77] In the same way, while they were not advocating revolution, they were "advocates of truth and peace", and if anyone rose up against them in their mission, they were permitted to defend themselves.[78]

Al-Banna believed that the Egyptians would be in a position to demand their independence from the British by the end of the Second World War, having utilized the time and space afforded by the preoccupation with international issues. At a meeting held in 1945 addressing influential leaders from differing localities, al-Banna once again clarified that the Brotherhood were working to correct "the understandings Muslims have of their religion," and "serving society [...] by purifying it against ignorance, illness, poverty and debauchery," which could not be achieved "except under the shade of a reformed state." The seventeen years of preparation since the founding of the Brotherhood had been focused on making people understand that "politics, freedom and honour are orders from the Qur'an." The chief cause of this corruption of society, as identified by the Brotherhood, was the "interference and rule of the foreigner." The solution remained working alongside current governments, calling for "a general Islamic Arab conference to unify the efforts."[79] This cooperation extended to the issue of the Palestine question and how the British mandate there would be concluded so that when meeting with the British American investigation committee taking opinion on the issue of how to resolve the question, al-Banna proclaimed that "in the name of the Muslim Brothers, I support what the Arabs and their leaders and their representatives in the Arab League have proclaimed,"[80] evidence of his continued good faith in them.

This good faith had been largely abandoned by 1948, as a result of the reluctance or inability of the Egyptian establishment to take a strong stance against the British in contradiction to the Brotherhood's announced position of confrontation, coupled with the belief that the Arab armies were preparing to simply surrender Palestine without a fight.[81] At this time the Brotherhood announced the "struggle for the Qur'an" in an article entitled "Where is the Rule of Allah?" which stated that the obligation of the state was to implement *shari'a* legislation. If the government neglected this objective "it would not be counted as an Islamic state," and if the people under the rule "were content with this neglect and agreed to it they would also not be considered to be an Islamic *Umma* whatever they claimed with their tongue."[82] As al-Banna also mentioned in an article written in May of the same year, quoting the Qur'anic reference "Do they desire the rule of *jahiliyya* (ignorance)" proves that "it is not enough in defining the law according to what Allah has revealed for a state to simply announce in its constitution that it is a Muslim nation and that the official religion of the state is Islam [...] or to say that the members of the government are Muslims," but rather the state has to implement and embody Islamic teachings as well as promoting them to the world.[83]

The atmosphere was not simply one of heightened rhetoric. At the time there was widespread political unrest in Egypt and regular acts of violence directed against the British and their interests or civil unrest, rioting and physical conflict between differing political factions. In this period the relationship between the Brotherhood and the government developed into an open confrontation, ending with the ordered dissolution of the group by Prime Minister Nuqrashi, due to the belief that they were planning an imminent revolution.[84] On December 28, 1948, Nuqrashi was assassinated by a young member of the Brotherhood acting independently of any instruction from al-Banna, symptomatic of how the situation had spiraled beyond his control by this stage. On 12 February, 1949, al-Banna was shot dead, most likely in retaliation, though the culprits were never identified. In his final pamphlet, written shortly before his death, he stated that those who had killed Nuqrashi "were not *Ikhwani* and not Muslims,"[85] as well as rejecting the charge that the Brotherhood were intending to overthrow the state, due to the consideration that the constitution recognized Islam and its basis was democratic and representative of the will of the people.[86] Taking a conservative stance that has characterized the Brotherhood repeatedly in its history, their pragmatism and conservative approach, whether wittingly or otherwise, buttressed the status quo even when there was upheaval around them. It can therefore be argued that their gradual method of working within the status quo, thereby maintaining it, became an end in itself rather than a means to an end.

The Inheritance of Hassan al-Banna

Due to the nature of al-Banna's personal leadership of the Brotherhood, his assassination was a paralyzing blow. The British government had previously identified that the major weakness of the organization to be their reliance on their leader,[87] and with no obvious internal candidate who could command the respect of the whole group, they remained rudderless for two years. As a symptom of this situation, when leading member Mahmoud Abdul-Haleem happened to meet the young Indian scholar Abul-Hasan al-Nadwi while on the pilgrimage to Mecca, he proposed that he take on the role vacated by al-Banna's assassination.[88] Though the Brotherhood by this stage had opened offices in Damascus, Palestine, Sudan and Jordan (with the apparent blessing of King Abdullah),[89] trying to convince someone from as far away both geographically and administratively as al-Nadwi, who had never had the opportunity to meet with the Brotherhood previously, shows the reliance placed on individual charisma rather than any internal ideology or culture. It also indicates the nature of the internal divisions which meant that an outside candidate was preferred to bring the factions together.

It was the Brotherhood's openness and vague ideas which invited the charge commonly leveled at the organization that it did not have any clearly defined political programme. This increased after al-Banna's death, leading some of the members to release books attempting to detail more systematically the details of the Islamic state that was at the heart of the Brotherhood's call. The two major contributions were Abdul Qadir Auda's book detailing the Islamic criminal justice system and Mohammad Ghazali's refutation of Khalid Muhammad Khalid's "From Here We Begin," which reopened the ideas first explored by Raziq almost thirty years earlier. Ghazali, as well as refuting those arguments that conflated the caliphate with theocratic rule, also described the caliph as "the leader of the prayers and arbiter of conflicts," while also believing that the constitution of the time (1950) had the right basis to bring about Islamic governance.[90] So, during this time it is clear that there were no new ideas emanating from the Brotherhood, and no new direction as a result of the loss of their leader; instead, the caliphate remained as an ultimate objective while the national polity remained a legitimate system in which to work.

By 1951, an Egyptian judge called Hasan al-Hudaybi, who had a close personal relationship with al-Banna but was not previously a member of the group, was convinced to fill the void left by al-Banna, with the hope that his political connections would help the Brotherhood repair their relationship with the monarchy, regain official legitimacy and reduce the pressure upon them from the authorities.[91] This rapprochement was soon achieved, and when the government announced the dissolution of the 1936 Anglo-Egyptian treaty, the Brotherhood "took the first step to reach the goals of its Islamic program, which was to free the Islamic nation from the noose of occupation, and cutting it from the binds of the colonialist."[92] Al-Hudaybi announced that the Brotherhood was "waiting for the decision of the government" as to what path would be taken, and "if the government decided to fight (against the British), then the whole people are behind it."[93] This eventuality never took place, with the Palace seen as too compliant and weak in front of the British, cut down by the Free Officers movement in a revolutionary coup, who had finally reached breaking point after warning King Farouk five years earlier that "the army will not allow itself to be used as an instrument for any reform movement, out of concern for the future of our country which is placed in the hands of weak and irresolute men." Their own opinion mirrored that of the Brotherhood, that the Egyptians had "sunk into a moral, social and economic morass," but unlike al-Banna they stressed that there could be "no escape by means of evolution, but only through radical change".[94] Ironically, while al-Banna, the leader of a group ostensibly working outside the constraints of the system, saw the government as legitimate, the army, which was an institution of the government, did not.

The revolution had some support from within the Brotherhood and several of its members had ties with the Free Officers Movement dating back to the time they had fought in the war over Palestine in 1948. However, the relationship between the two soured with the arrest of members of the group and their subsequent terrible treatment in the prisons of Gamal Abdul-Nasser, now well documented. It is during this period that the only other major personality comparable to that of al-Banna within the Brotherhood emerged. That man was Sayyid Qutb—a graduate of the same university as al-Banna, Dar-ul-Ulum, and who had also memorized the Qur'an from an early age. It is worth noting that, although Qutb was to become a major personality for the Brotherhood, he was not a product of their culture, having joined the movement in the early 1950s.

The circumstances that Qutb faced were radically different from that of al-Banna. The previous *ijtihad* of al-Banna held that foreign occupation was the major cause of the inability to carry out societal reform, jihad was the only path to liberation, individual reform was required in order to carry out the jihad and that, crucially, the government was a victim of the circumstances rather than the perpetrator. In the case of Qutb, the land had now been liberated and so the problem was no longer that of a foreign occupation preventing the full implementation of Islamic reform. At last, the government was ostensibly fully independent and able to make its own decisions, and it turned to a secular form of Arab nationalism rather than the Islamic state as proposed by al-Banna, let alone any steps to re-establish the lost caliphate.

From within the jail cells and hospitals of Nasser's prisons, having witnessed brutal torture of many members of the Brotherhood as well as suffering it himself, Qutb wrote prolifically, producing his two most influential works—the first being a complete exegesis of the Qur'an and the second his seminal work "Milestones," attributed as the factor behind Nasser's decision to have him sentenced to death in 1966. Neither book mentioned the caliphate much in its political form, a notable absence from Qutb's other work.

One of the reasons for this is that Qutb, as an Arab Linguist and literary expert rather than Islamic jurist, used the term *khilafa* in its Qur'anic literary meaning rather than the definition given to it by the *'ulama'*. The literal meaning of *khilafa* is "succession", and in its Qur'anic usage it means succession upon Earth, as a trust and responsibility, such as when the Qur'an mentions "and when your Lord said to the angels, I will create a *khalifa* (successor/viceroy) on the Earth."[95] In his use of this verse, Qutb extols that ruling according to the system laid down by God was "from the obligations of man from the start since Allah entrusted him with the *khilafa* in the Earth."[96] This *khilafa* was not deserved on the basis of material advancement, but on attaining the ability to adhere to the correct belief and apply the correct method in organizing ones life.

The understanding of the *khilafa* accordingly was a more general meaning which encompassed the political aspect without being confined to it. In this manner, "the *khilafa* necessitates the establishment of the *shari'a* of Allah on Earth to realise the heavenly system,"[97] with the leadership on Earth being a chain which extended from the first Prophet Adam until it reached the Muslim nation. The full responsibility and correct application of this succession on Earth relied upon belief in God, since "belief in Allah leads to the good *khilafa* on Earth, and the good *khilafa* on Earth is making it a place of dwelling and the enjoyment of its pure benefits."[98]

In this sense the *khilafa* is not a political order but a responsibility that can only be correctly fulfilled if the correct political order is applied. In other words, humanity generally and the Muslim nation specifically is charged with this *khilafa*: to apply Islamic systems would be to fulfill its conditions while neglecting the rule of the *Shari'a* would constitute a failure to fulfill its requirements. And so each person will be measured by what they did "with this *khilafa* from good and evil,"[99] with any deviation from the application of God's Law being "a deviation from the universal law upon which the heavens and earth are built."[100]

The naming of the political order was of no concern to Qutb, who simply stated that "there is one system which is the Islamic system and what is other than that is *jahiliyya* (ignorance)," and that "there is a single abode which is the abode of Islam, within which the Muslim state is established and the *shari'a* of Allah dominates over it, and the *hudud* (proscribed limits) are established within it." Anything that fell outside of this was considered "the abode of war."[101] The various terms used to describe Islamic polity in Qutb's "Milestones," considered a sort of political manifesto even though it was only intended as an introduction to a much larger work, were phrases such as "abode of Islam," "Islamic system" or "Islamic state" rather than the caliphate, but it is clear that Qutb's work was much more direct and did not reflect al-Banna's accommodation of the system which supposed several stages in the creation of an Islamic state, from national polity to international groups of polities, until finally a single united nation is formed with a caliph at its head. Rather, according to Qutb, if a state implemented Islam in its totality then it was an Islamic State, an Islamic State was unitary by its nature, and anything that fell outside of it or worked contrary to it would be *jahiliyya*.

It is argued that Qutb's ideas were not reflective of the Brotherhood's ideology, with the book "Preachers, Not Judges," written in 1969 by al-Hudaybi, considered to be a refutation of Qutb's stance. Some years later, the third leader of the Brotherhood, Umar al-Tilmisani, openly stated that Qutb spoke for himself. In particular, Qutb's description of the Egyptian society as one of *jahiliyya* is a point of major contention, with analysts seeing this as tantamount to an excommunication of all Egyptian Muslims, since it was used within Islamic sources and discourse to refer to pre-Islamic idolatrous practices. The phrase *jahiliyya* was actually borrowed from Qutb's reading of a book by Abul Hasan al-Nadwi entitled "What the World has Lost Due to the Decline of the Muslims," where in a foreword he had written for it in 1952 he praised the term as "an exact expression" which differentiates clearly "between the spirit of Islam and the spirit of materialism which dominated the World before (Islam), and which dominates over it today after Islam was removed from the leadership," and therefore "(it) was not (referring to) a specific time."[102]

As far as the charge of *takfir*[103] is concerned, Qutb is recorded as saying that he did not "charge the Muslims with disbelief," but rather that the Muslims "have come to be in their *jahl* (ignorance) about the correct implication of the Islamic creed" analogous to "those of *jahiliyya* before Islam."[104] Though Qutb's words indicate that his intention in using the term *jahiliyya* to describe society was not to judge people by their belief as individuals but rather to characterize the nature of ruling, customs and traditions between the people, the way in which it was used in "Milestones" left it open to interpretation. The discussion of whether the rule of disbelief could be applied to rulers or the whole society raged within Nasser's prison cells in the immediate aftermath of Qutb's execution. A new strand of thought emerged based upon a reading of "Milestones" that effectively saw Egyptian society as one of disbelievers, rather than simply Muslims who accepted living under a non-Islamic government and system either due to compulsion or ignorance. This debate involved al-Hudaybi and other senior members of the Brotherhood against a young Azhar graduate, Ali Abduh Ismael, and though Ismael was subsequently convinced to relinquish his ideas, they were adopted by Shukri Mustafa, who went on to form the group widely known as "al-Takfir wal-Hijra." It was during this period that al-Hudaybi's book "Preachers, Not Judges" was written, and though some, like Kepel, inaccurately cite the book as a refutation of Qutb,[105] its real purpose was to refute the *takfiri* ideas of Shukri by explaining that the ignorance of the masses meant that they could not be held accountable for the situation of Egyptian society at the time. That al-Hudaybi stated "this book has confirmed all my trust in Syed, may Allah preserve him," and that "Syed, Allah willing, is now the awaited hope for *da'wah* (the call to Islam),"[106] when asked about "Milestones," only further supports this argument. Moreover, al-Hudaybi had no problem with the characterization of society as being one of *jahiliyya*, but warned that to identify any particular individual as a disbeliever required a greater degree of evidence.[107] The book was published for the first time in 1977, immediately after Shukri's group had carried out the kidnapping and assassination of an Azhari scholar who had previously refuted their ideas,[108] further indicating that the target was not Qutb but rather this small offshoot group born out of the desperation of the circumstances faced in prison at the time.

Al-Hudaybi's own political ideas were clearly laid out in the book, describing Islamic government as one which embraces Islam as a religion and implements the *shari'a*. Much of the book reads very similar to the tracts produced by the Azhari scholars writing to confirm the obligation of the caliphate in their refutations of Ali Abdul-Raziq, but in line with al-Banna the caliphate was seen as the "symbol of Islamic unity" and the "expression of the connection between the Islamic peoples," which meant it was "imperative upon the Muslims to think about it and be concerned over it."[109] Within the context of Islamic politics all these points seem fairly typical in terms of academia, and yet the instruction to put thought into the issue and to have concern for it suggested that the serious steps for this particular objective were for another time.

There is no doubt that with the execution of Qutb and other senior members, as well as the extensive torture and extreme conditions in jail, the Brotherhood were left traumatized by their experience during the harsh repression of the Nasser period. With the relative ease enjoyed in the time of Presidents Anwar Sadat and then Hosni Mubarak, the Brotherhood have moved from being a party initially formed with the goal of liberation that was willing to work pragmatically and accept the shortcoming of the incumbent government, given the constraints of occupation and the need for a broad based unity against foreign interference to working fully within the status quo for gradual change while largely discarding the stated aims of al-Banna. Al-Banna's *ijtihad* was based upon the understanding that the British occupation was the barrier to the development of an Islamic society and the establishment of an Islamic state, and therefore the government was actually a potential ally in this cause and should be accommodated and worked with to achieve the goal of liberation.

Subsequently, Qutb reevaluated the situation, considering that occupation was no longer a factor and therefore the problem was the government itself, and so the opinion of al-Banna, that the governments were ultimately Islamic but prevented from fully applying Islam due to the circumstances, no longer applied. Qutb's method remained the same as that of al-Banna, with his claim that "the first aim is to change ourselves so that we may later change the society" being compatible with al-Banna's call for moral reform, with the only difference being that to "change the *jahili* system at its very roots"[110] was now the main aim given that the occupation was no longer a reality preventing what he considered as necessary political changes.

After Qutb, the Brotherhood reverted to the *ijtihad* of al-Banna even though the reality was completely different, and largely reconciled itself to working within the status quo, considering it Islamic in essence and in need of reform rather than replacement. Hence they had no problem in entering the Egyptian parliament and voting to keep Mubarak in power, as they did during the 1987 assembly. In this last evolution of the Brotherhood, the caliphate no longer seems to stand as a true goal, with al-Hudaybi's son, Ma'moon al-Hudaybi, who also became head of the Brotherhood towards the end of his life, stating in 2001 that "there is the caliphate of the status quo, and the Imam of Necessity" which, if in place, has to be obeyed, since otherwise "the outcome of armed resistance would be social turmoil" and so "this is the case of our President,"[111] Mubarak. Hence when protests which ultimately ousted the President from his position began in January 2011, the Brotherhood refused to support them initially, and then withheld themselves from any official participation, though they were reasonably quick to engage with the regime in negotiations when invited to do so, opening them up to accusations once again of being agents of the status quo. While a sizeable number of people were demanding revolution, the spokesmen of the Brotherhood were still writing about gradual, steady reform.[112] It would be a fair conclusion to submit that the Brotherhood today have adopted al-Banna's methods of pragmatism and gradualism, while ignoring the change in circumstance since the beginning of the post-colonial era.

This does not mean that the Brotherhood will completely ignore the issue of the caliphate. In fact, it would likely be unable to do so while retaining most of its internal membership support, given its position within both normative Islam and its symbolism as the proclaimed ultimate goal of al-Banna. With the more open political discourse in the Middle East in 2011, the issue of the caliphate has been raised by numerous groups and individuals within Egypt, and has been the focus of discussion shows on satellite television and in other forums. At the peak of these discussions in December 2011 (which were provoked by the ruling Egyptian military council's response[113] to an accusation against them made by Hizb ut-Tahrir), the Brotherhood's Supreme Guide sent out an internal message to all members where he exclaimed that the ultimate goal of al-Banna, the establishment of the caliphate, was nearing fruition[114] (as a result of the controversy around this statement, it was explained by senior member Dr. Abdul Rahman al-Barr to mean unification of the Arab states rather than a return to the classical orthodox system).[115] Though this may be explained away as simply rhetoric to satisfy internal expectations, thus ensuring its own constituency was not attracted to other movements who were more forceful in their calls for Islamic government, and as a cynical attempt to dampen any fears from the grassroots that the movement was forsaking their call to an Islamic state, it indicated that the movement did not intend to fully relinquish this symbol, acknowledging its resonance among the Brotherhood in particular and Muslims in general.

In conclusion, contrary to the radical change al-Banna envisaged, which he argued could be achieved through a jihad to liberate the country, today's Brotherhood more closely resembles the party politics declared as impermissible by al-Banna. It could therefore be argued that the Brotherhood of al-Banna in fact died with Qutb, and rather than Qutb being an anomaly and deviation from the original ideas of the founder, he was responsible for a more forceful and direct articulation of the methods to achieve the Brotherhood's original political goals, having understood that working within the status quo would ultimately be counterproductive in the post-colonial era. Though this is a contentious point and requires further exploration in its own independent study, it is worth noting that in the last period of his life al-Banna and the Muslim Brotherhood were in almost open confrontation with the Egyptian government, and that the benefit of the doubt they had given to the regime in the preceding years was clearly waning, as evidenced in their writings and actions at the time.

The dilution of the concept of the caliphate in the discourse of the Brotherhood is not surprising given that it appears that al-Banna was not concerned with it as a pressing issue in practical terms. Since the institution was seen by some as a tool in the hands of the British soon before it was abolished, and subsequently viewed as a trophy cynically competed over by the Arab leaders such as King Fu'ad and Sharif Hussain in order to increase their respective influence, people such as al-Banna perhaps found it difficult to call for it directly. Al-Banna had also witnessed the futility of the actions of those advocating the restoration of the caliphate like al-Dijwi, and likely thought that to retread such a path would be ineffectual and irrelevant. Therefore the discourse of al-Banna focused upon the principles of Islamic politics rather than the form they took, leading ultimately to a continuation of the weakening of the idea of the caliphate as the Islamic method of rule while strengthening the modernist, even apologist, strand of thought which claimed that other structures, such as parliamentary democracy, were seen as compatible with Islam. This was aside from the fact that in his opinion the issue of the restoration of the caliphate was not something practically achievable before several other steps had been taken, including the general elevation of the moral situation of society, the liberation of the land from the British, the reform of government and finally increasing unity between the various independent Muslim states.

Given the priority and order of the implementation of the aims of the Brotherhood, the caliphate as a specific term appeared in their discourse consistently as a long term goal with no current reality, and its appearance became more apparent at a time when it was implicitly rejecting the manoeuvring of leaders like Farouk to possibly use the caliphate title to strengthen their own position within the dynamics of Egyptian and Arab politics. Though the caliphate was a symbol of unity, and the ultimate proof of the strength and universality of Islam, al-Banna saw it as a figurehead that would be re-established after the re-emergence of Islamic politics, which itself was reliant on the ascension of the Islamic individual in society, and not as the essence of any political revival.

The Brotherhood was formed at a time when the few existing attempts to reconstitute the caliphate were floundering, largely due to the fact that its original appeal at the time was the theoretical political expression of Islamic independence, unity and power, while efforts to elect a caliph were either to install a spiritual pope-like figure or as a vanity title for one of the region's monarchs. Neither of these options would confront the political realities of the day that needed addressing, and so al-Banna set about finding other ways to achieve these same objectives, but by working within the polity he found before him, seeking to re-establish a global Islamic society through a liberated nation-state. By the time of al-Banna's death the caliphate was long departed as part of the wider political discourse, and the age of the nation-state and pan-Arab unity was dawning.

4

CALIPHATE AS LIBERATION

HIZB UT-TAHRIR—THE PARTY OF LIBERATION
IN THE POST-COLONIAL ERA

The thoughts of any nation are the greatest wealth it possesses.

Hizb ut-Tahrir, 1953[1]

On 14 May, 1948, a year prior to the assassination of Hassan al-Banna, the British mandate in Palestine was terminated. This was followed on 15 May by the proclamation of the State of Israel by Ben-Gurion. With the establishment of Israel quickly recognized by the major powers, the remaining tasks were to expel the Arab Palestinians in order to create a more homogeneous population within the territories taken, along with ensuring survival against the Arab armies entering Palestine who apparently harbored the objective of destroying the fledgling state. However, the intentions of the Arab rulers were not clear considering that these states "only sent an expeditionary force into Palestine, keeping the bulk of their army at home."[2] When Arab nationalist thinker Sati' al-Husri was asked about how seven Arab armies managed to lose against the single army of the fledging Israeli state, he would reply that "the Arabs lost the war *precisely* because they were seven states."[3] Though the primary concern continued to be unity in the region, as noted at the end of the last chapter, the dominant expression of that unity was seen in ethnic or pan-nationalist terms.

The competing personal interests and vanities of the multiple monarchs and presidents meant there had been no unified command, and each was concerned with preventing the others from gaining any regional advantage. Even if there had been a unified command, King Abdullah of Jordan did not intend to liberate since any independent state would most likely be led by Mufti Amin al-Husseini, apparently an avowed enemy of the British and therefore also of the King. Rather than see an independent Palestine run by a rival, Abdullah negotiated the idea of a Greater Transjordan with the Jews, suggesting that the United Nations-proposed Arab state be annexed by Transjordan, and the rest be occupied by any Jewish state. This became the basis of British policy towards the Arab-Israeli conflict in 1948,[4] and was formulated during the Anglo-Transjordan negotiation in February of 1948. A series of meetings between Golda Meir and Abdullah confirmed this agreement.[5]

This and other similar issues were known to those involved in politics at the time. Soon after the *nakba* (catastrophe), members of the Muslim Brotherhood in Damascus who had been travelling to secure weapons and support the fight for liberation heard their leader Hassan al-Banna claim "there is no use, (the Arab rulers) are all either cowards or conspirators."[6] Military officers such as Gamal Abdul-Nasser returned home humiliated and angry with the Egyptian rulers who had provided them with weapons that more often hurt those using them than those they were used against. In the first few years of this new era of discontent, anger and feelings of impotency, Sheikh Taqiudeen al-Nabahani, the grandson of the renowned Ottoman-era Sufi Sheikh Yusuf al-Nabahani, gave emotional public sermons winning support in al-Aqsa and Hebron, where he attacked the politicians and rulers of the region. In turn he was called by the King to his court where Abdullah praised his grandfather in an attempt to win the loyalty of this seemingly influential individual.[7] According to one report, at the end of the sitting the King extended his hand to al-Nabahani, asking him to pledge allegiance by saying "I pledge to be an ally of your allies and enemy of your enemies," perhaps hoping to use his religious influence against other opponents such as secular Arab nationalists and communists in the same vein as the unofficial understanding the Monarchy would have with the Muslim Brotherhood throughout the 1950s. The Sheikh did not reply, forcing the king to repeat his sentence three times until he finally responded saying "I have already pledged allegiance to Allah to be the ally of His and His Messenger's allies, and the enemy of His and His Messenger's enemies," an affront to the king which saw al-Nabahani jailed for a short period.[8]

Subsequently, on 17 November, 1952, al-Nabahani, along with four other men, made a formal application to the Jordanian government for recognition of the establishment of a political party, Hizb ut-Tahrir (the Liberation Party), whose stated aim was to "restart the Islamic way of life" through the establishment of "the single Islamic State which implements Islam and calls the world to Islam."[9] The goals of the organization went against the grain of the political discourse of the time, with Arab nationalism and socialism considered the only serious ideologies suitable for the contemporary era. The application was promptly rejected as being unconstitutional, since it refused to acknowledge hereditary rule, rejected Arab nationalism, and asserted that the Islamic bond was the basis of solidarity rather than the bond of nationality.[10] An attempt at recognition as an association under old Ottoman law in the same manner as the Brotherhood was also rejected.

The clampdown on the party was swift, with the circumstances so difficult for members that some people were compelled to emigrate out of Jordan within the first year.[11] From the beginning of the clampdown, prison was a common destination for leaders and supporters alike, with al-Nabahani and Sheikh Dawood Hamdan, another of the original founders, arrested and jailed as early as 1953.[12] Unlike the Brotherhood, the Hizb did not accept the legitimacy of the Hashemite entity[13] or any of the other governments in the Middle East, leading to immediate and persistent tension between the State and the party. Despite the limitations placed on it, in the ten years since the turn of the century Hizb ut-Tahrir has actively promoted its ideology in several countries, with members operating, and often arrested, as far afield as Uzbekistan, Turkey, Bangladesh, Egypt, Syria and Pakistan. In the summer of 2007, a crowd of 100,000 people filled Jakarta's Gelora Bung Karno stadium to "push for the creation of a single state across the Muslim World,"[14] the largest in a series of conferences and rallies that spread across diverse locations from the United Kingdom to Palestine to Ukraine, all organized by Hizb ut-Tahrir—evidence of a global presence and continuing propagation of its central message.

What also sets them apart from the Brotherhood is that Hizb ut-Tahrir have consistently aimed to establish a caliphate. Emmanuel Karagiannis states that they are the sole party that systematically and persistently advocated the establishment of such a state, such that the caliphate is their hallmark,[15] while Husain Haqqani claimed that the emphasis placed upon it is what differentiates the group from others who may have referred to the Islamic State before being assimilated into their own national political structures.[16] Highlighting this, when commenting on the slogans used by his own group during the years of insurgency before settling as a domestic political party, Mohidin Kabiri of the Islamic Revival Party of Tajikistan commented, "do slogans about the establishment of Islamic state or 'Islamic society' that the IRPT sometimes proclaimed during the armed insurgency have something in common with the ideas of establishing of the caliphate? I think not."[17] Both of the aforementioned comments were made during a conference entitled "The Challenge of Hizb ut-Tahrir," organized by Zeyno Baran of the Nixon Center as part of American efforts to assist the Uzbek regime led by Islam Karimov in coming up with strategies to deal with the spread of the party's ideas in Central Asia.

There is very little academic work on the group prior to 9/11, and due to the highly politicized discussion around it, attributed to fears that it could destabilize central Asian allies of the US,[18] almost all of the work around the group in the immediate post-9/11 period is inaccurate, polemical in nature and rarely undertaken academically, with singular web pages, interviews with unnamed sources and unsubstantiated claims. As noted by Jean-Francois Mayer, the Hizb is the "perfect candidate" for being seen as a threat since there are no known experts on it and yet it has a radical discourse which can be used judiciously by commentators.[19] After the overtly politically-driven analysis emanating from the American think tank circuit, even the more independent work has, in response, revolved around security-driven questions such as whether it will remain peaceful or not or how to neutralize its threat to American interests. For example, Mayer comments on how "remarkable" the "considerable restraint" shown by "Islamic militants" in the face of repression of local regimes is,[20] which he puts down to ideology. Karagiannis also considers that understanding their ideas is critical to "understanding why Hizb ut-Tahrir remains peaceful,"[21] since his framing of theory could not explain why the Islamic Movement of Uzbekistan and Hizb ut-Tahrir have taken opposing pathways even though both groups use identical frames which would, in his view, justify violence against the state, concluding that ideology must be the determining factor. John Horton noted that the party recognized the decline of Islam, and their ultimate aim was to reverse it. Rather than this decline being a result of Western actions, Horton claims that al-Nabahani attributed the decline of Islam, and ultimately the caliphate, primarily to a failure within Islam itself; therefore the establishment of the caliphate is a higher priority than "simply striking down those it sees as the enemies of Islam."[22]

If one turns to the period before 9/11, there are in fact two studies of Hizb ut-Tahrir that have been largely overlooked by the majority of policy driven analysts, perhaps helping to explain how they have arrived at what Karagiannis calls their largely "unfounded conclusions."[23] The older of the two is the Arabic book *Hizb ut-Tahrir al-Islami* by Auni al-Ubaidi written in 1993, which is the most comprehensive historical study of the party to date, using multiple internal and external sources. Suha Taji-Farouki is the author of the first complete study of the party written in English, which is the most complete work detailing the historical background, ideological foundations and internal structuring of the group. Al-Ubaidi states that the group was formed by one of "the elite of [Palestine's] *'ulama',*"[24] while Farouki states that the ideology of the Hizb was "the response of an Islamic scholar and talented intellectual to the break-up of the Ottoman empire, the fragmentation of its territories into nation-states, the creation of Israel and the impotence of Muslim societies in the face of neo-colonialism."[25] Farouki's study is the more analytical of the two, investigating al-Nabahani's ideas and concluding that his keenness to create an authentic Islamic alternative to other modern ideologies in contemporary political terminology meant he was engaging in a certain form of apologetics.

Though the Hizb is most widely known and characterized by its persistent call to the caliphate, it did not feature prominently in its public discourse for at least the first ten years following its inception. According to senior member Sheikh Taleb Awadallah, the term "Islamic State" was usually used, initially due to the overwhelming image in people's minds that the caliph was a "holy Sheikh" and "historical legend" consigned to history.[26] Seemingly, the personalization of the position of the caliph to a spiritual, "secularised" individual separate from the State had become even more entrenched over the thirty years since its formal abolition, and the lingering image in the minds of the people was closer to that of the last official Ottoman caliph Sultan Abdul Majed, who occupied the seat after its separation from its temporal powers in 1922, and not that of the more strident figure of Sultan Abdul Hamid II. The failed caliphate conferences and congresses had reduced the position of caliph to a title competed over by the elites of the time, and even as the election of a token caliph failed, the term appeared consigned to history in the minds of the people, and no one with a political program would frame it within such a paradigm.

By examining the literature and public discourse of the Hizb it can be seen that it was not initially engaging in an explicit and direct public call for a return to the caliphate, but rather arguing for a liberation from the intellectual legacy of colonialism, which according to them would be achieved by establishing a public consensus within society such that Islam becomes the reference in all societal relationships. It would be at this point that society would demand that the State applies the *shari'a* to regulate those relationships in a manner in accordance with Islam, which would be through the caliphate system of government. This required a rehabilitation of the image of the caliphate from the ineffective Ottoman system that was overtaken by the West to a single solution for the revival of the Muslim peoples. In other words, they were not seeking to build the legitimacy of the caliphate as a political program upon the tradition of the last known example, but rather upon a legal basis which would build credibility in the proposed political system.

Understanding what the caliphate means to Hizb ut-Tahrir requires an understanding of its ideology and how their *ijtihad* was constructed in light of the situation facing its founders in the late 1940s and early 1950s, and how this altered and affected its discourse throughout that period. To the scholars of al-Azhar University, who issued their verdict against Ali Abdul-Raziq, the caliph was a representative of Islam whose presence was a legal obligation placed upon them by Islam, with little concern for the role of the caliphate in reform or revival. Subsequently, al-Banna posited the caliphate as the ultimate objective for Muslims to work towards. Its achievement would be the crowning moment for a reformed and united community, and was peripheral to that community's political revival, as foremost in his mind was the development of a generation of Muslims who would rise and liberate Egypt from the influence of the British. Neither of these two points of view would reverse the image of the caliphate as unable to deal with contemporary political realities, with the vision of al-Banna contributing to this perception. The founders of Hizb ut-Tahrir, who were Islamic jurists as well as activists, viewed the caliphate both as a *shari'a* obligation and as the necessary political structure required to reform and unite the community. Emerging in an era when the physical restrictions of colonial control were being removed, their *ijtihad* led them to conclude that the necessary revival was one of an intellectual nature, requiring fundamental changes in the concepts carried and worldview held by the Muslim community, and that the caliphate was not the final goal but rather the vehicle for change in the world. Though the caliphate had a role in their discourse, the aim was initially to demonstrate the idea that Islam has a unique governmental structure responsible for implementing and promoting Islam in the domestic and international arenas, and that without it there would be no true liberation. Over time, as the party believed these core ideas had gained legitimacy, the public call for the caliphate became their primary identifier.

Hizb ut-Tahrir—The Liberation Party in the Era of Revolution

Taqiudeen al-Nabahani was born in 1909 to a religious family in the village of Ijzim in the Haifa district of Palestine. He was brought up in a scholarly household, with both his father and mother being scholars of Islamic jurisprudence. He was very close to his maternal grandfather, Yusuf al-Nabahani, a famous Sufi scholar and prolific writer who authored more than forty-eight works on various Islamic subjects.[27] This close relationship, which included spending childhood summers with Sheikh Yusuf, who had worked as the head judge in several of the Ottoman courts and had close links to the political classes, meant that he was raised in a political environment and was affected by the awareness and involvement of his grandfather in the political issues of his time.[28] He had memorized the Qur'an by the age of thirteen, and by the age of nineteen he was simultaneously enrolled at both al-Azhar and Dar al-Uloom, sent to complete his Islamic studies in Egypt, fulfilling the wishes of a grandfather eager for him to utilize his full potential. In 1920s Egypt, while studying and after graduating with exceptional marks,[29] al-Nabahani used to attend poetry recitals by Ahmed Showky lamenting the end of the Ottoman caliphate,[30] which his grandfather used to believe was a protector of the Islamic faith, a symbol of the unity of the Muslims and the defender of their essence.[31] Upon his return to Palestine, he worked as a teacher and then a judge in Haifa. During his time in Haifa he was apparently impressed by Sheikh Muhammad Izz ad-Din al-Qassam[32] due to his political awareness that the British were the central problem and therefore should be the focus of resistance in Palestine rather than the Zionists, as opposed to al-Husseini who was still seen as close to the British.[33] The *nakba* of 1948 forced him to flee to Syria, before returning to work in Jerusalem, until 1951 when he travelled to Amman to work as a lecturer and to pursue his political activities.

Although Hizb ut-Tahrir was formed after the trauma of the establishment of the State of Israel and the dislocation of the Palestinians therein, the true roots of its reason d'être lie in the period of decline before 1924. While the Muslim Brotherhood was formed on the back of the eager requests of al-Banna's followers, who put their trust in his judgment and leadership, the Hizb was formed by al-Nabahani after he had actively sought to win over many people to his ideas, amongst them other scholars from al-Azhar. The path necessary for the formation of a party capable of the required Islamic revival was mapped out meticulously in one of the first books of the party, "*al-Takattul al-Hizbi*" (the Party Formation), where the starting point is described as when one man of heightened sensation and elevated thought is "guided" to "the ideology (*mabda*)."[34] This suggests a very idiosyncratic experience leading to the formation of the party, though the Hizb claims that this does not mean that the personality of this initial individual, or his charisma, would be the basis of the group, but that he would soon find other similarly-minded individuals who would form the first circle based upon a shared intellectual foundation.

In such a scenario, the ideas of the party rather than the individual were considered central. For example, the Hizb does not consider any of the books written by al-Nabahani prior to its establishment as formative of the group's ideas. While several of the initial books were actually written as joint projects between the founding members, they were published solely under al-Nabahani's name due to the ban on the party.[35] One of the distinguishing characteristics of the group is its insistence upon an adherence to its defining culture and ideas, which have remained largely unchanged since its inception.[36] Any alterations that have been made have been to details rather than the core ideas and beliefs held by the party, while its strategy has remained consistent despite varying political circumstances and conditions.[37] While al-Banna emerged as leader of the Muslim Brotherhood based upon his charisma and political activity, he did not fully develop a program of ideas, goals and methods.[38] His non-confrontational and inclusive style, which aimed to generate co-operation between the different parties meant that up to and after his death their program remained vague and based upon slogans rather than a defined ideology, leaving the group in chaos and searching for substance after his death, with its gradualist approach making the movement more pragmatic than ideological.[39] The death of al-Nabahani in 1977 had little substantial impact upon the ideas of the Hizb,[40] with internal legitimacy being conferred upon the corpus of material left behind rather than his charisma, though there was some internal dissatisfaction around the selection of the next leader, eventually leading to a split in the party in the mid-1990s.

This does not mean that the personality of al-Nabahani was inconsequential as he came from a well known political and religious family. Since his death in 1977, the Hizb has not had such an established personality as its leader, perhaps partially explaining their lack of apparent movement during the 1980s. Previous members mention that al-Nabahani's forceful nature meant that he would rarely accept disagreement in discussion.[41] The initial membership of the Hizb, which included strong personalities of similar social stature to al-Nabahani, such as Dawood Hamdan, clashed with him over issues linked to policy and direction, notably which areas should be targeted for work to establish the caliphate. These and similar conflicts led to the expulsion of a number of high profile members of the party and renunciation by others due to al-Nabahani's insistence that the party required full adherence to the groups adopted ideas and decisions taken by the leadership. Though his death was a blow for the Hizb from the point of view of losing its founder and most established figure, the party's intellectual culture, which had been articulated under his leadership, has remained the central focus of the party.

This is exemplified by the manner in which the Hizb was formed. Al-Nabahani, like his contemporaries, had seen the rise of several Islamic groups in the region around Egypt, the majority of which had the aim of combating Westernization and reviving the *shari'a*,[42] and yet none had succeeded in bringing any real form of religious-based politics into reality. Expulsion from his home in Palestine by the Zionist forces further motivated him to look into the causes of this catastrophe, asking whether it was a fundamental issue or a symptom of a wider malaise, and if there was a wider malaise to identify it, its causes, its solution and what the required vehicle to bring that solution about might be. In the process he studied other social and Islamic movements in detail, concluding that the solution lay in the return of the caliphate and the need for a group to stridently work towards achieving that goal. This process, constitutive of the initial formulation of the Hizb, is described in its literature as one of "severe shocks" in the *Umma* producing a "vitality," which in turn generates an environment of common feelings. In al-Nabahani's time, this was likely the humiliation of the loss of Palestine and the impotency of the regimes at the time.

After studying the history of Muslim civilization, along with the contemporary political situation of the *Umma* compared to what they understood to be the rules of Islam, individuals would emerge out of this environment seeking to reconcile the two.[43] They would subsequently study "the movements that were established to bring salvation to the Muslims," in order to ascertain "whether they were based upon Islam" before concluding with a "clear, crystallized, particular thought" that the only method for true revival would be through the establishment of a caliphate by forming a party which would work to achieve that aim, following a specific *ijtihad* based upon the example of the Prophet.[44] A critical foundation of their idea was that previous movements had mistakenly separated the *shari'a* as a corpus of legislation from the concept of the state, which was required to implement it, believing that the establishment of the *shari'a* could be achieved through any form of government. It should be noted that the individuals who emerged to form this party would by necessity have to be politically engaged Islamic scholars, capable of making a comparison between their religious obligations and the current political situation.

This process of study and discussion has led to claims and counter claims about the relationship between al-Nabahani and others such as the Muslim Brotherhood and Mufti Amin al-Husseini. With respect to al-Husseini, Awadallah claims that the rumors of his relationship with al-Nabahani were incorrect, resulting from the Mufti's closeness to Sheikh Abdul Qadeem Zalloom, an early member of Hizb ut-Tahrir, who had originally been with the Brotherhood. Indeed, al-Nabahani's son claims that his father was suspicious of al-Husseini due to his proximity to the British in the 1930s.[45] As for the Brotherhood, the only confirmed direct contact between al-Nabahani and senior central Brotherhood leadership in Egypt at the time was with Hassan al-Banna's son in law, Saeed Ramadan,[46] at a meeting arranged by Dr. al-Khayyat who had been a Brotherhood member in Palestine.[47] Al-Khayyat claims to have discussed issues with al-Nabahani around the renewal of Islamic work and the adoption of the most appropriate goals and styles, and was drawn to his thoughts. After several attempts to convince the Brotherhood of the ideas and methods of al-Nabahani, which he claims failed largely due to the lack of willingness on behalf of Saeed Ramadan, he left the Brotherhood to join al-Nabahani. Though no longer with the Hizb, he denies that al-Nabahani was ever involved with the Brotherhood directly, as a member or otherwise, and as confirmed by other internal sources the attempts to bring about a merger between the two movements was a result of his endeavors within the Brotherhood and nothing to do with al-Nabahani.[48]

It is clear that numerous prominent members of the Brotherhood, such as Zalloom and al-Khayyat, did indeed leave and join the Hizb. Though Awadallah claims that there were no members of the Brotherhood in the first circle of the Hizb, which would have been primarily responsible for the articulation and clarification of its ideology, this can be contested. A number of early members of the Hizb were previously members of the Brotherhood; others had been communists, but most of those who had prior allegiances came from a group known as "Movement 313".[49] Details regarding the group are scant, but it was apparently established by a Palestinian truck driver called Sheikh Hamza Abdul-Ghaffar Tahbob which called for the caliphate believing that it would be re-established when their membership level reached 313, since this was the number of supporters of the Prophet Muhammad who established the Islamic State in Medina. Soon after the formation of the Hizb, Movement 313 was dissolved as the majority of its members joined the new party.[50] According to Awadallah, this was the only group before the Hizb which had the explicit aim of re-establishing the caliphate, its emergence in the same locality perhaps indicating a stronger connection of the area to the Ottoman State in some way, possibly due to the previous presence of prominent local personalities who had been involved with the State, such as Yusuf al-Nabahani.

Whatever the case, there is no doubt that al-Nabahani and those who established the Hizb with him felt that the other movements had failed in their efforts to bring about necessary change and the revival of the fortunes of the Muslim states. Though the Brotherhood was without a doubt the dominant Islamic party in the Middle East in the immediate post-War period, al-Nabahani felt that although al-Banna was "an intelligent scholar, renewer and *Mujtahid*," the area in which the Brotherhood was lacking was "political Islamic thought,"[51] particularly given that the Brotherhood have never posited an alternative state structure or constitution than whatever was in existence at the time. This was all the more evident in the period of upheaval, change and uncertainty that intensified after independence, with the movement caught between the opportunity for revolution and working within the status quo. The Brotherhood were in any case experiencing a period of weak and divided leadership after the assassination of their founder.

In what could be termed the era of the coup d'état, Hizb ut-Tahrir was formed in between numerous coups and counter-coups in Syria, beginning with that of Colonel Husni al-Za'im, and the July Revolution in Egypt in 1952, which overthrew the monarchy and subsequently led to the formal installment of Abdul-Nasser as the President of the Republic by 1954. In its first year the Hizb grew rapidly[52] despite an immediate post-revolution crackdown, which exiled, jailed and generally harassed its members, and banned the publication of its books and journals. They garnered greater attention and an increase in membership in 1953 with the release of eight books detailing the ideology of the party,[53] with early members listed from areas such as Hebron, the West Bank and Amman, including several Islamic scholars and judges, teachers, traders and barbers.[54] With a network of activists that included numerous Islamic personalities, they were able to take advantage of their position to address the masses through public sermons and talks in mosques, helping to attract new followers. In 1954, the Hizb put up numerous candidates on an independent platform for election to the Jordanian Representative Assembly, but only succeeded in getting Ahmed Da'ur elected. His tenure was marked by consistent criticism of the Jordanian government's domestic and international policies,[55] and he was even an opponent of the relatively permissive al-Nabulsi government.[56] According to Azzam al-Tamimi, a prominent Hamas sympathizer and critic of the Hizb, Hizb ut-Tahrir had become the primary

Islamic party in Palestine and Jordan during this initial period of limited success.[57]

This was not to last, with the political circumstances in Jordan worsening for all illegal opposition to the King, irrespective of its ideological bent, with communists, nationalists and the Hizb all facing efforts by the security services to prevent them from establishing any kind of effective leadership.[58] Government stipulations that meant any mosque preachers required an official license curtailed much of the party's public activity and cut off their primary point of contact with the masses. These measures were later extended to ban teachers from teaching political subjects in schools in 1955, which saw the exile of members into neighboring countries such as Syria, leading to a first round of internal disputes with al-Nabahani, which ended in the expulsion of several founding members including Dawood Hamdan. Their differences apparently hinged on two issues—the first being the call on one side that the decision making within the Hizb should be undertaken as a collective, against the insistence of al-Nabahani that the leadership and decision making was unitary. This argument was sparked by the second issue— the suggestion of some of the members to exclude Syria as a target for the Hizb's work, and instead adopt it as a form of a safe sanctuary to operate from, similar to how the Brotherhood treated its relationship with the Jordanian regime while it focused its struggle against Nasser in Egypt.[59] Their expulsion was a prominent example of al-Nabahani applying what he considered to be the consistent application of the Hizb's principles, which viewed all individual Muslim countries as one and all current regimes as illegitimate, against more pragmatic considerations of ensuring a safe base to work from by gaining the patronage of one of the region's regimes.

Other members left the Hizb over the decision to contest the elections for the consultative council, while another was expelled for pulling out from the elections in favor of a government candidate under pressure, described as the "carrot and stick" approach.[60] Similarly, al-Khayyat was expelled for writing a flattering letter to the King while serving a jail sentence due to his membership of the Hizb, and was subsequently "rewarded" by the government with the position of Minister for Religious Affairs.[61] These were the greatest internal divisions to occur under the leadership of al-Nabahani, while the leadership of Zalloom was also afflicted by internal division at the hands of a group led by senior member Mohammad Nafi', who was apparently originally disgruntled over the choice of Zalloom as leader and was subsequently expelled for trying to engineer an internal coup in the mid-1990s.[62]

However, internal conflict and increased security measures were not the only hurdles preventing the advancement of the work of the Hizb in its first decade. Rather, the environment of revolution and dissatisfaction which led to numerous changes of leadership and systems in a region facing interference from both the Western and Eastern camps during the height of the Cold War witnessed the rise of the charismatic leadership of Gamal Abdul-Nasser and pan-Arabism, ultimately embodied in the merger between Egypt and Syria and the establishment of the United Arab Republic in 1958. In the charged atmosphere after the claimed Arab victory of the Suez Canal, it was easier to mobilize Arab masses behind slogans of Arab unity, nationalism and anti-colonialism.[63] The nascent Arab nationalism and pan-Arabism was emerging in all its strength in this period, meaning that the emergence of the Hizb during the rise of anti-colonial struggles in the region ultimately detracted from its initial spread as a consequence of other events and meta-narratives overtaking and sidelining it, with legitimacy being conferred upon a secular ideology and discourse.

Whether the unification of Syria and Egypt was a response to genuine public demands is irrelevant, the fact being that such events, which included revolutions in Lebanon and Iraq, meant that the Hizb found that the public stopped listening to their call, believing that they had been truly liberated from the influence of colonialism. According to Awadallah, Nasser reached the stage of "being worshipped by the people," while at the same time the Hizb distributed leaflets declaring him an "American agent" which led to "wide-spread hatred against the Hizb."[64] As a result of this unpopular stance, the Hizb failed to gain any new supporters for years while simultaneously losing 75 per cent of its own membership due to their distrust of the party's analysis of the situation.[65] It is this kind of black and white proclamation couched within a paradigm that viewed the Middle East as an Anglo-American struggle for influence that can leave the Hizb open to accusations of an oversimplified analysis and discourse regarding the politics of the region. However, irrespective of information that has since come to light, such as CIA Director Allen Dulles' fondness for Nasser[66] or the truth behind claims that the CIA had "developed an intimacy with Nasser's revolutionary regime" and considered that their "first priority was to keep Nasser in power,"[67] by making statements in the heat of the rise of pan-Arabism and challenging the legitimacy of Nasser, the Hizb was demonstrating its belief that whoever advances the separation of religion from the State or politics is following a path trodden by "foreign intellectual leadership" and is therefore an agent of the imperialists, regardless of their intentions and position towards Islam.[68]

This wave of emotion and subsequent devotion to the various rulers proclaimed as saviors of the Arab people, wrestling them from the grip of colonialism, did not last, and by the late 1960s and early 1970s there was an optimism that the party was close to establishing its goal, shown in an open letter asking King Hussein of Jordan to "save the country and yourselves with the return of Islam and the establishment of the caliphate by handing the ruling over to Hizb ut-Tahrir," after a number of members had been arrested accused of planning to take "material actions" against the regime.[69] This optimism was misplaced and internal sources claim that the Hizb undertook a small number of failed attempts to engineer coup d'états simultaneously in Jordan, Iraq and Syria in the same period, which ultimately led to nothing other than the arrest of some of those involved.[70] A few days before his own death, al-Nabahani was left astonished at the passivity of the Palestinians to Anwar Sadat's visit to Jerusalem in 1977 after his "betrayal" of the Palestinian cause, contrasted to the way they had reacted to the visit of King Abdullah in 1951, claiming that although he "knew the *Umma* had declined," he did not realize it had "declined to this level."[71]

This pessimism continued during the first few years under the second leader, Zalloom, with a leaflet written during Israel's invasion of Lebanon in 1982 lamenting that it was only "the absence of the caliphate" which had given Israel the chance to "undertake the barbaric, disgusting slaughter of Palestinians and Lebanese," and that "the establishment of the caliphate has been delayed, for a reason that no-one other than Allah knows."[72] While al-Nabahani had been primarily engaged in bringing about the caliphate by trying to engineer coup attempts through influential army and tribal contacts, it may be that Zalloom, not having the same social and political stature of al-Nabahani, was unable to utilize such avenues if they continued to exist. If this is the case, then irrespective of the intellectual corpus of material of the party and its understanding among its members, the willingness of individuals within the military to apparently consider conferring consent on al-Nabahani was linked to his credibility as a leader as much as ideology. This meant that the party was forced to return to a focus on spreading its core message in an attempt to widen its constituency among the masses and to cultivate new personalities, a difficult task given the environment in which it was operating and its own lack of flexibility on ideological matters.

By the late 1990s and at the turn of the century the Hizb had spread globally, extending its reach well beyond the Middle East where, as yet, it had been unable to achieve and maintain deep penetration in society across the region. By 2009 it claimed to operate in over forty Muslim countries in conditions varying from illegality, facing severe security crackdowns such as in Bangladesh, to the more permissive atmosphere of somewhere like Indonesia. News reports seem to confirm a wide geographical spread of its membership, with arrests reported in Bangladesh, Pakistan, Palestine, Turkey, Uzbekistan, Kazakhstan and Kyrgyzstan within the last year, and public activities such as conferences and demonstrations held in Indonesia, Lebanon, Tunisia and Yemen amongst others. In the areas where the Hizb is banned, the focus is restricted to personal contact to convince individuals to study with the party while utilizing public events such as the Friday prayer to distribute their literature to the masses, as circumstances permit. Where they are able to operate publicly, their activities may also extend to hosting public talks and conferences, utilizing venues ranging from mosques to universities to propagate their call for a return to the caliphate on a public level while continuing with personal contact for more detailed discussion. In all cases, the Hizb does not idealize mass membership but rather mass support for its ideas, as the members are expected to gain the leadership and trust of the *Umma* as a result of their political and ideological beliefs, with membership to the party theoretically based upon adherence to its core literature and ideology. Their public activities are carried out with the aim of undermining the confidence of the people in incumbent political regimes, while building a critical mass of support for their political program, such that their envisaged call for the return to an Islamic system of governance will build momentum, drawing political and military figures to throw their weight behind the group. An independent branch of the party operates within each country, labeled "governorates" of the future caliphate, and adopts different styles of activity according to local circumstances, though the ideology presented is consistent across borders. They also have a presence in majority non-Muslim countries such as the UK, Australia, USA and Ukraine, among others, though they do not seek to undertake any political struggle against the governments of these countries owing to the belief that the natural returning point for the caliphate is the Muslim world.

Emerging out of the rupture of the *Nakba*, the Hizb was an anomaly in that it sought to reverse the events of 1924 while other anti-colonial, nationalist and pan-Arabist movements were mainly concerned with ideas of regional unity to reverse the events of 1948. It survived the initial clampdown in Jordan, internal ruptures, and a period in which it was seemingly operating in the wilderness, to spread its membership base and establish itself to an extent sufficient to address contemporary political issues such as the "clash of civilizations,"[73] the current global economic crisis,[74] and even international proposals to deal with climate change.[75] This is in keeping with the *ijtihad* of al-Nabahani that Islam has a viewpoint and solution for every issue confronting man, and is pursuant to the rebuilding of the legitimacy of Islam as a practical idea applicable to contemporary issues, with the caliphate providing the executive method for the implementation of these solutions. In doing so, the Hizb has continued to promote the caliphate as the only vehicle for true liberation from the forces of colonialism, and as a comprehensive solution to the issues facing not only Arabs or Muslims but also the whole of mankind after the failure of communism and the proclaimed "self destruction of global capitalism."

Intellectual Revival—Ijtihad for a "True Liberation"

Having been both displaced and having witnessed the failure of the "independent" Arab states firsthand, al-Nabahani embarked upon a study in his capacity as a jurist to understand why previous movements established with the aim of revival had as yet been unsuccessful. The independence of other countries from the apparent manifestations of colonialism was of little comfort given that his home was now occupied by the fledging Israeli state, and the circumstances gave him the opportunity to consider deeply the root causes of the political malaise in the region. This approach to analyzing the situation was mentioned in one of the original eight books published by the Hizb, stating that "it is dangerous for humans to jump from sensation to action without thinking" as "such behavior will never change the reality" but rather the person will in fact "succumb to reality and become reactionary" by making "reality the source of the thinking rather than the subject" of it.[76]

While others had been engaged in nationalistic and patriotic movements to attempt to secure liberation, the Hizb considered them to be engaging the people in a "cheap struggle" and a reaction to the suffering under colonialism, which "lacked any serious thought to define their course of action." The leaders of these struggles were also considered unwitting agents of imperialism since they had adopted foreign ideas such as patriotism, nationalism and secularism. The discussions of the period around the establishment of either an Islamic or an Arab League were dismissed as "colonial projects" which were used to take attention away from addressing the crucial issue of the Islamic state, while other movements had failed because "they were established upon a general undefined idea which was vague," without detailing a "method to implement their idea." Instead, the only correct philosophy to achieve revival would be an "ideology that combines the idea and method,"[77] with the "idea" meaning the laws and principles derived from the foundations of the ideology, and the "method" being the vehicle that would be responsible for executing them (in other words, the state).

In the first paragraph of the first book in the series released by the Hizb shortly after its inception, it states that man moves forward in accordance with what he understands to be the purpose of life. Therefore, for man to revive, it would be necessary to "comprehensively change his current thought" replacing it with another since "human behavior is linked to man's concepts," and to change the declined man's behavior "it is imperative to change his concepts first." This is explained by the verse of the Qur'an, "Allah does not change the circumstances of any people until they have changed what is within themselves." It would be that intellectual basis that forms what is described as the "comprehensive thought" which solves the "biggest problem for man," the question of his creation and the purpose of life, since all his actions and decisions ultimately return to that basis.[78]

In other words, the revival and decline of a people are linked to their intellectual state. The decline of the Muslims is identified as occurring from around the eighteenth century, with the cause identified as the "severe weakness" which "destroyed the ability of the minds in understanding Islam."[79] This, in turn, resulted from three factors. The first was the detachment of the Arabic language from Islam, which resulted in a weakness in *ijtihad*, and since *ijtihad* was the manner by which problems are resolved in accordance with Islam, it is the key which would keep the ideology alive. As a result of this, by the mid-nineteenth century Islam was being used to justify non-Islamic rules (such as the constitutions adopted by the Ottoman State) which resulted in the "detachment of Islam from life." The second factor was the influence of Indian philosophy, which engrained the idea of spiritualism and "self-deprivation" among Muslims leading to the adoption of a "passive life." Finally, the Western cultural invasion had led Muslims to adopt material interests ahead of everything else.[80]

It is this final cultural invasion which is seen as the true colonialism, since it is a colonization of the intellect which therefore prevents the possibility of any revival. As Western nations progressed through an intellectual and industrial revolution, the Ottoman caliphate remained paralyzed in the face of the development of the sciences due to the lack of capability of true *ijtihad*. There was a confusion which led to a failure among Muslims to distinguish between industry and inventions which "Islam encourages Muslims to acquire" irrespective of their source, and "culture and ideology," which must be adopted from Islamic sources alone. As a result, European achievements were seen by Muslims in general and by the religious establishment in particular as being antithetical to Islam, and consequently their adoption was prohibited. This created a dichotomy in society between two camps, one rejecting technological advances like the printing press while accusing "every intellectual of being a disbeliever," the other made up of those who had been educated in the West and wanted to adopt Western cultural facets along with scientific advancements wholesale.[81] It was this "industrial revolution," emerging in a "remarkable manner," which left Muslims "confused," and ultimately saw a shift of the balance of power toward Europe. Once intellectually dominant, a new set of "crusades" took place, which were to be more than just military invasion into Muslim lands, and were designed to "uproot the Islamic state" and "uproot Islam from the souls of the Muslims," leaving behind only "spiritual rites."[82] It was this lack of clarity between what could be adopted by Muslims irrespective of its source, meaning technologies without any intrinsic ideological values, and what had to be rejected as contrary to Islamic teachings, such as the ideas of nationalism, secularism and democracy, which the Hizb identified as the core reason why the Islamic State was unable to generate a coherent position in the face of the rise of the European powers, as evidenced by the Ottoman State's adoption of Ottomanism, pan-Islamism and nationalism at different junctures during its decline.

In addition to this decline towards the end of the caliphate, three further problems were identified as emerging at the beginning of the twentieth century. Islam was studied in a purely academic manner, with the religious scholars more akin to missionaries than seeking to practically resolve issues in accordance with Islamic law. Secondly, the West pursued an attack on the laws of Islam while the scholars "allowed Islam to stand accused" and consequently adopted an apologetic stance, which "caused them to misinterpret the rules of Islam." Finally, the destruction of the Islamic State and the occupation of the Muslim lands led to a perception of the Islamic State as an "impossibility" in the minds of many Muslims. They then accepted the legitimacy of un-Islamic rule, not seeing "any harm in this as long as the name of Islam was kept."[83]

Consequently the role of the group would be to reverse this decline and put the Muslim *Umma* on a path to revival, with the Hizb working "for the liberation of the Islamic *Umma*" from "slavery" in all aspects,[84] as it was necessary for an Islamic movement to be formed which understood Islam correctly and worked for the resurrection of the "Islamic way of life." This was necessary as even though in the first few years that followed the Second World War there was an "apparent autonomy" which was "enjoyed by some areas of the Islamic World," it remained "completely subjugated to the democratic capitalist intellectual leadership,"[85] with their rulers considered agents of the imperialist powers as they adopted foreign paradigms such as nationalism and secularism. Though society may be composed of majority Muslim populations, they remained dominated by un-Islamic thoughts, emotions and systems.

Hizb ut-Tahrir held that this decline would not be reversed so long as society was thought to consist of individuals alone, and that "the community is corrupted by the perversion of individuals,"[86] which led people to believe that change would come about by improving the moral and ethical state of the people, as had been the initial goal or method of most other groups, including the Brotherhood. The Hizb believed that reforming the individual would not lead to societal reform since they understood that a society would emerge when individuals in a group were "bonded" by "other components" which were the common "thoughts, emotions and systems."[87] Therefore if people complained about the loss of morals in society leading to widespread sin such as alcoholism and stealing, they should be made aware that this was the "result of the absence of the *shari'a*," since the "sanctities of Allah" could only be protected through the implementation of the proscribed punishments.[88]

Accordingly, society would only be changed if the thoughts and emotions which existed between the people were changed, and the systems implemented upon them were removed and replaced. It would be this remodeled society which would reform the individual, and not vice versa. This could only be achieved if what are described as "partial solutions," such as establishing educational and charitable associations and organizations, are rejected in favor of political work, and if the Islamic "thought and method" formed the exclusive basis of that work rather than the politics of compromise imposed from the West such as submission to the status quo and pragmatism.[89] This has invariably meant that the Hizb has found itself unable to take advantage of political opportunities to open a space for itself within state controlled political arenas, unlike other Islamic movements, such as the Brotherhood in Egypt and the AKP in Turkey, who have been better able to create political space for themselves because of their willingness to work within the confines of incumbent political systems. Conversely, it is this consent that prevents such groups from being able to talk about the caliphate as an alternative, and rather restricts discussion to some form of Islamic state utilizing the existing political framework.

Built upon their view of society, the call of the Hizb is defined as being a "collective *da'wa*" addressing "public opinion" in an attempt to change the prevailing consensus, which held that living under an un-Islamic system was permissible, to one whereby a new opinion was established which would subsequently necessitate the creation of an alternative system to regulate society's affairs in accordance with the *shari'a*. Therefore if the people in an area are "bonded" by a public opinion in which Islamic thoughts and emotions were dominant, believing that Islam should be the regulator of their societal affairs and awarding sole legitimacy to the *shari'a* even though individuals in that society may remain irreligious in personal conduct, the natural next step would be to establish a system which would enforce and protect that regulation and consequently reform individuals within that society. It is at this point that the Hizb would then seek to engineer the establishment of that system through either mobilizing popular support or by calling upon the military establishment to enforce a change in power in line with public opinion.

The Hizb summarized its work as being composed of three main stages based on their *ijtihad* and derived from how the Prophet went through various stages while establishing a state in Medina. It would begin with the intensive ideological culturing of individuals who would form the party, carrying its ideology before then entering the public arena and engaging in discussion to address and mould public opinion, and finally engaging in political struggle when they would seek support for a radical change, uprooting and replacing the current political system. This would be the "Islamic state" or caliphate, which the Hizb defined as "a caliph implementing the *shari'a*,"[90] or the "political entity which governs the affairs of its citizens in accordance with the *shari'a* rules."

The Caliph, Caliphate and Constitution

This understanding of the caliph differed from many of the prevailing ideas of the time that saw it as a title or position to be filled by a charismatic leader rather than a unique form of government, such as the Brotherhood, who first envisaged making the national state Islamic (hence their understanding of the construction "Islamic State") before the formation of some loose form of coalition or unity to appoint a figurehead caliph. The Hizb rejected this conception as it considered it to be built upon the Western definition of the state as a "collection of territory, inhabitants and rulers," whereas they considered the Islamic understanding of the state to be expansive and encapsulating people of multiple ethnicities, races and languages. Rather, "any mass who respond" to the call of Islam and believe in it "become a part of its subjects, and their land becomes a part of its land".[91]

Their concept of the Islamic State is one completely different to other political systems, as set out in the Hizb's explanation to the Jordanian government and public at large in a leaflet published in 1953, after it was initially refused a permit to operate. In it, mirroring the argument between Ali Abdul-Raziq and his opponents, it completely rejects the idea of the state being theocratic, since it is neither "holy" nor "sancti-fied," but rather it "derives its authority from the *Umma*" who are "represented by the state" which acts as the "implementer of the *shari'a*" rather than as "a sanctified ruler." The position of caliph was thought to be a human, civil position to which one was elected by the people rather than an infallible, ordained representative of God on earth, and so the-refore it was only obligatory to obey the ruler if he implemented the rules of Islam given that his legitimacy was derived solely from his adhe-rence to enforcing the *shari'a*. Any deviation from this would incur an obligation on the part of the people to hold him to account and correct him.[92] In addition, the laws implemented would also not be considered as sanctified since they are rules derived from Islamic jurisprudence and are therefore "open to discussion" and to "change, correction and remo-val according to correct *ijtihad*."[93]

Any comparison to other systems of governance was also rejected, whether republican, federal or otherwise. The caliphate alone was the only valid expression of statehood recognized by Islam, and was there-fore the only possible model for an Islamic state. Though the state was also defined as not having fixed borders, and therefore open to expan-sion, it was claimed that it was not imperialist since "the Islamic way of ruling is to establish equality between the subjects in all regions of the state," whether Muslim or otherwise. This insistence upon the unique-ness of the caliphate as a political structure meant that although the word "caliph" was important, it was not indispensible, on the condition that any other term used in its place had to convey a meaning that would be similarly understood and not confused with any other political system. The terms Sultan, Leader of the Believers and Head of State were all acceptable, whereas President of the Republic or King were not, as they represented un-Islamic political systems.[94] This concern for dif-ferentiation and "authenticity" extends throughout their understanding of the caliphate, another example being that "it is not permitted to make the *shura* (consultative) council analogous to the parliament," as it would detract from the "visualization" and therefore the uniqueness and practicality of the Islamic rule.[95] Paradoxically, the use of thoroughly modern terms such as *mabda* (ideology), *dawla* (state) and *dustor* (constitution) to articulate the Hizb's ideas has prompted the accusation that they are in fact engaging in a form of apologetic politics similar to other "modernists" who adopted democratic discourse, as argued by

Farouki. The Hizb frequently respond to this charge by arguing that such words are neutral terminological definitions rather than ideological expressions and the importance is not the form of the word or its origin but the meaning that it represents. Accordingly, while the terms constitution and state do not represent a specific type of constitution or state and are therefore ideologically neutral, the word democracy has ideological connotations which are seen as contradictory to Islam.

For any system to be considered truly Islamic, the Islamic belief (*aqida*) must form the basis of the state, which meant that its constitution and laws had to be derived from Islamic sources—the Qur'an and Prophetic narrations. The Islamic state was founded upon four principles: that *shari'a* law is sovereign and not the will of the people as in a representative democracy; that the authority for electing, holding to account and removing the ruler belongs to the Muslim *Umma*; that the election of a single leader over all Muslims is a religious obligation; and that it would be the leader of the state who would decide which *shari'a* rule is to be followed where differences arise. He would be the one who prescribes the constitution and the rest of the laws,[96] a point contested by other modern proponents of Islamic governance who suggest that a more consensual approach to legislation is mandated to circumvent the dangers of the accumulation of power in a single individual encompassing both executive and legislative power.[97]

The Hizb has written and updated several books on issues such as economic, judicial and social policy to propose its own *ijtihad* of what this system would look like, detailing the fundamental principles and structure of the basis of the state and its constitution in order for its "visualization" as a practical entity be demonstrated to the *Umma*. They suggest that the caliph should restrict his adoption of laws to the minimum level required to regulate societal affairs and propose that the constitution should formalize this. The latest copy includes articles regarding the process for the election of the caliph; the structure of the state—detailing powers and limitations of Executive and Delegated Assistants (*mu'awin al-tanfidth/tafwid*); Governors (*wula*) and the Consultative Council (*majlis al-Umma*); details of the judiciary (which they divide into three areas: resolving disputes at the personal, public and state level); details of revenues, expenditures and economic policies of the state including taxation policy and differentiation between state, public and private ownership; and sections on the industrial, educational, media and foreign policies of the state.[98]

The caliph is to be elected by the *Umma* and after being elected he undertakes a specific contract or pledge of allegiance (*bay'a*) with them to implement *shari'a* and run the affairs of the state according to Islam while they in turn give him their support and obedience, a form of social contract between the two. In the case of complaints against the caliphate itself, there is a specific court (*madhalim*) established to deal with any issue pertaining to the state up to the level of the caliph, with the judges given the authority to ultimately remove the caliph or any other person in a ruling position if deemed to not be ruling in accordance with Islam. In effect, there is a contract of consent, articulated in the *bay'a*, between the caliph and the *Umma*, with the *madhalim* court as the final arbiter in resolving conflicts.

The organization of the caliphate is based upon centralized ruling authority with a decentralized administration. It is to be divided into provinces (*wilaya*) with each province ruled by a governor (*wali*) who is appointed by the caliph. Provinces are then further sub-divided into smaller administrative regions. The Hizb divides the possible types of governorship seen in Islamic history between "general" and "specific" roles. General roles are those in which the governor is given full control over all aspects of governorship in his province while a specific role is where the responsibility for tax collection, for example, is separated from that of controlling the judiciary. Both types of role are claimed to have precedence in the practice of the Prophet and his early companions. Citing the problems encountered in Islamic history as a result of overly powerful governors, notably during the Abbasid era, which saw the caliph reduced to a symbolic figurehead mentioned in congregational prayers, the Hizb holds that each province should appoint separate governors to control the army, judiciary and responsibility for revenues. These governors will have the general capability to run the affairs within their area of jurisdiction in accordance with their *ijtihad* but within the overall limits of the constitution adopted by the caliph.

The caliph also has the ability to appoint two types of assistant. Executive Assistants are given the responsibility for executing the orders of the caliph, making it primarily an administrative rather than ruling position. The other type of assistant is the Delegated Assistant, who acts as a deputy to the caliph in that he is given the authority to make decisions acting on behalf of the caliph, carrying responsibility for the management of regions of the caliphate, giving him the same capability as the caliph to appoint the governors and other ruling positions within his appointed region. However, the caliph is still considered to be the sole person responsible for the subjects of the state, and therefore must review and monitor the actions of his Delegated Assistants to maintain control over his actions and their consequences.

Citizenship within the Islamic state is awarded according to residency, with any person who takes up permanent residency within any of the lands of the state becoming a citizen. A Muslim who decides to live outside of the state would not be considered a citizen, and the rules and laws of the caliphate as a coercive entity would not apply to him, whereas a non-Muslim who chose to live within the state would be subject to the rules and laws except those specifically conditional upon Islamic belief (most prominently paying the *Zakah* tax on wealth, instead they pay a *jizya* which is a head tax). This goes against the generality of the "universal" authority claimed during the Ottoman era, with Muslims who choose to remain outside of the territory of the state subject to the government they reside under. Though their primary allegiance is still expected to be to Islam, and by extension its political entity, this is considered to be a creedal issue rather than a legislative one.

This centralized power, delegated through the structure and institutions of the Islamic state, is reflected in the organization of the Hizb itself. The leader of the Hizb is restricted according to the party's core ideology and can be held accountable to it, but he holds the final decision on any party action or adoption within that framework. At the same time the group is divided into several geographical provinces, each run by an elected member, with sub-committees appointed by the provincial leader responsible for the administration of activities in regional sub-divisions. The provincial leadership runs its province independently and is responsible for the authoring and publication of any local materials, the administration of public and private cultural activities and interaction with local media and politicians, with the central leadership taking a monitoring role. The leader of the Hizb also appoints assistants who can be sent across regions as his representative or to carry out executive tasks on his behalf. In the same manner as the *madhalim* court within the state, there is a parallel office within the Hizb which deals with complaints regarding members and the leadership. The administrative structure of the party is closely aligned to the envisaged structure of a future caliphate and provides a suggestion of how aspects of the caliphate would operate if implemented according to their lite-rature,[99] though there are obvious differences between a political party and a state.

The attention to detail in mapping out the structure of the state at the inception of the party, along with detailed explanations of various Isla-mic principles and issues within jurisprudence and a comparison of Islam to capitalism and communism, was in line with the belief that the primary cause of the decline of the Muslim was an intellectual one, and that the path to revival was a renewal of *ijtihad*, thereby practically demonstrating the applicability of Islamic law for all times and all places. The call to the revival and propagation of Islam was to be based upon thought, and "it should be delivered as an intellectual leadership." This meant they believed that the promotion of ideas within the people had to be solely based on Islam, even if this led to rejection and conflict with the dominant modes of thought at the time, since the person adhe-ring to this would not be seeking the praise of the people or rulers, but rather his belief would "mandate that the sovereignty belongs to the ideology" alone.[100]

The Islamic state could only be established if these ideas gained legi-timacy in society. As peoples' views in life change, their interests would also alter, and since the state is charged with the "guardianship" and "management" of society's interest,[101] their emergence would naturally necessitate a change of executive power since the previous regime would no longer be considered legitimate and therefore no longer have the consent of the people. Elections were rejected as a method by which to achieve this consent, in part because al-Nabahani believed, for example, that "socialism could not reach power in a country under the influence of the West through elections" and so in the same way "Islam cannot attain authority in a country under the influence of the West through elections," meaning that the State would prevent its own apparatus from being used to bring about its own downfall. Therefore participation in elections was to be used simply as a way to disseminate ideas. The only way to achieve the radical change required would be "to spread the idea to the masses until there is mass support" leading to "a revolution car-ried out by the masses," or through "a coup d'état by the military" enfor-cing the will of the people against the old established order.[102]

The Hizb's conception of the caliphate is based upon a certain type of social contract and a type of constitutional theory which could be described as falling between the two poles of legal and popular constitutionalism. The social contract is between the ruler, or caliph, and the ruled, or *Umma*, whereby the *Umma* consents to be ruled by the caliph who is elected by them on the agreement that he will govern them according to the constitution, derived from Islamic sources. It could also be described as a form of contractualism, with the *shari'a* providing its normative force in place of a rationally derived morality. Since the elected caliph has the final say in the constitution, it could be argued that the system is an autocratic one with unrestricted power concentrated in the hands of the ruler. The counterargument would posit that the caliphate is more closely related to a form of constitutionalism which would constrain the ruler, in that although he has responsibility to take the final decision upon most constitutional and legislative matters, he is restricted by the Islamic sources. The interpretation of these sources can be challenged by any person, akin to a type of popular constitutionalism, though the final arbiter in such disputes would be the *madhalim* court, which could overrule the caliph, a form of legal constitutionalism. Hence there exists a form of accountability and balance invested in the separate court system which would check the power of the caliph. The other critical aspect is that there is no concept of popular sovereignty in the legislative sense, but rather sovereignty lies in the *shari'a*, meaning that, as mentioned, any interpretations can be challenged by anyone and overturned if found to be invalid. This could be termed a type of Islamic constitutionalism, where the rule of law is paramount, state power is restricted and political participation is considered a duty under the overall Islamic tenets of enjoining good and forbidding evil.

The caliphate is therefore the Islamic state initially established on the back of public support that gives legitimacy to the *shari'a* as the source of legislation, and consent to a caliph to apply it across society. The Hizb's initial literature warns against taking the leadership prematurely, which they believed could occur as a result of people handing them consent based primarily upon their agreement with the party's prognosis of the imperialist designs on the region, but that "the masses would not have lost their previous emotions," and thoughts such as "racism", "tribalism" and "freedom" would soon re-emerge.[103] This did not, however, mean there was a lack of optimism within the group, with Dawood Hamdan reportedly believing that the party would garner enough support to achieve its objectives within three months, a wildly optimistic forecast that he soon recalculated.[104]

The price paid for proclaiming the regimes in the Middle East as illegitimate and ultimately undermining the very basis upon which they were established was for the Hizb to be confronted and harassed as a security threat in the West Bank from the outset in the same manner as the other groups perceived to threaten the Hashemite entity. The price for not compromising on their ideas and methodology was to miss any opportunity to work with the rest of the opposition in the face of that oppression, leaving themselves isolated and at times seemingly irrelevant as events passed them by.

The Road to Liberation—Conflicts and Confrontation

According to Hizb literature, effective political movements do not emerge "when affluence prevails," when "natural rights are secured" or when "people are selected to hold important positions based on their competence," but rather the success of any collective movement is "measured by its ability to instigate resentment amongst the masses."[105] After one year of working in Jordan, since its founding members were all based there, it published four further booklets on top of the eight initial books released, explaining in more detail the next stage of entering and imposing itself on the society as a political entity. It stated clearly that "the one weapon in the hand of the Hizb is Islam" with the "intellectual aspect" the only weapon for the party.[106] This would lead to an intellectual confrontation where the party warns against conflict with the general public and to carry the *Umma* with it such that the "conflict against colonialism" is between all of them "and not the Hizb alone."[107]

With the physical vestiges of colonialism mostly gone, this meant conflict to undermine the legitimacy of foreign ideas and culture, upheld primarily by "a Western influenced and educated group" which emerged towards end of the nineteenth century, and made up the majority of those who became politically involved in government in the Middle East. These "graduates" of the "imperial process" were educated "with a culture which teaches them how others thought" rather than their own authentic thoughts and ideas, and hence they became "strangers to the *Umma*, unaware of themselves and their *Umma*."[108] In other words, they were in effect carrying on as the agents of the imperialists, even though they were people of local origins and may have had other intentions.

A clash between the Hizb and the ruling classes was therefore inevitable since they were seeking to undermine their legitimacy, and after tiring of Ahmed Da'ur's constant criticism of the Jordanian government in the Representative Council, he was expelled in 1958 with the consent of all but one member of the council, stripped of his immunity and given a three year jail sentence. A similar process occurred in Lebanon in 1962 when the Hizb's application for a permit was rejected, a move decried by the Hizb as an "attack on Islam" since the party's only activities were "spreading its ideas," "holding public and private gatherings," "sending delegations," and the publishing of books.[109] Intolerance of the Hizb peaked in 1963, when a member of the Hizb was tortured to death in Iraq.

The perception of the incumbent rulers as representing foreign ideas and the systems of imperialism, forced upon the people, was central to the call for the caliphate, since the "political struggle" was considered to be "commanding the good, forbidding evil and questioning the rulers," and as such these the most important actions for liberation and carrying the call to Islam once the party had become more established in society.[110] A quick survey of Hizb literature from the 1960s onwards shows a fairly consistent application of this principle, coupled with a constant call for the establishment of an independent, unified caliphate established upon Islamic law. In 1967, a leaflet criticizing then Turkish Prime Minister Sulaiman Demeril accused him of hypocrisy by opening an Islamic center one day and a large alcohol factory the next, calling him an "employee" in the "hands of the military," and informing him that without a doubt "the Islamic State and the caliphate are going to return."[111] King Husain of Jordan was labeled as a traitor for cooperating with the British and the Israelis, and accused of pulling the army out of Palestine in 1967 in some areas without firing even a single shot.[112] In 1975, Sadat was characterized as a "sincere American agent" who "should be thrown out against the wall."[113] Libyan leader Muammar Gaddafi was contacted in 1978 after the publishing of his "Green Book," in which he detailed his "Third Universal Theory" as an alternative to capitalism and communism, and debate ensued on the role of politics in Islam and how his call ran contradictory to the beliefs of Muslims. He was urged to "drop his call," give up his "greenness" and to hand over rule to those who would "announce the establishment of the caliphate of Islam, and to appoint the caliph," to whom Muslims would pledge obedience.[114] While some of these moments of contact were undertaken in the hope of a positive response, they were often intended to publically expose the positions of the rulers of the time, with details of the meetings published and distributed, including the Hizb's detailed refutation of Gaddafi's rejection of the *Sunna*, which had been presented to him directly.

Other governments which claimed to be Islamic were also scrutinized. An internal leaflet in 1970 addressed the question of whether King Faisal was ruling in accordance with Islam or not. It was stated that Saudi Arabia was historically a monarchical system which was fundamentally un-Islamic, and the pledge of allegiance given in the country to the ruler was merely a formality, and in any case illegitimately given to the monarch as head of a nation-state and not as the caliph of the Islamic state.[115] Khomeini and the Iranian government were contacted and urged to establish the caliphate, and were criticized because the constitution of the Islamic Republic was not derived solely from the Qur'an and *Sunna*, the Republic system was "not an Islamic form of government," and nationalism contradicted Islam.[116] It appears that this was the last time a delegation was sent directly to address a ruling faction for some time, with a leaflet in 2008 stating that the Hizb had refrained from continuing this activity due to the belief that any positive response was beyond hope.[117]

Also targeted for criticism by the Hizb, at least in substance if not with respect to their intentions, were those Islamic movements who campaigned for an "Islamic state" within the existing political system. A prominent example outside of the Brotherhood was Abul Ala Maududi's Jamaat-i-Islami, which was characterized as one of the "most sincere" and "most aware" movements. He was criticized for "election campaign papers" which "[did] not call for the establishment of the caliphate," but instead for "Pakistan to be an Islamic state," which would not act as a starting point for expansion but rather remain within its national borders. As such, Islam had been utilized in nationalistic terms, and Pakistan would be "a national Islamic State" and nothing more.[118]

Nationalism of all types was rejected from the outset by the Hizb, including any wider form of pan-Arabism. The call to nationalism was considered to be a call to imperialism, as it was thought of as alien to Islamic teachings and was unknown in Islamic lands before "the disbelievers brought it there." In one of his addresses to the Jordanian parliament, Da'ur mocked the government's "deep belief" that the "Jordanian people are part of the Arab nation," proclaiming that they were simply words without any real meaning behind them. The call to nationalism was seen as a call to disunity, and the people should not "consider each state as a sister state" but rather as part of a single entity, and therefore all talk of "co-operation" between "sister states" was in fact propagating division.[119] This is ironic as the government at the time was adopting both nationalist and Islamic discourse to undermine the threat of a secular pan-Arabism and parties such as the Arab Nationalist Movement (ANM), who were agitating for a union with Egypt, but the Hizb's uncompromising stance meant there was no real chance for cooperation with either side given their refusal to accept any space for the legitimacy of unity of Arabism nor consent for the King, leaving it on the fringes of the events in post-Nabulsi 1957.

This rejection of nationalism and pan-Arabism also extended to the question of Palestine. While its position that any peace or colonial presence in the land was considered a crime was similar to that of the ANM, like the Brotherhood they would stress that it was an Islamic question. The establishment of the Palestinian Liberation Organization (PLO) was seen as a ploy to make the issue a local, nationalist one rather than one concerning all Muslims. As such, though its members may have been considered sincere in some cases, the idea behind its creation made it a "traitorous" organization, which was being used as "tool" to bring about recognition of the Israeli state in the region, and that throughout the history of Palestine the British had never been able to achieve its plans without the complicity of some of the natives.[120] In its literature, the Hizb classed the issue of Palestine as an Islamic rather than Arab issue, a confrontation "between the Muslims and the West" rather than "the Arabs and the West." Israel is seen as having been established and supported by external states, and so the "true enemy" was the British and Americans, and Israel was merely a "bridgehead" used by others to maintain control and influence within Arab lands. The "solving of the Palestinian problem" by "the removal of Israel" from its roots through a "jihad" to "save Palestine" could only be achieved through the establishment of the caliphate.[121]

The growth of the Hizb in its contemporary form can be traced back to the beginning of the 1990s, soon after the fall of the Soviet Union, which led to the belief among some people that the era of ideology had finally come to an end. Currently there is a combination of growth in a belief in the failure of nationalism and the nation state across the previously colonized world, the crisis of legitimacy suffered by some Muslim governments and the recession of the universality of Western thought after its reinvigoration at the end of the Cold War, due in no small part to the legitimacy of its claims to economic and social superiority being undermined by events from Guantanamo Bay to the bailout of the banking system. With pan-Arabism largely dead, the era of the charismatic leader seemingly over and Arab nation-states continuing to fail their local populations both in immediate economic and social terms as well as in the ongoing occupation of Palestine, the caliphate as part of Islamic ideology, as an authentic alternative to a universal "liberal democracy", may be an alternative vision in which legitimacy is conferred upon the *shari'a* instead, though increased reference to it may simply be a return to tradition after the failure of "alien" or "modern" ideologies. With increased conflict between Arab states and increased sectarianism, the caliphate is the model that would "gather the Muslims" and "unite their lands," and guarantee the "protection of the Muslim lands" and everyone, "irrespective of whether they were Muslim or not," would "have the full rights of the citizens, and enjoy the rights and obligations of the *shari'a*."[122] However, until now the Hizb has not established itself in critical Arab countries such as Egypt, possibly due to the strength of the Brotherhood there. Their true size and influence is hard to gauge, but indications of their presence in parts of the region include the mass arrest of hundreds of activists in Syria at the turn of the century, an economics conference in Khartoum in January 2009 which reportedly attracted thousands of attendees, and since 2005, a growth in membership in the West Bank, with a rally in Ramallah in August 2007 bringing 20,000 people onto the streets according to official estimates.[123] As a result of the more open political environment post-2011, members of the party began to appear on local and satellite television in countries like Tunisia and Egypt, an indication of their presence in the region which was previously not apparent due to the state security apparatus in place.

In other regions like Central Asia, new nations were born with unrepresentative governments that applied even harsher repression than the communist regimes before them, and with no ideology or even a shared identity to build legitimacy upon, the ground was fertile for the expansion of the Hizb in spite of the security climate, which has reportedly seen the arrest and imprisonment of thousands of activists in the region.

Though far away from the issues of Palestine and the troubles of the Middle East, the Hizb has maintained the same stance in these regions, but focused upon explaining the solutions offered by Islam and their conception of the caliphate to the specific social and economic problems in the region. In Indonesia, the growth and visibility of the Hizb has increased over the past decade, with questions raised as to whether the independence of the country "is a real independence" or whether it was "still languishing under colonialism," with the answer being that "colonialism is still hovering over the country through intellectual dependency, political subordination and economic dominance, and even in many aspects of military subordination." Through the establishment of the caliphate, "the Muslims will become powerful anew" and would "put an end to all the oppressors and despots who are pressing on the necks of the Muslims," which would lead to "Indonesia and the rest of the Muslim countries" being "freed from the influence of the disbelieving colonialist nations such as the United States which plunders the countries' wealth."[124]

The liberation targeted by Hizb ut-Tahrir is one from the intellectual chains of colonialism, which according to them will be achieved by intellectively elevating Muslims such that Islam becomes their reference in all societal relationships, until they demand that the state applies Islam upon them to regulate those relationships according to the Islamic system. The caliphate is the practical embodiment of that demand, since the Islamic state is not simply made up of the rulers, but rather, according to the Hizb, it is "the *Umma* practically under the authority of the caliphate," which in their construction means that "the whole of the *Umma* is the State."[125] The use of the term "caliphate" was initially avoided as the Hizb did not want to build legitimacy around the legacy of the failed Ottoman State, but rather upon the capacity of Islam to provide its own comprehensive legal and political system. Over time, the Hizb has used the term more as a signifier for the ideas it is promoting as it felt those ideas had been understood and accepted by the people. Though the caliphate as a term has begun to enter parts of mainstream Muslim political discourse once again, as modern failure has allowed it to be re-imagined, it is usually still a reference to a vision of Islamic solidarity which existed in the past such as the Head of the Organization of the Islamic Conference (OIC), claiming they were its inheritor in the contemporary era in order to confer legitimacy upon themselves.[126]

The intellectual revolution which was sought supposedly prevented al-Nabahani from accepting offers of power during that first decade, with the Hizb claiming to have had offers of support from members of the military establishment in Jordan in 1953, 1957, 1961 and 1963, rejecting them since it "felt that the society in Jordan had not embraced the Hizb,"[127] in other words because they considered that the people were not ready to award sole legitimacy to the *Shari'a*, though they may have consented to the rule of al-Nabahani. Given the lack of success of future attempts, this may have been an overly optimistic reading of what such offers could have possibly led to. The Hizb considered that it was the absence of the caliphate that was the root physical issue and that if left unaddressed it would lead to the perpetuation of other problems. According to their *ijtihad*, this executive structure was the correct expression of a popular will that was liberated from the legacy of colonialism and submitted to Islamic rule, which would then work to carry it to the rest of the world.

The Hizb believes that since the mid-1960s the intellectual elevation has been achieved within the *Umma* to a sufficient extent that it would now consent to the establishment of the caliphate, and according to internal sources, the Hizb has attempted to engineer coup d'états in Jordan, Iraq and Tunisia, but the process has arguably been reduced to seeking military support rather than instigating civil unrest. Though the group has in the past addressed the rulers directly, only one such leaflet has recently been produced, consisting of four pages, delivered to governments in 2008. It explains to them that although the Hizb realizes they may consider the establishment of the caliphate as a dream far removed from reality, they were being called to establish the caliphate in what they considered to be an opportune time of Western inability to consolidate their occupation of both Iraq and Afghanistan, along with a rise in the support for the call to a caliphate as evidenced by the increased attendance and visibility at events held by the Hizb around the world. The message ends by stating that the Hizb realizes that they will not respond positively, but that the call was being delivered "in compliance" with the Qur'anic injunction of delivering the warning of a punishment for those who stand to block the path of Islamic revival.[128]

Several contemporary leaflets produced by the Hizb end by encouraging and commanding the "people of power," in other words the military, to fulfill the wishes of the people by removing whatever current regime exists and establishing the caliphate in its place. In Pakistan in May 2010, a long media campaign was waged ahead of a "Declaration to the People of Power," calling upon the military to "uproot the agent rulers" and "establish the caliphate." The declaration took place in the Islamabad media club, where a statement was read out in front of the assembled journalists by a single member, with a large security presence waiting outside to arrest him.[129] The Hizb remained relatively unknown amongst the masses in Pakistan. However, the arrest of a brigadier accused of having links to the group in 2011[130] has subsequently raised their profile in Pakistan as an active opposition party seeking to remove the incumbent government. In the Middle East, though the party was not especially visible in the media during the uprisings, they were accused by the Syrian regime of playing an early role in the uprising by distributing leaflets which led to the initial demonstrations against the regime.[131] Though the party has iterated its belief that the *Umma* is ready for the establishment of the caliphate, it has not yet shown itself capable of establishing its own legitimacy amongst the masses, and could simply be retreading the path of al-Nabahani's original optimism and subsequent disappointment.

While to al-Banna the caliphate was the ultimate goal to be established after all reform had been achieved, and was seen as an aspiration for the future, the caliphate as conceived by al-Nabahani is what would actually lead to the comprehensive reformation of the individual since the individual must be reformed by society and not vice versa. The intellectual repression of the *Umma* was the true legacy of the colonial occupation in the view of the Hizb, and its liberation could only come about by adopting an authentic ideology as derived from Islamic sources, which would lead to the implementation of an authentic form of government over Muslims.

This academic approach, combined with party activism that rejects the legitimacy of any of the regimes in the Middle East, is one of the most prominent characteristics of Hizb ut-Tahrir. Al-Nabahani was perhaps the natural combination of the political involvement of his grandfather, the dynamism of al-Banna and the Brotherhood, and the precise academic approach of al-Azhar scholars such as Sheikh al-Khidr Husain, who had refuted Ali Abdul-Raziq in 1925, a few years before giving al-Nabahani the formal *ijaza* (qualification as an Islamic scholar and permission to teach), having taught him at the university. The party emerged at a time when people's hopes for liberation, independence and honor were increasingly articulated in terms of Arab nationalism and unity of a secular nature. Many anti-imperial activists were adopting socialism as a framework through which to articulate their demands and politics. Against this backdrop, the Hizb appeared as an anomaly. Though it has been considered a security threat from the moment of its inception, it remains a non-violent movement eschewing material actions in favor of "*da'wa*", the result of adherence to their ideology and *ijtihad*, while their call for the re-establishment of the caliphate has since emerged in the discourse of others as the failure of alternatives and lack of legitimacy of local regimes has left space in which it has been re-imagined.

5

INSPIRATION FROM THE PAST

OSAMA BIN LADEN AND AL-QAEDA—THE DISCOURSE OF RESISTANCE

So where is democracy? Where is freedom? Where is human rights? Where is justice? Where is justice? We will never forget! We will never forget what these criminals have done.[1]

Ayman al-Zawahiri[2]

The loss of legitimacy of one of the major Middle Eastern states would have grave consequences internationally, and would lead more people to invoke the symbolism of the caliphate as a defender and representative of Islam. This was the legacy of British colonialism in the region, with one consequence being the creation of the sovereign state of Kuwait, which was given its formal independence from British control in 1961. This independence was immediately contested by Iraq, another mandate creation patched together in the aftermath of the First World War. The dispute had been simmering for a number of years, with numerous botched agreements of varying value such as the 1913 Anglo-Ottoman convention which somehow managed to recognize Ottoman sovereignty over Kuwait while agreeing to not interfere with British control, quickly discarded at the outset of war and followed afterwards by the 1922 Uqair agreement which established "neutral" zones between Saudi Arabia and Kuwait. This was followed by an agreement the next year between Iraq and Kuwait which failed to specify the precise location of the border between the two countries, a somewhat crucial omission given the subsequent oil discoveries in the disputed region.[3]

Attempts by Iraq in 1961 to exert their perceived right over the land were met by Kuwaiti appeals to the British to come to their aid. The country was subsequently admitted to the Arab League, with the Iraqi delegation storming out of the meeting at the time. Almost thirty years later, facing heavy debts after a decade long regional war of attrition with Iran, Iraqi forces amassed by President Saddam Hussein along the disputed border entered Kuwaiti territory on August 2, 1990. Within two days, the small Sheikhdom was under Iraqi control, with most of the ruling royal family fleeing by helicopter to neighboring Saudi Arabia. Taking place in the immediate aftermath of the formal end of the Cold War, the move created the opportunity for the United States to forge a broad international coalition against Iraq, with President George Bush Sr. addressing a joint session of Congress on September 11, 1990, announcing that "the crisis in the Persian Gulf, as grave as it is, also offers a rare opportunity to move toward an historic period of cooperation," and a move toward the objective of "a new world order."[4]

The arrival of an international coalition of troops in the Arabian Peninsula was the final provocation that sparked a rupture between a young Saudi man, Osama bin Laden, and the Saudi regime. Bin Laden had returned to Saudi Arabia from his heroic exploits fighting the Soviets in Afghanistan, and claimed that the veterans who had helped bring about the downfall of the Communist power should be used to expel the invading Iraqi Ba'athist army from Kuwait. Writing in the *Daily Telegraph* in 2005, Anton La Guardia claimed that "for Osama bin Laden and his followers, the end of the caliphate was the moment of historic rupture."[5] An examination of the roots of Bin Laden's grievances indicate that the real rupture was the first Gulf war. The split that occurred between Bin Laden and the Saudi regime was compounded by the arrival of non-Muslim troops in a land where, according to Bin Laden, they should never have been allowed to enter. If other areas of the Middle East had still been under the chains of a cultural and political colonialism relying upon or submitting to Western traditions and interests for its direction, relying upon Western forces could in turn be construed as a return to a more obvious physical form of colonization.

Ten years after his father had talked about forming a "New World Order," another event of seismic consequence would afflict America on its own soil. Addressing Congress and the American people nine days after 9/11, President George Bush Jr. declared that "the enemies of freedom," in this case a "collection of loosely affiliated terrorist organizations known as al-Qaeda," had "committed an act of war" against the United States. Al-Qaeda was described as terrorism's mafia, but with the caveat that their goal was not "making money." Rather, their aim was "remaking the world—and imposing its radical beliefs on people everywhere."[6] Five years later, Bush began to articulate what he believed that aim was. Remaking the world meant the establishment of a "totalitarian Islamic empire across the Middle East," in other words "a caliphate."[7] The American administration had shown little interest in the word before 2006, but there was a clear shift in emphasis within the administration in the months preceding this radio address. In 2006 alone, the "caliphate" was mentioned more than fifteen times by Bush, including, on one occasion, four times in a single speech.[8] The day after the President's radio address, Vice-President Dick Cheney stated that al-Qaeda wanted to "recreate the old caliphate,"[9] and, prior to his resignation, Defense Secretary Donald Rumsfeld told Pentagon employees that the goal of extremists was to "establish a caliphate" on the back of the destabilization of "moderate mainstream Muslim regimes."[10] Erstwhile allies helped promote this discourse, including British Home Secretary Charles Clarke, who told his American audience "there can be no negotiation about the re-creation of the caliphate" or "imposition of *shari'a* law" since in his understanding they were contrary to the values "fundamental to our civilization," which were "simply not up for negotiation," a strident position for a Minister whose remit was, at least theoretically and in the post-Imperial age, concerned with the domestic issues of Britain and not the Middle East.[11]

A cursory glance at the statements of al-Qaeda show that allusions to and calls for the caliphate have become a prominent part of their public discourse. During a speech aired in mid-2006, Bin Laden admonished his "brothers in Jihad" in "Baghdad, house of the caliphate" that they "must not miss this opportunity to establish the nucleus of the caliphate."[12] However, they have not produced any detailed written work explaining the structure of the caliphate, how it would function, nor even how the leader would be appointed,[13] indicating that they consider this goal as either too far off for these details to be deemed necessary, or representing something other than the detailed understanding of a particular government structure, as outlined, for example, by Hizb ut-Tahrir. Consequently, in order to better understand the statements of the former leader of al-Qaeda, they need to be read in context, as part of a discourse spanning more than twenty years.

Much of the secondary material about al-Qaeda produced around and in the aftermath of 9/11 is of debatable quality. Most of the "experts" either have their own political agenda, which obscures any meaningful analysis, or lack a nuanced understanding of Middle Eastern politics and Islamic scholarship. Among professional analysts, the search for intelligence often detracts from any serious consideration of what is actually being said. As former CIA officer Michael Scheuer mentions, in the event of a new Bin Laden tape being aired, the actual words spoken are the most overlooked part of any review.[14] Notable works that have attempted to analyze the *words* of Bin Laden include Bernard Lewis' "License to Kill" article, which analyzes the 1998 fatwa entitled "Declaration of the World Islamic Front for Jihad against the Jews and the Crusaders" from a religious and political perspective. A more detailed study of Bin Laden's two *fatawa* is Rosalind Gwynne's "Usama bin Laden, the Qur'an and Jihad," which examined the Qur'anic verses mentioned in both Bin Laden's 1996 "Declaration of War" and 1998 fatwa, with reference to and in comparison with an understanding of the fourteenth century exegete Abu Abdullah al-Qurtubi. Both Lewis and Gwynne analyze Bin Laden's words from a doctrinal and scriptural perspective, and are limited to his two major declarations. Scheuer's "Through Our Enemies' Eyes" is a more expansive analysis. Among the main themes identified by Scheuer are the articulation of America as the main enemy, the betrayal of the Muslim governments and the Islamic duty of self-defense.[15] A further addition to the collection of Bin Laden portraits and analyses is Mohammad-Mahmoud Ould Mohamedou's "Understanding al-Qaeda," which identifies the earlier years of al-Qaeda as being a time of strategy development and asserts that Bin Laden's goal of undermining the Saudi government and displacing the state's military function was fixed from the beginning.[16] A report written for Congress in early 2007 entitled "Al-Qaeda: Statements and Evolving Ideology" gives an overall perspective on the strategy of the group's public discourse.

Most academics have understood the caliphate as a long-term "strategic" goal for al-Qaeda. Gene Heck positions the call of Bin Laden for the establishment of the caliphate as a purely utopian ideal within a tradition of political Islam that can be traced back to the Brotherhood via Sayyid Qutb, as part of the work to abolish globalization and bring about the destruction of the "decadent" West.[17] This type of analysis, similar to that of Lawrence Wright,[18] falls into the trap of drawing straight and somewhat lazy lines between Islamic scholars, thinkers and movements, usually beginning from Ibn Taymiyya through Mohammad Abdul Wahhab until Qutb and finally al-Qaeda is reached, without making any differentiation between ideas, context, goals and methods along the way. Bruce Riedel believes that the caliphate is their "ultimate goal," one of (re)creating the state from Indonesia through to Spain, but that they have no plans detailing how it would be governed, making the imposition of *shari'a* law on the model of the Taliban a more than likely outcome.[19] If this is the case then the question that arises would be how seriously al-Qaeda themselves take the caliphate as an alternative form of governance at the present time. Explaining this in more detail, Devin Springer considers the caliphate to be a "core strategic goal" of al-Qaeda, but argues that the caliphate, in their conception, is not based on leadership or territory. Rather, it symbolizes the ultimate goal to be achieved by the waging of a successful global jihad, the final point of victory after which people would live under God's authority without interference from corrupt elements.[20] On the other hand, some academics, such as Saudi expert Madawi al-Rasheed, consider Bin Laden's call for a caliphate to be "just part (of al-Qaeda's) war of slogans,"[21] and therefore their adoption of the word within their discourse is driven more by utility than ideology.

By reviewing the changing public discourse of al-Qaeda over a number of years, the calls to and for the caliphate can be analyzed within their proper context, allowing a proper assessment of the word in al-Qaeda's discourse and propaganda. Though the American government now claim that the caliphate is a major political goal of al-Qaeda, the liberation of what al-Qaeda perceives as occupied land, the reform of despotic local regimes, independence from outside interference in local politics and control over resources all feature higher on Bin Laden's list of priorities. In reality, the caliphate is at most a distant aspiration used by al-Qaeda for motivational and doctrinal purposes rather than a true political goal. The reason this warrants discussion is that the caliphate has entered public consciousness in the West as a result of the claims of Western governments, and particularly the American administration post 9/11, that it was a central goal of al-Qaeda, and accordingly should be considered a threat. As a result, the introduction of the caliphate into public discourse simultaneously linked the caliphate to terrorism in the minds of the general public, while also serving as a way to deflect attention from the actual political grievances of Bin Laden and others. For al-Qaeda, the caliphate was a way to globalize the struggle against the West by entering into a civilizational struggle that extended beyond immediate military conflict. By disentangling the caliphate, the goals of al-Qaeda and its methodology, it should become clear that the caliphate is not linked exclusively to al-Qaeda, and that it is not unusual that the group—like most other Islamic movements—have adopted it as part of their discourse even if it does not constitute an immediate goal.

To Bin Laden the caliphate is the antithesis of what he perceived as the corruption of the Saudi regime, who gave up Islamic brotherhood for the sake of worldly gain, and surrendered the purity of the Arabian peninsula to foreign soldiers. Consequently, the figure of the caliph is represented by a pious, independent leader in the mould of Mullah Umar, who would unite them under a single banner establishing a moral society based around the teachings of Islam. This attitude was illustrated when he was asked by Robert Fisk what kind of Islamic State he would like to live under, his simple reply being that "all Muslims would love to live under true *shari'a*,"[22] without any further explanation. His right hand man, who replaced him as leader after his assassination in 2011, Aymen al-Zawahiri, widely considered to be al-Qaeda's ideologue, pays a little more attention to the idea in both his writing and public statements, but ultimately continues to provide only minimal details or new complexions about the caliphate beyond the scope of his former leader's understanding.

The *ijtihad* of al-Qaeda does not view the problems of the Muslims through a cultural or political lens, in the sense that it is not the morals or individuals subjugated under foreign colonialism, nor the intellectual decline and subservience to a political and cultural colonialism which is the root problem; rather, the issue facing them is one of physical colonialism manifest in the presence of non-Muslim troops in the Arabian Peninsula, carried out either by or with the acquiescence of local regimes.

Over time, three main themes developed which characterized Bin Laden's changing public discourse and goals, beginning with his attempts at addressing domestic grievances, primarily targeting reform of the Saudi regime. Subsequently, his focus moved to justifying global jihad against America and its allies, while there has been a constant undercurrent in the discourse of al-Qaeda, namely the "Battle for Hearts and Minds" within the global Muslim *Umma*, competing with the draw of the West, and for jihadist sympathizers, with the caliphate playing an inspirational and doctrinal role in those messages directed at an Islamic audience. Consequently, Bin Laden's attempts at positing a global Islamic movement did not depend upon the construction of a caliphate, but upon the engagement of wider elements of the Muslim population in a global jihad against America and its allies. Religious authority is therefore not invested within a political entity, but instead is part of a discourse of struggle, with those participating in the jihad being recognized as a legitimate source of authority on Islamic matters, rather than discredited scholars and supporters of the region's incumbent regimes.

Addressing Domestic Grievances

While al-Zawahiri spent his days in an Egyptian jail after the assassination of Egyptian President Anwar Sadat, Bin Laden was busy providing logistical and financial support to the jihad in Afghanistan, having travelled there for the first time only days after the arrival of invading Soviet troops in 1979.[23] One was a political detainee who had plotted to overthrow the Egyptian government from the age of sixteen, inspired by the execution of Sayyid Qutb by the regime of Gamal Abdul-Nasser to go down the path to either martyrdom or victory against the corrupted elite.[24] The other was the youngest son of a family with close ties to the Saudi Arabia's rulers, motivated by the opportunity to fight Jihad against a foreign infidel invader, and who had spent time listening to the lectures of Mohammad Qutb, the elder brother of Sayyid Qutb, who was Professor of Islamic Studies at King Abdul Aziz University.

The differing trajectories of the two men cannot be understood without recognizing the differences in the basis of legitimacy on which the Egyptian and Saudi regimes are based, coupled with a reading from two different books, one known as *The Absent Obligation* and the other as *Defence of the Muslim Lands*. Though both books shared the subject of the obligation to wage jihad, they proffered very different conceptions of the nature of that obligation. One was written by Abdus-Salam Faraj and became a core text for al-Zawahiri's Islamic Jihad group, the other was authored by Abdullah Azzam, who was recognized as the head of the Afghan-Arabs and one of Bin Laden's former teachers in Saudi Arabia.

Azzam's book encouraged Muslims to take up arms against the Communist Soviet invader in defense of their religion, since "Jihad today is individually obligatory [...] on every Muslim," until "the last piece of Islamic land is freed from the hands of the Disbelievers."[25] On the other hand, Abdus-Salam Faraj's *The Absent Obligation* called for a struggle against the "near enemy," meaning "the present rulers," who "have apostatised from Islam,"[26] since "fighting the enemy that is near to us comes before that which is far."[27] Alternatively, Azzam held that "violence should not be used against Muslim regimes no matter how far they had deviated from *shari'a* principles."[28]

The Egyptian regime was considered the near enemy, a government whose leader had apostatized from Islam due to a series of actions thought to be blasphemous, most importantly the failure to rule by the *shari'a* and the signing of a peace treaty which recognized the state of Israel in 1979. Living in Egypt and growing up under the shadow of Qutb's execution and the subsequent failed Military Academy coup of 1974, al-Zawahiri had been arrested, tortured and thrown into jail with his co-defendants because they had, in his words, tried their best to "establish an Islamic state."[29]

The situation in Saudi Arabia was very different, with the al-Saud family basing their legitimacy on Islam and the fact that they were the "guardians of the two holy places" (*haramain*). The Wahabi clerical establishment has consistently provided doctrinal support for the regime since the supposed eighteenth century promise of Mohammed Abdul-Wahhab to Ibn Saud that "you will be the *imam*, leader of the Muslim community and I will be leader in religious matters."[30] With the apparent application of parts of the *shari'a*, prominent parts of the punishment (*hudud*) system in particular, Saudi Arabia had traditionally been considered an Islamic state by many Muslims and Saudi citizens. Bin Laden and those around him in Saudi Arabia were not living under the "near enemy," and were quite content in their conviction that they had no religious obligation to rebel against the state at that time. The last prominent case of such a rebellion was the military occupation of the

Grand Mosque in 1979 by a small group of Muslims of differing natio-nalities under the leadership of Juhayman al-Utaibi, who allegedly pro-claimed himself to be the *mehdi* or guided one.

Though Saudi Arabia claimed to be an Islamic state, it never claimed to be the seat of the caliphate which would represent unitary rule over the entire *Umma*. While Sharif Hussain had made a claim to the title in a bid to bolster his position regionally, the position held by Ibn Saud, of which he had previously informed the British, was that "the Wahabis recognized no *Khalif* after the first four," a useful understanding since "should the Sharif assume the title it would make no difference to his status among other ruling chiefs,"[31] with this lack of consent put into practice soon after. It should be noted that throughout the statements of both Bin Laden and al-Zawahiri reference is made to both the cali-phate and an Islamic state. Though the words have been used interchan-geably in some modern political tracts, particularly by those Muslim thinkers, scholars and movements who advocate that the caliphate is the only valid system of governance in Islam, such as Sheikh Taqiudeen al-Nabahani and Hizb ut Tahrir, they have not been used as such by al-Qaeda's two major leaders, who rather followed the terminology as originally promoted by Rashid Rida and then later adopted by Hassan al-Banna, which differentiates between an Islamic state and the cali-phate. This is rooted in their belief of the permissibility and legitimacy of multiple national Islamic states which do not claim to be the cali-phate, often referring to them as "emirates," such as Afghanistan under the Taliban, with Saudi Arabia presenting a further example before it lost legitimacy in Bin Laden's opinion.

This approach is evidenced by a number of statements, including when al-Zawahiri claimed in 1982 that he had tried to establish "an Islamic state and an Islamic society,"[32] not a caliphate. In his book *Knights Under the Prophet's Banner*, he talks of the "emergence of two Islamic states," referring to Chechnya and Afghanistan, which he also refers to as the "Islamic Emirate of Afghanistan."[33] In 2001, Bin Laden claimed that it was obligatory for Muslims to "establish an Islamic state that abides by God's law," and went on to point out that one had already been established, "the Islamic Emirate of Afghanistan."[34] When inter-viewed later in the same year, only days before the start of the American invasion of Afghanistan, he stated that "America is against the establish-ment of any Islamic state."[35] Such references to existing Islamic states indicates Bin Laden and al-Zawahiri's view that it is permissible to have multiple smaller Islamic states as opposed to a caliphate which would be a unitary system under a single leader, in stark difference to the nation state model. The thinking that lies behind such a differentiation can be seen in Faraj's text when he states that the establishment of the caliphate "depends upon the existence of its core, the Islamic State."[36] In conclusion, according to Bin Laden and al-Zawahiri, there is a difference between an Islamic state and a caliphate. Unlike a caliphate, an Islamic state is, in origin, analogous to a national government within set territorial borders that implements some form of *shari'a* before either expanding or uniting with other similar states until a caliphate is formed.

Even though Saudi Arabia was not considered to be a caliphate, its position as an acknowledged Islamic state gave it legitimacy and meant that during a period of increased activity against the regime in nearby Egypt by those accusing it of infidelity, the Islamic-oriented youth of the Arabian Peninsula would not question the religious legitimacy of their own state. With establishment scholars such as Abdul-Aziz bin Baz and Mohammad bin Uthaymeen supporting the government with their Islamic credentials, most of the revolutionary zeal of the Saudi youth was focused on jihad elsewhere.

It is not surprising that while in Afghanistan Bin Laden saw no problem in liaising with representatives of the Saudi government. The first time, reluctantly addressing a camera after the battle of Jaji in April 1987, he took the opportunity to "thank God for giving us the blessing of Jihad in the Path of Allah," whilst claiming that "this obligation (jihad)" has "been forgotten today."[37] There was no mention of the caliphate or any questioning of the legitimacy of Arab regimes. Bin Laden remained focused on the jihad against the Soviet Union, returning back to Saudi Arabia as a hero after the withdrawal of Soviet troops from Afghanistan in 1989.

As previously mentioned, the roots of Bin Laden's grievances lay around the conduct of the Saudi government at the time of the Gulf War in 1990. The split that occurred between Bin Laden and the Saudi regime happened as a result of the rejection of his offer to provide troops to help defend Saudi Arabia against Iraqi leader Saddam Hussein, who had just sent his army into the neighboring state of Kuwait. This humiliation was compounded by the invitation extended to the Americans to establish military bases in Saudi Arabia, considered a sacrilegious act considering that the Prophet Mohammed was reported to have said "two religions shall not co-exist in the Arabian Peninsula."[38] Though a number of junior and middle-ranking clerics protested this move, such as Salman al-Auda and Safar al-Hawali, the establishment clergy produced a fatwa under pressure from the ruling al-Saud family, which gave legitimacy to the presence of American troops as "they deserve support because they are here to defend Islam."[39] This verdict was formulated in August 1990 by a state appointed committee led by Bin Baz, who was subsequently elevated to the status of Grand Mufti in 1993, which could be construed as a reward for his support of the official Saudi stance throughout the Gulf war. The rupture between Bin Laden and Saudi Arabia later widened as the religious and political spheres of the establishment rapidly lost whatever prior legitimacy they had in Bin Laden's eyes. After he had left Saudi Arabia for Sudan in 1991, he began to call against both sides of the establishment from afar, at first using the Advice and Reform Committee (ARC) to privately advise and hold the regime to account before taking his agenda into a more public arena.

Bin Laden believed that the Saudi regime derived its legitimacy from its claim to uphold Islam and therefore "bases itself upon its *'ulama.*"[40] As he was not from a scholarly background, he was not able to hold the government to account directly, and as long as the official clerical establishment carried weight in the eyes of the average Saudi citizen, any calls for change would fall on deaf ears. The early communiqués released by Bin Laden addressed the clerical class in Saudi Arabia, attempting to expose those who supported the government as lackeys while encouraging those who felt estrangement from the regime to align themselves with him, thereby increasing his credibility as a result of the religious legitimacy conferred upon them.

The first publicly available letter from Bin Laden initially focused on Bin Baz and the fatwa he issued legitimizing the Oslo Accords in 1993, in order to undermine his position among the general public. The letter begins by berating Bin Baz, stating that "no one can be unaware of the tremendous spread of corruption, which has penetrated all aspects of life," thereby challenging any possible benefit of the doubt given to the Mufti due to his status and reputation as a blind and isolated man who was given inaccurate information by those around him. The rest of the letter paints a picture of Bin Baz as a government stooge, pointing out that when the "forces of the aggressive Judeo-Christian alliance" decided to "occupy the country in the name of liberating Kuwait," he had "justified this act with an arbitrary judicial decree," in reference to the 1990 fatwa. Also criticized was the support Bin Baz gave for the treatment meted out to Safar al-Hawali, Salman al-Auda and their supporters, claiming that he had "issued a juridical decree condoning everything suffered by the two sheikhs." Having done enough to expose the Mufti's domestic betrayal, Bin Laden then mocks him, claiming that "it seemed as if you were not satisfied abandoning Saudi Arabia, […] until you had brought disaster upon Jerusalem,"[41] with his support for the Oslo accords made to look even stranger by the fact that the Mufti himself had given an opposing verdict years earlier. By removing opportunity to plead ignorance and then pointing out Bin Baz's contradictory stances on various issues, Bin Laden made a direct attempt to undermine the legitimacy of the state by questioning the credibility of its 'ulama'.

Because of the prominence of Bin Baz both inside and outside Saudi Arabia, he continued to be singled out as the main clerical personality targeted by Bin Laden, notably during a 1996 interview with *Nida ul-Islam* magazine, in which the government was described as using "the cane of Bin Baz" to strike "every corrective program which the honest scholars put forward." Bin Laden also warned against the "organisation of the scholars of the authorities," which was being used "to lead the people astray."[42] By simultaneously encouraging other "honourable and righteous scholars" to "come and lead your *Umma*" by calling them to a jihad against the "Crusaders" occupation of Saudi Arabia," with the advice that "if you cannot do so in your own country then emigrate for the sake of Allah,"[43] Bin Laden was effectively calling for the mutiny of the clerical class in Saudi Arabia and a break in the centuries old alliance between the al-Saud ruling family and the religious Wahabi establishment.

Though both Bin Laden and al-Zawahiri continued to warn against the establishment scholars of both Saudi Arabia and al-Azhar in their more recent statements, the discourse that followed was aimed at discrediting those who disagreed with their call to jihad against the Americans and their allies, whereas the original intent was specifically to undermine the legitimacy of the Saudi regime.

Having exhausted the channels of private admonishment and the public addressing of members of the clerical establishment by way of open letters, Bin Laden "took a decision" to "begin to speak the truth and forbid the *munkar* (open sin)" directly. Acknowledging his own lack of clerical authority, he maintained that he had only done so "after the Saudi government exerted pressure upon the scholars" and "forbade the distribution of their cassettes."[44] These words, in his first major interview with an Arab newspaper after the release of the 1996 "Declaration of Jihad," are a reflection of the sensitivity of Bin Laden to show his adherence to the accepted cultural convention and formalities. This is particularly pertinent with respect to Saudi Arabia, where it is not considered within the remit of a relative religious layman to question the regime or the clerical authority that backs it.

Fully aware of his own limitations, Bin Laden adopted the views and interpretations of recognized Islamic personalities as part of his discourse against the Saudi government, in an attempt to overcome his lack of credibility and religious legitimacy. In an open letter published in July 1995 addressing King Fahd directly, the first accusation leveled at the Saudi leader was his "ruling with other than what God has revealed."[45] Such an accusation would carry no weight if it was from Bin Laden alone, so a litany of scholarly references are used from twentieth century personalities such as Egyptian scholar Ahmed Shakir and former mufti of Saudi Arabia Sheikh Muhammad bin Ibrahim al-Sheikh, to more classical references such as Ali bin Ahmad ibn Hazm al-dhahari,[46] Taqiudeen ibn Taymiyya[47] and Abul Fida' ibn Kathir.[48]

Bin Laden's second accusation was that the King's "allegiance to the infidels and hostility towards Muslims," with the contradiction highlighted between the Saudi "support for Muslims against the communists in Afghanistan while championing the cause of the communists in Yemen against the Muslims," in reference to his belief that members of the Saudi government had given financial backing to the Yemeni Socialist Party to fund an attempt to split from the unified Yemeni state in 1994. A further issue mentioned was that of the "deception of the Palestine cause," pertinent after the "surrender" of the 1993 Oslo Accords, a particularly grave matter given that Palestine was considered "the mother of all Islamic causes."[49]

The second part of the 1995 letter addresses the "collapsing economic situation," the failure to "provide proper maintenance for the hospitals" and the "catastrophe" in the "status of education." The failure of the state to provide the Saudi public with acceptable social services is contrasted with the personal corruption of Fahd, whose ability to "spend the people's wealth on those palaces and houses inside and outside the country is an astounding and scary one."[50] Of particular note given the Saudis' limited ability to defend themselves in the face of Saddam's aggression in 1990 was the rhetorical question of where the money spent on the military went, given that it constituted a third of the national budget. This link between military spending and the taking of bribes by various princes and members of the ruling family played into the sense of resentment felt by average Saudis regarding their inability to field a viable defense force, independent of an external power. These are all domestic concerns revolving around the performance of the state in providing for its citizens while also maintaining the sovereignty and independence of the nation.

Fahd's worst transgression remained that he had transformed "the nation to an American protectorate" in order to protect his "crumbling throne."[51] The King is mocked for the imperial manner in which then American President Bill Clinton dealt with him during visits to the country, as well as allowing oil prices to be dictated according to foreign interests.

The first two accusations, made at the start of the letter, are of an ideological nature, and attack the Saudi regime for neglecting their domestic responsibility to implement the *shari'a* as an Islamic state as well as their perceived capitulation to external interests in their foreign policy, thereby relinquishing their position as propagators of the faith. However, it is too easy to draw the incorrect conclusion that Bin Laden's primary problem with the government was ideological, just as it is inaccurate to conclude that his oppositional discourse focused mainly on external rather than domestic factors, as Mamoun Fandy contends.[52]

Domestic problems could not be addressed as long as the state remained ideologically legitimate, with any dissent related to internal politics rejected with the refrain that, according to Islam, the leader must be obeyed even if he is oppressive or tyrannical. Once the religious credentials of the regime had been challenged and the ruling elite had been stripped of their ideological protection, Bin Laden then goes on to address practical domestic grievances in the second part of the letter.

The same format was used in the 1996 "Declaration of Jihad." By first claiming that "the Zionist-Crusader alliance resorted to killing and arresting the truthful *'ulama',*" *and* that the Saudi government, under orders from the United States, "also arrested a large number of scholars,"

Bin Laden explained to his audience why the onus of speaking out had fallen upon his shoulders rather than on someone more qualified in Islamic scholarship. He went on to state that "the regime has torn off its legitimacy" by the "suspension of the Islamic *shari'a* law and exchanging it with man-made civil law,"[53] thereby legitimizing subsequent dissent.

Once the formalities are completed, a study of the actual grievances that Bin Laden lays against the Saudi regime reveals that the majority of the complaints are not ideological in nature. Notable issues mentioned include the "abuse and confiscation of human rights," the "miserable situation of the social services," the "state of the ill-trained and ill-prepared army" and the use of the media as a "tool of truth hiding and misinformation." Of the nine complaints listed, only two can be labeled as ideological, and one of these two was related to foreign policy.

Since his core issues with the Saudi regime appear not to be fundamentally ideological but rather a protest against the surrender of sovereignty and irresponsible governance, it is not surprising that Bin Laden continued to hope for the reform of the government for some time. In 1995, though Bin Laden stated that giving "support to the infidels against Muslims" meant that the teaching of Islam "demand[s] that you (King Fahd) be revolted against and removed," he was content to merely call for Fahd's abdication. Even with the release of the 1996 and 1998 *fatawa* against the Americans and their allies, al-Qaeda had not yet moved into total open conflict with the Saudi government. In an interview published soon after the release of the 1996 declaration, Bin Laden held out the possibility of "reconciliation" between the regime and the "different sections of the public," with their first demands pursuant to this being the release of imprisoned scholars, implementation of Islamic law and "to practise real *shura*,"[54] a form of consultation and advice between the ruler and his followers. In mid-December 2004, Bin Laden addressed Saudi scholars to "do everything you can to diffuse the crisis" between al-Qaeda and the ruling elite, since they had "not yet launched a war against the regime," even though he claimed that it would be justified to rebel against the "apostate ruler."[55] Such words indicate Bin Laden's acceptance that the Saudi state could regain its legitimacy as an Islamic state through reform.

It is clear that Bin Laden sought a reformed Islamic state and was not calling for Saudi Arabia to become a caliphate. Throughout the early discourse of both the clerical establishment and the ruling elite, no reference is ever made to the caliphate or its necessity. Nowhere among the various complaints leveled at the Saudi regime is it mentioned that they did not establish or represent the caliphate; rather, after ideological formalities are dealt with, the main grievances listed revolve around sovereignty of the government, independence from outside powers, social services, eradication of corruption and the right to consult with and advise the ruling classes freely without fear of oppression.

With reform of the Saudi government still unrealized, and forced to leave Sudan, where he had taken refuge from intense pressure applied by the American and Saudi governments, the 1995 call for abdication was abandoned in favor of a call to Jihad in 1996, issued from the mountains of Afghanistan, but it was not directed primarily against the Saudi regime. Since both the clerical and ruling establishment were seemingly content with the status quo of American and foreign troops remaining in the Gulf, Bin Laden took it upon himself to reassert the lost sovereignty of his home country by justifying war against what he considered to be an infidel occupying force.

Justifying the Global Jihad—For a Caliphate?

The call for jihad against the United States and its allies went through three distinct phases. The first phase, as announced by the 1996 declaration, targeted foreign troops stationed on the Arabian Peninsula, while the second fatwa released in 1998 by the "World Islamic Front for Jihad against Jews and Crusaders" expanded the target to include all Americans and their allies. The third phase was not announced by a specific fatwa or declaration, but rather by 9/11 and its aftermath, which led to the call for a global clash between the Muslim world on one side and America and her allies on the other. It was only in this third phase that the use of the caliphate symbol became prominent as part of a propaganda campaign to globalize the conflict between al-Qaeda and America in an attempt to involve the wider Muslim population and bolster al-Qaeda's position.

The localized nature of the 1996 declaration is clear from Bin Laden's claim since even though he and his compatriots used the freedom afforded them in the mountains of Afghanistan to spend time "talking and discussing the ways of correcting what had happened to the Islamic world in general," the main concern was "the Land of the two Holy

Places in particular." As mentioned previously, a large part of the declaration focused on domestic grievances leveled at the Saudi regime, and an explanation of how all the "advocates of correction and reform movement were very keen on using peaceful means in order to protect the unity of the country" as well as "to prevent blood-shed."[56]

Bin Laden shifts the onus onto the regime for rebuffing all these attempts and thus pushing "people toward armed action," a reference to the perpetrators of the Riyadh and Khobar bombings of 1995 and 1996, which targeted American troops based in Saudi Arabia. However, he warns against falling into an internal war, asking whether the government was planning "to play the civilians against their military personnel and vice versa, like what had happened in some of the neighbouring countries," a clear reference to the conflicts in both Algeria and Egypt. Perhaps having learnt from the failings of the jihadi movements which attempted to rebel against their own states, a number of reasons are elucidated as to why civil war would be counter-productive. Bin Laden makes it clear that the problem does not lie with the average Saudi or with those in the military or the civil service, but rather with the agent of the "American-Israeli alliance,"[57] the Saudi regime.

According to Bin Laden, "everyone agreed that the situation cannot be rectified unless the root of the problem is tackled," and even though "the regime is fully responsible for what had been incurred by the country and the nation," it is apparent that "the occupying American enemy is the principal and the main cause of the situation."[58] In other words, as he explained to Peter Arnett in 1997, the "main problem is the US government, while the Saudi regime is but a branch [...] of the US."[59]

Rather than engaging in an open confrontation with the Saudi establishment, the expulsion of foreign forces took priority since "after *iman* (belief) there is no more important duty than pushing the American enemy out of the holy land," a statement echoing the fatwa proclaimed by Ibn Taymiyya against the Mongol invaders more than seven centuries earlier. Bin Laden believed that the Americans imposed themselves on the Saudi regime, which did not instruct "the army, the guards, and the security men to oppose the occupiers" but instead used them to "protect the invaders."[60] By relinquishing their role as the upholders of Saudi Arabia's sovereignty, they had lost their legitimacy and were considered nothing more than a branch of the occupying nation. Armed with a fatwa, Bin Laden was able to follow the expected convention of adherence to religious scholars in giving legal opinions, and the ruling gave Bin Laden the opportunity to claim that "our trusted leaders, the 'ulama', have given us a fatwa that we must drive out the Americans," holding that "the solution to the crisis is the withdrawal of American troops."[61] The religious legitimacy conferred upon these 'ulama' rather than those in Saudi Arabia, or indeed any others who did not support their call, was derived from their agreement with the process and aims of jihad as well as their independence from the Fahd regime.

Though it has since become apparent that al-Qaeda had no operational role in the bombing of American targets in Riyadh and Khobar that occurred prior to the release of the declaration, it seems that Bin Laden was trying to capitalize on what he thought was a simmering undercurrent of discontent in Saudi society, ready to explode at any moment at the indignation and humiliation of having non-Muslim troops violate the sanctity of their homeland. Most of his exhortations in the declaration are focused on the men and women of Saudi Arabia, calling them to either take up arms against the Americans or, with respect to the women, to aid the cause by boycotting American goods.

A litany of international grievances are leveled at the United States, including the killing of Muslims in Iraq and Palestine, the death of Iraqi children as a result of sanctions, the intervention in Somalia and even their perceived role in dividing "the *Umma* into small and little countries," an unusual accusation given that the United States had no apparent part in the Sykes-Picot agreement, though it may be the case that he was expressing his opinion on the role of President Woodrow Wilson in confirming the division of the spoils. However, the *casus belli* for the 1996 declaration was none of the above, but rather the "latest and the greatest of these aggressions, incurred by the Muslims since the death of the Prophet," namely "the occupation of the land of the two Holy Places." At this stage, even though the Americans were accused of numerous crimes, liberation and reform of Saudi Arabia was still the main concern, with the hope that if left intact its economic power could form the base of the "soon to be established Islamic state." The reasoning for this was that "clearly after belief there is no more important duty than pushing the American enemy out of the holy land," and while the Saudi regime was "fully responsible for what had been incurred by the country and the nation" it was considered that "the occupying American enemy is the principal and main cause of the situation."[62]

Though the 1996 declaration was restricted to a call for jihad against foreign military forces based in the Arabian Peninsula, by 1998 the "rule to kill every American and their allies, civilians and military" had become a religious obligation, "until *al-Aqsa Masjid* (the main mosque in Jerusalem) and *Masjid al-haram* (in Mecca) have been liberated from their grasp."[63] In addition to differences with respect to the widening of the scope and the globalization of the jihad, a third difference was that Bin Laden was not alone among the signatories. Along with other scholars and personalities, Ayman al-Zawahiri had also aligned his Egyptian Islamic Jihad group with the Saudi.

In Bin Laden's case, the arrival and subsequent settling of American troops in the Arabian Peninsula proved to be the last straw. Al-Zawahiri's Islamic Jihad did not appear to have any concern for the events in Saudi Arabia for the practical reason that they were, theoretically, involved in a material struggle against the "near enemy," meaning the "apostate" Egyptian regime. As late as 1997, al-Zawahiri claimed in an interview with the Associated Press that the military conflict between the *mujahideen* (those engaged in jihad) and the Egyptian regime would continue until "the regime hands the rule to Muslims."[64] However, by 1998 al-Zawahiri openly aligned himself with Bin Laden's World Islamic Front in a declaration of war against America. Muntasir Zayyat argues that al-Zawahiri's change in methodology was due to a number of factors ultimately adding up to the failure of the armed insurrection against the Egyptian regime to yield any positive results.[65] Fawaz Gerges claims that those around al-Zawahiri believe that financial dependency drove him into the arms of Bin Laden.[66] A serious analysis of what caused al-Zawahiri's ideological change, such that the focus of his jihad shifted from the "near enemy" to the "far enemy," requires its own independent study, but his own claim is that the Egyptian regime had no option but to internationalize the battle with his movement after "America became convinced that the regime could not stand alone against this jihadi campaign."[67] However, it should be taken into account that at the time of al-Zawahiri's merger with Bin Laden, he had little (if any) of the operational capability needed to carry out attacks in Egypt. In other words, irrespective of his financial position, it is likely that there was simply no other option available to him.

With the large number of signatories for the fatwa coming from Egypt, Saudi Arabia and the Indian sub-continent, wider political goals were also adopted. By incorporating the liberation of *masjid al-Aqsa* as an aim, the struggle against America and its allies was globalized, framing Palestine's position as the central cause that resonates most widely in the heart of the Muslim world. This is not to suggest that Bin Laden and al-Zawahiri never had any previous concern with Palestine, or were insincere in their call as the liberation of *al-Quds* (Jerusalem) had always been a long-term goal with reports stating that Bin Laden had given public speeches as early as 1990 calling for the cutting of relations with America over their support of Israel.[68] Rather, the announced widening of goals to include the liberation of Palestine was to further internationalize the struggle in order to weaken the United States and its allies to the point that the original goal of the expulsion of American influence in the region could be met.

Though the aims of the 1998 fatwa were more expansive than those of the 1996 declaration, they did not contain any call to the caliphate or any mention of its necessity. In order to internationalize the issues and widen its possible support base, it was sufficient to mention the liberation of Palestine as a stated objective. Indeed, from 1996 until 9/11 there appears to be no substantial talk regarding the caliphate, except for an interview in 1997 with Hamid Mir in which Bin Laden urged Muslims to unite and establish a "pious caliphate,"[69] giving the impression that the concept was linked to the ruling individual rather than a political system. However, the issue is not touched upon in any of the major interviews that Bin Laden gave during that period with major Arab and Western media outlets including CNN, ABC, al-Jazeera and al-Quds al-Arabi.

The core ideas that were propagated in the Arab media by Bin Laden at the time were to "seek to instigate the nation to get up and liberate its land," by explaining world affairs as a clash of civilizations between "World Christianity" and "Zionist Jewry" led by the "United States, Britain and Israel" against "the Muslim world."[70] The key feature of this discourse was the construction of the jihad against America as defensive in nature, and therefore an obligation incumbent upon every Muslim.

When interviewed by the Western media, Bin Laden took the opportunity to explain that the fatwa was a response to America's role in spearheading "the crusade against the Islamic nation" by its stationing of troops in Saudi Arabia. When questioned about the targeting of civilians, the explanation was that "the Americans started it" and "retaliation and punishment should be carried out following the principle of reciprocity, especially where women and children are involved." On the other hand, he asserted that Islam "forbids us from killing innocent people such as women and children."[71]

The Ideology of Reciprocity—Ijtihad without a Mujtahid

While Hassan al-Banna considered foreign occupation as the primary problem facing the *Umma*, he was willing to consider local political forces as Muslims constrained by the limitations imposed by the occupiers. Thus he sought a moral revival among Muslims to allow them to throw off the physical yoke of colonialism and establish an Islamic state once independent of colonial influence. In the post-"independence" era, Hizb ut-Tahrir concluded that the cause of the decline of Muslims was an intellectual one, and re-establishing Islam would require an intellectual revival which would naturally lead to the establishment of the caliphate, according to the popular will. This stage was supposedly reached by the mid-1960s and the Hizb have been seeking power since. The reality in Saudi Arabia from the mid-1990s onwards, as understood by Bin Laden, is neither that of a foreign occupier subjugating a naïve political class nor an intellectual colonialism, but rather occupation by a foreign power aided and abetted by a local elite who had surrendered their Islam for the sake of protecting their political position. The local elite would not survive without the help of this foreign support, who were now physically occupying Muslim lands in order to prop up these regimes while preventing any return to Islam. Moral and intellectual issues were irrelevant; the immediate issue confronting the *Umma* was the presence of foreign troops which had to be rectified if they were to remove illegitimate regimes.

The permissibility of the killing of civilians in their attempts to eject the perceived occupiers of Muslim lands has proven to be the most controversial aspect of al-Qaeda, with even Khaled Fawwaz, the former media representative for Bin Laden in London, expressing his opposition to the 1998 fatwa targeting civilians.[72] This is not surprising given that the position goes against what is considered to be a consensus in Sunni scholarship that it is not permitted to target women and children who are not fighting you. This *ijtihad* is perhaps the ultimate exemplification of Faisal Devji's opinion that the real meaning of al-Qaeda is not found in its violence but in its overturning of contemporary religious *'ulama'*, thereby following in the path of certain Muslim liberals. Howe-ver, al-Qaeda have taken this far beyond what the original liberals had managed to achieve in the fragmentation of traditional religious autho-rity,[73] in this case by the existence of a leader (Bin Laden) not formally trained in Islamic sciences overturning not only contemporary, but also a corpus of established classical scholarship on the issue.

This ideology was introduced in stages by Bin Laden. When asked about the targets of the 1996 fatwa, he replied that "we have focused our declaration on striking at the soldiers in Saudi Arabia." This was quickly followed with the qualification that "the United States is responsible for any reaction (targeting civilians), because it extended its war against troops to civilians," such as in Iraq, by imposing sanctions which led to the deaths of large numbers of children.[74] By 1998 the warning was given that if Americans "do not wish to be harmed inside their very own countries," then they should "seek to elect governments that are truly representative of them."[75] By making such declarations and other similar statements in the Western media, Bin Laden was articulating his justifi-cation for attacks within the United States using his own doctrine of collective responsibility, holding any sign of consent conferred by an American citizen upon their government, such as paying taxes or voting, as giving legitimacy to and therefore aligning themselves with their government's actions. Such a mentality is not restricted to a particular religion or educational class, as seen by academic and self-professed "Jewish practitioner" Geoffrey Alderman's view that "every Gazan citizen who voted for Hamas" would qualify as a "rodef" whose life could be taken pre-emptively according to his understanding of Jewish scriptures.[76]

With the attack on the Twin Towers, al-Qaeda operatives put that doctrine into practice on a spectacular scale, something they believe to be the natural inverse and reaction to what they saw as Muslim suffering in Iraq and Palestine. The ideology of reciprocity had now overtaken any Islamic justifications, with the claim that "what the United States tastes today is a very small thing compared to what we have tasted for tens of years."[77] In other words, "we treat others like they treat us," meaning that "those who kill our women and our innocent, we kill their women and innocent."[78] This is their attempt at an *ijtihad* which justifies the position of al-Qaeda, based upon a literal, de-contextualized understan-ding of verses which can be translated as "so whoever transgresses against you, then transgress against them in the same manner," even though it contradicts established readings based upon holistic understandings of Qur'anic text such as the thirteenth century Maliki scholar Abu Abdullah al-Qurtubi, who states in his exegesis that "even if (the disbelievers) kill our women and children and afflict us with sorrow, it is not permissible for us to act likewise with the intention of making them feel grief and sorrow."[79]

This event marked the climax of al-Qaeda's preparation for the forthcoming "clash of civilisations," with Bin Laden asserting that the battle was not one between al-Qaeda and America, but rather it was one between "the peoples of Islam and the global crusaders." Given that the world was now divided into two regions, one of faith and another of infidelity, the call for the establishment of "the righteous caliphate of our *Umma*"[80] began to emerge as a symbol of unity in the battle for hearts and minds.

Though the British and American governments began talking about the "battle for hearts and minds" after 9/11, Bin Laden had been engaged in a propaganda battle to convince others of the righteousness of his cause long before this. The main audiences were initially the general Muslim population and the West, but also jihadi sympathizers—particularly after the overthrow of the Taliban, which led to a dispersion of all operatives previously resident in Afghanistan as well as a general questioning of the wisdom of al-Qaeda's strategy. Though the Muslim audience had always been the main target, addressing the West began as early as 1993.

Bin Laden's initial interviews with Western journalists, such as Robert Fisk in 1993 and Scott MacLeod in 1996, generally confirmed his opposition to the Saudi regime whilst belittling any accusations of terrorism. Though the full extent of al-Qaeda's activities in the pre-1996 period is not known, other than their claim to have participated in fighting American forces in Mogadishu, these initial encounters with Western audiences seem to be an attempt at reducing the pressure brought by accusations of terrorism that were directed at the Sudanese government at the time, whose officials were present, monitoring the interviews as they were given. A similar scenario occurred in Afghanistan post-1999, when Bin Laden agreed to avoid addressing the media for the sake of relieving the pressure on the Taliban regime hosting him and his associates since expulsion from Sudan.

Whenever al-Qaeda has been able to address the Western media freely, they have made it clear since the 1996 fatwa that they "declared jihad against the American government, because the American government is unjust, criminal and tyrannical," as well as being "the leader of terrorism and crime in the world."[81] Bin Laden warned *Time* magazine that "thousands of millions of Muslims are angry" and that the American people "should expect reactions from the Muslim world that are proportionate to the injustice they inflict."[82]

These and other similar statements should be understood through al-Zawahiri's maxim that "the one who warns bears no guilt."[83] Just as Bin Laden went through the culturally expected formality of addressing the Saudi regime privately at first, the detailing of the case against the United States and its allies was generally for the benefit of letting his wider Muslim audience know that the declared target had been forewarned of action against them and the reasons for that action.

The most detailed example of the (post-) rationalization for 9/11 came in the form of a response to a letter signed by sixty American intellectuals entitled "What We're Fighting For." The fact that such a letter had to be written by patriotic Americans to justify their President's decision to embark on a "war on terror" is perhaps indicative of how far Bin Laden's stated grievances reflected certain quarters of international opinion against aspects of America's foreign policy, and in particular their unflinching support for Israel at the expense of the Palestinians. In his response to the letter, Bin Laden lists American aggression or support for attacks against Muslims in Palestine, Somalia and Chechnya. Then he mentions official backing for local regimes that act as American "agents" by attacking, torturing and jailing their citizens, as *casus belli*, since "our fight against these governments is not separate from our fight against you." Detailing his own particular doctrine of collective responsibility, the targeting of civilians is due to the fact that the American people freely choose their government, "a choice that stems from their agreement to their policies." Further proof of this was that American civilians are the ones "who pay their taxes" that "funds the planes," "the tanks" and "the armies that occupy"[84] Muslim lands.

Once the *casus belli* has been re-explained, Bin Laden covers a second theme: the double standards set by America. The Americans are "the last ones to respect the resolutions and policies of international law," and are mocked for claiming "to be the vanguards of human rights" which "vanished when the *mujahideen* hit you," with Guantanamo Bay being "a historical embarrassment to America and its values."[85] The intention behind undermining the United States' claim to "freedom," "justice" and "human rights" was not only an attempt at destroying the morale of the enemy, but also an effort to again highlight the bankruptcy of Western civilization's use to the Muslim world, undermining not only its own legitimacy but that of those regimes in the region seen as aligned with Britain and America.

The final section of his response was dedicated to explaining what was expected from America for hostilities to cease between the two sides. This included an end to their support for governments dealing aggressively with local Muslim populations, such as Israel, the Philippines and Russia, as well as a demand to end their support for regimes across the Middle East in general.

These three themes form the basis of most of al-Qaeda's subsequent discourse directed at the West, particularly after any major international terrorist attack, namely restating the *casus belli*, highlighting the hypocrisy of those governments pursuing al-Qaeda and explaining what must be done for future attacks to cease. After six attacks carried out worldwide, including those in Bali, Bin Laden released an audio message stating that "the time has come to settle accounts […] just as you bomb, so you shall be bombed, and there will be more to come."[86] Al-Zawahiri appeared in a video after the July 7 bombings in London, claiming that the attacks in London, New York and Madrid had "brought the battle to the enemy's soil," while mocking British Prime Minister Tony Blair for repeatedly claiming, in al-Zawahiri's paraphrase, that "what happened in London has nothing to do with the crimes he perpetrated in Palestine, Afghanistan and Iraq."[87]

The reiteration of these three core points was mainly for the benefit of their own constituency, the *Umma*, as a matter of formality intended to undermine any claims made against them that they had not given necessary warning before announcing hostilities. A further notable example of al-Qaeda's sensitivity to convention can be seen in a video featuring both al-Zawahiri and American al-Qaeda member Adam Gadahn, in which a formal presentation is made inviting the American and Western masses to Islam. This was apparently released as a reaction to the complaints of many jihadi sympathizers who criticized the 9/11 attacks for having taken place before an open call to Islam was extended to the American people, one of the prerequisites of declaring jihad. In reality, al-Qaeda had no real doctrinal reason to pay attention to such opinions since they claim to be fighting a defensive jihad, which does not have such conditions attached to its prosecution, but the tape can be taken as evidence of their sensitivity to criticism from what they consider to be their key support base.

In order to garner greater legitimacy for their cause and actions, al-Qaeda has tried to position itself as spokesperson for the Muslim world in the absence of any independent, sovereign leadership from local regimes. Both Bin Laden and al-Zawahiri articulate general grievances, present political demands, outline their own program for action and even offer truces with Western leaders, but without any real expectation of being taken seriously.

In a similar vein, just as Bin Laden and al-Zawahiri talked over the leaders in the Muslim world in an attempt to represent the *Umma*, they also began to talk over the leaders of the Western world with messages directed at the general Western population. Scheuer notes that there is a definite sense of a foreign policy in al-Qaeda's statements that is "delivered over the heads of the US and Western leaders to voters in non-Muslim countries."[88] Though a study of the kind of psychological warfare employed by al-Qaeda is worthy of more space, it is sufficient here to mention that allusions to the caliphate have not appeared prominently in any of their propaganda aimed directly at a Western audience, just as it played little part in those messages nominally addressing the West but intended for Muslim consumption.

Convincing the Umma *and Religious Authority*

As already explained, the main target for al-Qaeda messages are Muslims around the world. It is therefore unsurprising that the three themes that remain constant through their discourse nominally addressing the West—reaffirming their *casus belli*, exposing the hypocrisy of those "waging war" against al-Qaeda and explaining their political demands—also remain constant themes in the bulk of their discourse aimed at the *Umma* after the declaration of 1996.

Bin Laden consistently made efforts to explain the difference between blameworthy and praiseworthy terrorism, and to argue that the Americans as aggressors were terrorists deserving blame, whereas whoever struck back against them were terrorists deserving praise. Though this may seem obscure to someone not aware of the details of Arabic morphology, the word for terrorism in Arabic, *irhab,* is derived from the same root as other words which do not possess the same negative connotation as they do in English. A variation of the verb form is used in a verse of the Qur'an related to the material preparation of power in order to "strike fear" in the hearts of the enemy. Linguistic gymnastics aside, al-Qaeda's arguments have thus far gained very little traction among the wider Muslim population, irrespective of Bin Laden's own interpretations, since, as already mentioned, in Islamic scholarship "there is no difference between (the Muslim scholars' opinion) that it is not permitted to kill (the enemies) children, nor to kill their women as long as they are not fighting."[89] In other words, the weakness of his *ijtihad* added to the lack of support for the methods used by al-Qaeda, though the political grievances which they sought to address were almost always shared.

With Bush's declaration of a "war on terror," al-Qaeda was provided with all the necessary ammunition to move attention away from their own reprehensible actions and toward those of the "crusader" enemy. New themes emerged in their statements, including: a "fog of war" propaganda discourse, which attempted to highlight the weakness of the American military and economy in order to encourage the belief that it could be defeated; continuing calls for reform and change in their home countries; and advice to al-Qaeda sympathizers including regular updates on the political and military situation as seen through the eyes of al-Qaeda, and recommended possible targets, causing countless hours of misery and significant financial expense for Western intelligence and security services, a success that Bin Laden was quick to point out. The caliphate also began to feature in this discourse.

Leaning heavily on Islamic concepts of unity soon after a number of Pakistani citizens were killed while protesting President Musharraf's decision to align Pakistan with America against Afghanistan, a fax was sent to al-Jazeera exhorting the "Muslim brothers in Pakistan to give everything" in order to "push the American crusading forces from invading Pakistan and Afghanistan."[90] In an interview given a month later, Bin Laden called upon the *Umma* to unite and to "establish the righteous caliphate of our *Umma.*"[91]

Though the anticipated uprising never emerged and the Taliban regime was swiftly deposed with the help of their local enemies, the

Northern Alliance, the invasion of Iraq provided a second opportunity to portray the Muslim world as under siege from a newly-launched crusade. The position of Baghdad in Islamic history as the capital of the Abbasid caliphate and victim of the Tartar invasion is an emotive issue among Muslims in general and Arabs in particular. It is therefore not surprising that each time either Bin Laden or al-Zawahiri mentioned Baghdad, they mentioned its position as the "house" of the caliphate.

Prior to the invasion of Iraq, Bin Laden appears to have mentioned the caliphate only a few times in known public statements, but it becomes more common after March 2003. Some of these comments were simply linked to the mention of Baghdad as the land of the caliphate, while at other times the loss of the caliphate is mentioned to highlight the rise of un-Islamic states in their place or to indicate how the "crusaders" continue to try and prevent its re-establishment. In one of his last audio messages, in July 2006, Bin Laden warns the *mujahideen* in Iraq not to miss "this opportunity to establish the nucleus of the caliphate."[92] In 2007, al-Zawahiri stated that all the sacrifices of al-Qaeda have been to "restore its caliphate." But this restoration is to occur after winning back "dignity, honour, [and] freedom" for the *Umma*, and the proposed caliphate will "establish justice, spread the *shura*, protect the sacred things, and preserve the rights."[93] In other words, in a discourse of physical resistance the caliphate was an expression of independence, sovereignty and unity.

It cannot be denied that the caliphate remains an aspiration of al-Qaeda, but this is by no means unique to them. When questioned regarding the accusation that al-Qaeda wanted to establish a caliphate, al-Zawahiri replied that this is not unusual since it is something all Muslims wish for.[94] Though guilty of exaggeration, poll results released in 2007, showing that sixty-five per cent of respondents from across four major Muslim countries wanted to live under a single state,[95] indicate that the idea of unity on the basis of religion rather than race, one of the critical aspects of the caliphate and its use in modern discourse, has become a mainstream aspiration in the Muslim world today, and as such is an issue that few groups would ignore. Though it may suit some Western governments to link political programs like the establishment of the caliphate to terrorism in the mind of their constituents, its position in normative Islam means that it will invariably end with the alienation of many more Muslims than simply those supportive of al-Qaeda.

As demonstrated, the caliphate and its call plays a minor role in the discourse of al-Qaeda, and an equally small one in its ideology. Within their statements, it is used as an emotive historical symbol to motivate and incite the war against occupying forces, most notably in Iraq, where for a period al-Qaeda even broadcast a series of internet messages under the title "Voice of the Caliphate." While both Bin Laden and al-Zawahiri tried to convince the *Umma* that a great crusade was being waged against it, the caliphate is both a useful reminder of a symbol from the last crusades and a justification for a globalized jihad. As the conflict has moved beyond Iraq, the caliphate and its use in their discourse has been more limited, and Palestine more explicitly occupies the foreground, especially after events in Gaza since 2007, with Bin Laden again linking the motivation of the 9/11 operatives to Palestine in his address to President Obama in 2009 on Pakistan.[96] Another Bin Laden audio broadcast in January 2010 stated that America will never be secure "until security becomes a reality in Palestine," and that the Americans would not have enjoyment "while our brothers in Gaza live in hardship," in reference to the alleged failed attempt to detonate a passenger aircraft above the United States in December 2009.[97]

Given their lack of concern for the caliphate as a practical goal, it is not surprising that al-Qaeda have not made much effort in detailing it. Other groups who have at one time adopted the call for a caliphate, such as the Pakistani Jamaat-i-Islami, the Malaysian PAS and Hizb ut-Tahrir, have all written books describing it in differing degrees of detail. While al-Qaeda has produced manuals detailing military and terrorist techniques and papers discussing their theological position on the use of weapons of mass destruction, there is no book or paper detailing the caliphate they are supposedly seeking. Details are lacking because the main complaint of al-Qaeda, which underlines all their actions, is corruption and hereditary rule in their own countries that, in their words, "deprived the *Umma* of any political participation." While the Brotherhood considered that reformed individuals would in turn lead to the caliphate, and the Hizb believed the caliphate would in turn reform individuals, in Bin Laden's understanding the caliph is the reformed leader, the opposite of the failing of the Saudi regime, and an independent leader with morals needed by the Muslims to "unite them and establish a pious caliphate."[98] Hence they have no problem in labeling entities which are unsustainable, such as the Taliban regime in Afghanistan at the time of Mullah Umar or the fictitious Islamic State in Iraq "run" by Abu Umar al-Baghdadi, as "goalposts" along the road to achieving their aims. The goals they have repeatedly identified are the liberation of occupied lands, the eradication of corruption and dictatorial rule imposed from abroad, and political independence free from external interference. As stated by Mohamedou, "it is justice, and the yearning for it."[99] Indeed, the core complaints of al-Qaeda against America can be summed up in the manner Bin Laden himself was killed—an extrajudicial murder carried out by a hit-squad while simultaneously abusing the sovereignty of another country,[100] another unsurprising act constitutive of American exceptionalism and feeding the perception that the most powerful countries in the world are above the law.

In conclusion, the American and British governments have spoken frequently in public about the caliphate between 2005 and 2007, many more times than Bin Laden and al-Zawahiri twenty years after 1990. While the caliphate is marginal in the discourse of al-Qaeda's two main leaders, it seemed central to the discourse of some Western governments' attempts to address al-Qaeda during a period in which they sought elevated credibility from their constituents to prosecute the "War on Terror" with impunity. Rather than using the caliphate as a political program to reinstate religious and political authority, Bin Laden and his followers have sought to establish a global religious authority which is conferred upon those either physically participating in or supporting their jihad at the expense of government-supported 'ulama' who are seen to legitimize the un-Islamic rule of their regimes for the sake of patronage and position. While the extent of their support is limited, this is the natural outcome of the lack of any recognized Islamic political authority which has subsequently opened a space for other interpretations, whether within the bounds of the shari'a or not, with no recognized mechanism or authority to resolve disputes and differences.

6

BEYOND THE MIDDLE EAST

THE SUB-CONTINENT, THE DIASPORA, AND THE NEW MUSLIMS

The world that resulted from the tragic elimination of the Khalifate was a cluster of separated nations each with its own flag, constitution and central bank. None of these realities are acceptable in Islam.[1]

Umar Ibrahim Vadillo, 2003

While the caliphate appeared to briefly enter the lexicon of the Republican administration under George Bush Jr., arguably more for its negative resonance among the American public than out of strategic concerns, it appears to have a positive resonance amongst a substantial number of Muslims across various countries and regions. Research conducted by Gallup in 2007 found that an average of seventy-one per cent of those interviewed across four Muslim countries (Egypt, Morocco, Indonesia and Pakistan) agreed with the goal of requiring "strict application of *Shari'a* law in every Islamic country," with thirty-nine per cent agreeing strongly, while sixty-five per cent agreed with the goal of unifying "all Islamic countries into a single state or caliphate" in line with classical orthodox Islamic position that holds that there should be a single ruler for the entire Muslim community. At the same time, the research also found that seventy-four per cent wanted "to keep Western values out of Islamic countries," and yet seventy-five per cent held positive views of globalization while sixty-seven per cent believed that "a democratic political system" was a good thing,[2] which raises questions as to what the respondents understood by caliphate, democracy and *shari'a*.[3] Other research carried out in 2006 which covered ten Muslim countries found that seventy-nine per cent wanted *shari'a* incorporated as a source of legislation, while majorities in Egypt, Pakistan, Jordan, and Bangladesh wanted it as the "only source" of legislation,[4] what would otherwise be referred to as an Islamic state. A majority of African Muslims in ten out of fifteen Sub-Saharan countries polled in 2009 believed that they would see the re-establishment of a caliphate within their lifetime, while majorities in twelve countries favored making *shari'a* law the law of the land.[5]

The research detailed above is a small indicator of the kind of popular consciousness or revival for a polity based upon Islam that al-Qaeda's Ayman al-Zawahiri was referring to when he claimed that his wish to establish a caliphate was not unusual since it was something he believed all Muslims wish for.[6] An examination of the countries surveyed shows the resonance of the idea of *shari'a*-based governance, political unity and the belief in the caliphate beyond the Middle East in countries such as Pakistan and Indonesia in Asia to Morocco in the Maghreb and down to sub-Saharan Mozambique. Accordingly, it is not unusual that many groups beyond the Arab Middle East lay claim to or proclaim their goal of establishing a caliphate as being a fundamental part of their program. Given the history of advocacy for the caliphate in the Indian subcontinent and the depth of scholarship there, one should expect to find numerous movements emerging over time inspired by the activity and outlook of the Khilafat movement.

A subsequent blend of the crisis of Islamic authority within Sunni Islam, set off by the removal of the caliph, and the lack of legitimacy of artificially imposed nation-states across the region provide fertile ground for the emergence of individuals and movements who coalesced around the pivotal idea of the caliphate in an attempt to re-establish that authority. This vacuum of authority is not geographically restricted since the Sunni caliphate has always been held as the ultimate authority for Muslims, irrespective of where they reside. Though the coercive political authority of the state was always limited to the areas under its direct control, historically a form of leadership has been afforded to the position of caliph as exemplified by the inclusion of his name in the weekly Friday sermon throughout Muslim communities that extend beyond the borders of the caliphate, thereby engendering a sense of unity and belonging.[7] Since the 1960s, the failure of other transnational ideologies, whether pan-Arabism or otherwise, the perceived ineffectuality of regional and international bodies such as the Organisation of the Islamic Conference or even the United Nations, and the inability of the nation-state to build legitimacy for itself in the Middle East, have led people to reconsider a polity modeled on Islamic tradition and history. The disappearance of this symbol of political unity and sense of belonging to a wider community contrasted with the inability of the nation-state to provide an alternative model of governance, and over time this led to the emergence of individuals and movements in areas which were not governed by the Ottoman State prior to its dissolution and yet for whom the concept of the caliphate and its reinstatement is of central importance.

To give an overview of these other smaller and less well-known movements primarily based outside of the Middle East, and to examine their nature and the differing role the caliphate plays in their alternative frameworks and *ijtihad*, groups from three different areas encompassing at least some of the range of the Islamic community will be examined. The first of the three groups is the Tanzeem-e-Islami of Pakistan, founded by Dr. Israr Ahmad after his split from the Jamaat-i-Islami of Abul Ala Maududi, as a movement calling for the caliphate in the Indian subcontinent with a mainly Pakistani membership. The second group is the Jama'ah-tul-Muslimeen, a group led by Dr. Mohammad al-Rifaa'e, a Jordanian refugee resident in the UK, drawing its membership largely but not exclusively from the Muslim diaspora in the West. The third group is the Murabitun, a contemporary movement based around a Sufi order headed by Muslim convert Abdalqadir as-Sufi, born Ian Dallas, who founded the original community in Norwich, which has subsequently spread as far afield as Spain, Mexico, and Indonesia, while its current headquarters are in South Africa. The majority of its members are Muslim converts from various backgrounds and ethnicities. There are obvious gaps in this selection, the most notable being the rise of movements in the former Soviet Republics of Central Asia. This is because of their more localized nature and the fact that a substantial amount of their activity is linked to the emergence of Hizb ut-Tahrir in the region, discussed earlier. Other omissions include the irredentist movements in the Caucasus that were particularly active in Chechnya in the 1990s, and the discussions regarding the caliphate in the Balkans.

The movements identified here come from important areas of growing influence—movements based in Muslim countries which are non-Arab and groups emerging from within growing Muslim communities in the West, both indigenous and emigrant. By examining these different movements, which represent diverse elements of the Muslim community beyond the Middle East, it becomes clear that each has very different ideas about what caused the decline of Muslims worldwide and the method by which it may be remedied, and yet at the same time there exists a commonality between them. The continuing theme of the exchange of ideas across nominal national borders also becomes more apparent since even though each of these movements is geographically distant from the other, there is evidence of the transfer of ideas between them and the groups that preceded them.

Much like the movements studied previously, each of them embraces the call for the re-establishment of the caliphate as a primary objective. What sets them apart is their emphasis on personal leadership, which manifests itself in a different manner in each group and yet is noticeably more prominent than in the other movements. While Hassan al-Banna for example exercised his position over the rest of the Muslim Brotherhood in a forceful way, with his charismatic personality acting as the engine which drove them, there was no deep sense that he saw himself as destined for the position of the absent caliph. Similarly, while Taqiudeen al-Nabahani insisted that leadership was singular, the concern for the caliphate in Hizb ut-Tahrir was for the system of Islam to be implemented with the caliph as the mechanism by which this could be achieved, and did not focus on the embodiment of its personality. With respect to al-Qaeda, while various movements and individuals from disparate locations pledged their allegiance to Osama bin Laden or to Ayman al-Zawahiri after him, this is more of an association with the brand of global jihad than a true investment in following his personal commands and leadership, hence the need for their pledge of allegiance to be announced in the media rather than given personally. In contrast to these groups, Dr. Israr Ahmad took a pledge of allegiance from each of his followers in lieu of the pledge to a caliph, Dr. al-Rifaa'e went a step further and was given the pledge of allegiance as the actual caliph while Abdalqadir leads his group as the unquestioned spiritual head of a Sufi order who will only welcome new members into his order if they have first given a pledge of allegiance to an "Amir" (leader).

The reason for this extra investment in personal leadership may be linked to the origins of each of these groups, formed and based in countries outside of the historic lands governed by the Ottoman State, or indeed in some cases by any Islamic state. Their continuing lack of connection to any of the nation-states of the Middle East, specifically those areas covering the most revered Islamic symbols such as Mecca, Medina and al-Quds, along with their perceived lack of legitimacy and the absence of any meaningful authority in which Sunni Islam could be anchored globally since the abolition of the caliphate has meant that the primary objective of these groups is the establishment of such a unifying symbol. This would engender a sense of Muslim belonging wherever that community may have resided previously, whether under the authority of their temporal leader or not, and in its absence they have each sought to invest that authority in different ways, in anticipation of its return.

Tanzeem-e-Islami and Tehreek-e-Khilafat

By the First World War, opinion within Arab lands was divided with respect to the Ottoman caliphate, due in part to the machinations of the British in the area of the Hejaz. However the caliphate enjoyed considerable support outside of its borders, particularly with the rise of pan-Islamism as advocated by Sultan Abdul-Hamid II and also in the Indian subcontinent around the time of the First World War, where the Khilafat movement mobilized support from Indian Muslims and wider society for the beleaguered State. The abolition of the caliphate in 1924 led to the collapse of the Khilafat movement, since its proclaimed raison d'être of supporting the Ottoman State became obsolete, and so the Muslims of India were left without an external anchor to focus their activity around in their struggle against British colonialism, remaining a minority in a Hindu-majority land. With the end of the Khilafat movement, Islamic activists like Maududi were left to invest their efforts in other avenues of opposition to colonial rule.

In the years preceding British withdrawal from India, Muslim engagement in the political arena was usually either as part of the Indian National Congress, or after the 1930s as part of the separatist All-India

Muslim League established by poet Mohammad Iqbal and subsequently led by Mohammad Ali Jinnah, which sought the establishment of an independent Muslim state. The main body of Indian scholars, particularly those who had supported the Khilafat movement from the Deoband movement, were against the Muslim League and cessation. Some of them, notably senior member Abul Kalam Azad, had abandoned their support for pan-Islamism and had turned towards an inclusive Indian-based national polity by working within the Indian National Congress to find a place for Muslims within a united India.

Maududi, originally an activist from the Khilafat movement, was against the Muslim League—explained either by his resistance to the idea of cessation[8] or his belief that if there was to be a Muslim state, he should be the one to lead it.[9] Whatever the reality of his views on the idea of cessation, he was against the Muslim League's secular nature and wanted to invest his efforts in an Islamic party, to which end he subsequently established Jama'at-i-Islami in 1941 as the vanguard of a struggle that would result in the establishment of an Islamic state. His proposed method of change was incremental and non-violent rather than radical or revolutionary, and he believed that the future revolution would come from a conversion of society's leaders to the movement in a top-down rather than bottom-up approach.[10] He focused on convincing the elite to implement his ideal of an Islamic state on the basis that they would then apply this over the masses. This elite-led model was driven by his belief that the general public was lacking in influence and unable take matters into its own hands, but was already Islamically inclined and willing to accept such a state given that the rhetoric for Pakistan's establishment was based upon religious slogans.

Though the Jama'at was originally conceived as a religious community and movement, with reformation of the political order being considered secondary to individual reform, by 1957 Maududi had decided to make political reformation a primary aim. His argument was that since the party had been established to bring about Islamic governance, this aim would not be achievable if secular forces became too entrenched in power, which meant that they were compelled to contest and compete against them. It was at this point that a power struggle took place within the Jama'at, with several of the more than 200 scholars in the party leaving due to disagreements over direction and personality. While many of those who left made up a significant part of the established religious and intellectual weight of the party,[11] among them were other noted activists such as the young Dr. Israr Ahmad, disillusioned that after his time in prison Maududi then began to co-operate with the very government that he had previously criticized by accepting the legitimacy of the system and participating fully within it.[12]

Dr. Ahmad was born in 1932 in Hisar, a district of East Punjab in India, as the second son of a government official. Though he considered himself a "product of the dynamic teachings of Maulana Abul Ala Maududi," he also believed that his "dynamic and revolutionary conception of Islam" was also partly drawn from the influence of Abul Kalam Azad.[13] In addition, like many of his contemporaries he was also greatly influenced by the poetry of Iqbal, in whose writing he sought solace at a time when he believed that the decline of the Muslims worldwide "had reached its lowest ebb" with even the last symbol of "their global unity," the Ottoman caliphate, no longer there to "reassure the Muslims."[14] His formative years prior to partition were spent as a member of the Muslim League, where at a young age he became the General Secretary of the Muslim Students Federation in 1946–7. At the same time he used to read Jama'at literature, and often defended them from their critics within the Muslim League. While confined to his house during Muslim-Hindu rioting at the time of partition, he spent his time reading Maududi's exegesis of the Qur'an, which inspired him for the first time to read the Qur'an with understanding rather than simply recitation. After his family moved to Pakistan in November of 1947, he spent his student days as an activist within the Jama'at rather than the Muslim League.

After completing his studies, Dr. Ahmad became a member of the Jama'at, but soon became disillusioned with the "deterioration" in the moral behavior of its members and believed their attitudes had become "more like members of a purely political party than a revolutionary organisation."[15] It was this change that led to his resignation from the party in 1957, also prompted by the party's participation in elections. His understanding was that politics could either be revolutionary or electoral, and that while the Jama'at began as a revolutionary group pre-partition, it had succumbed to the possibility of achieving change through the "short-cut" of elections rather than working through the grassroots. His own understanding was that "elections are held to run the system" rather than to "change the prevailing system,"[16] and therefore by running for the elections the Jama'at had given up their call to radically change the status quo, replacing it with an Islamic system.

After waiting ten years for other more prominent and qualified members who had left the Jama'at to bring forward an alternative program based upon the original goals of the group, in 1967 Dr. Ahmad published a work entitled "Islamic Renaissance—the Real Task Ahead," in which he articulated his own view of the reality of the state of the Muslims, the problems they faced, his criticism of other Islamic movements and his proposed solution. His main contention was that Western thought and philosophy were so dominant and pervasive that those who were struggling against it were in fact often "greatly influenced by the West" themselves, and that by thinking "in terms of Western philosophy and ideology," they had lost the "impact and efficacy to oppose it." The central issue was that "science was [...] received with as much enthusiasm as should be accorded to Divine Revelation" which meant that "a large number of educated people in the Islamic world adopted a secular and materialistic point of view." In other words there was a spiritual void in the reaction against the two-fold Western attack on the Muslim world—ideological and cultural on the one-hand and military and political on the other. As "the European attack was primarily and initially political," the reaction against it, as seen from pan-Islamists such as the Khilafat movement, was a "revolt against political repression only" and not ideological and cultural.[17]

Dr. Ahmad concluded that the nationalist and self-rule movements launched across Muslim countries "invariably appealed to religious sentiments of the people for sparking off feelings of nationalism," since there was "no alternative to this" as "Muslim nationalism had no anchorage other than Islam." In this analysis, the Muslim Brotherhood and the Jama'at are both seen as part of the struggle against colonialism, without any real differentiation with other nationalist movements. The adoption of Islam by these two groups was seen more as a "slogan" than as "an existential concern for the Islamic faith," with neither achieving any remarkable success in his opinion. Rather, he felt that they seemed to have "outlived the span of their lives," with contemporary conditions not "ripe" for the realization of the "fond hopes for the renaissance of Islam." The Muslim Brotherhood, at that time suffering under the regime of Gamal Abdul-Nasser, had "met almost complete disintegration" while the Indo-Pakistani Jama'at had "fared no better," possessing "hardly any programme other than joining hands with various political parties in the struggle for democracy."[18]

The problem with the two groups was that their view of Islam was based on the Western standpoint of "preferring material existence and worldly pursuits to [the] spirit and the life Hereafter," with the metaphysical beliefs of Islam affirmed but not stressed enough. The focus was wrongly placed on Islamic teachings that related to the conduct of life's affairs leading to an understanding which affirmed religious belief but lacked deep faith. This was a result of the influence of the ideas of secularization from the West amounting to a "materialistic interpretation of faith and religion." In sum, the movements were seen as "more social and political than religious," or "more 'this-worldly' than 'other-worldly.'"[19]

It is clear from his critique of the two older movements that Dr. Ahmad believed their original intent to work as grassroots educational movements to affect change, was the correct path forward, but that the temptation to engage in elections and participation in the political process had effectively corrupted them and ensured their failure. His analysis appears to be profoundly affected by his disillusionment with Maududi's Jama'at and its decision post-1957 to effectively become a political party, with later works expressing his disdain for the "political game" of electoral politics in Pakistan, based around feudalism, meaning that anyone from outside the "capitalist class" who tries to engage within it "inevitably becomes the agent or instrument for the fulfilment of someone else's ambition of power."[20] Returning to the founding philosophy of the Jama'at, Dr. Ahmad suggested the establishment of a "high-powered academic movement" to effect change in "the educated elite and intelligentsia of the society," in order to take them from the "darkness of materialism and atheism" back to "the light of faith and belief."[21]

"Islamic Renaissance" ends with a suggestion to establish an organization dedicated to the dissemination of the message of the Qur'an in order to "revive and revitalize the faith of Muslims in general" and "provide practical training and guidance" for those who respond to its call. A complementary research academy was also suggested to "start a popular movement for learning and teaching the Qur'an amongst Muslims."[22] These ideas were inspired by the unfulfilled visions of Azad and Iqbal to establish seminaries dedicated to the promotion of the Qur'an. Dr. Ahmad gave up his medical practice in 1971 to dedicate himself to Islamic activism in order to achieve this vision, and by 1972 he had established a Qur'an academy in Lahore—the Markazi Anjuman Khud-dam-ul-Qur'an—while the organization Tanzeem-e-Islami was formed three years later in 1975 in order to work toward the re-establishment of the Islamic state.

The Tanzeem-e-Islami was to be the revolutionary organization that the Jama'at had initially positioned itself as, working with the elite and middle classes to affect change through academic discourse. For the first two years there was no organizational structure, as Dr. Ahmad was hoping that old Jama'at members would join his new venture before he formalized the movement. In the end a convention was held to resolve the issue, with Dr. Ahmad becoming the head of the movement, and members expected to sign a pledge of allegiance (*bay'a*) in which after affirming the tenets of the Islamic creed they also take the "oath of allegiance" to him, promising to "obey all his orders and accept them" as long as they were not outside the bounds of Islam, and to "never have a dispute with the responsible people of the organisation."[23]

This very structured and disciplined leadership seems at odds with Dr. Ahmad's criticism of Maududi as acting in a dictatorial manner in forcing out members who disagreed with him, but it appears that Dr. Ahmad recognized that the lack of clear authority invested in Maududi within the Jama'at ultimately created problems since his fellow members expected their views to be considered on equal terms. In fact, Maududi did originally imagine that the leader of the Jama'at should take a pledge of allegiance and noted this in a letter he wrote in 1941, in which he compared membership of an "Islamic party" to the Sufi follower giving allegiance—or bay'a—to the spiritual master who assumed the central role in a Sufi order and demanded complete submission from his acolytes.[24]

In the year before the establishment of the Tanzeem, Dr. Ahmad published an article in the *Meesaq* journal discussing his understanding of the reasons for the decline of the Muslim *Umma*. In essence the growth in material power and wealth of Muslims led to a parallel decline in enthusiasm for their faith. This decline was ultimately exposed by Western power and colonialism, the final result being the split of the central region of the Islamic world between the Arabs and Turks and the destruction of the "essential as well as symbolic institution of Islamic unity, the caliphate."[25] While recognizing that Muslims had ceased to function as a unified body and therefore assumed national status, he believed that after the achievement of real independence—even if it relied on the use of nationalism as a foundation for the struggle against colonialism—it was necessary to return to true Islamic beliefs, specifically the unity of the Muslim nation. Upon examination of some of his speeches delivered in the mid to late 1980s, it becomes clear that Dr. Ahmad was seeking ways to reconstitute the universal *Umma*, which had been reduced to an "abstract concept," his opinion being that this would be brought about by a smaller group, who would actively enjoin the good and forbid the evil.[26] This strong emphasis on holding the government to account mainly through the use of mass communication, coupled with his belief in the global nature of the Muslim nation and the ultimate goal of its reconstitution, meant that the Tanzeem aimed to present itself as a worldwide movement through the use of modern media,[27] even though its membership numbered less than 2000, of whom fewer than 300 were based outside of Pakistan.[28]

A third movement called Tehreek-e-Khilafat Pakistan was launched in 1991[29] as a result of the global activities and travel that Dr. Ahmad engaged in, prompting the exchange of ideas with others outside of Pakistan. This occurred soon after he met with members of Hizb ut-Tahrir in the United States who believed that prior to their meeting, Dr. Ahmad had been engaged primarily in calling for a more democratic Islamic state in Pakistan in a very general manner, while also trying to focus people on understanding the Qur'an, and that it was only as a result of their discussions that he became convinced of the correctness of making the revival of the caliphate the "vital issue" for Muslims and adopted it as a goal of his movement.[30]

The launch of the Tehreek movement took place in the Karachi Press Club, where a statement which urgently called for the "total change in the entire socio-political fabric" of Pakistan, along with "the establishment of Islamic system of social justice" was read out. No longer was a movement for the mass dissemination of the message of the Qur'an sufficient. This change now required "launching a mass movement," made up of "all that the aspirants of Islamic revival have got at their disposal" in order to achieve the aforementioned system, which could be "summed up as the system of caliphate." His initial understanding of this caliphate was based upon the normal fundamental tenet of any exposition of an Islamic state: that sovereignty belonged to Allah and that the legislatures are Muslim only. Islamic law is to be implemented, with the abolition of gambling and interest alongside the collection of the *Zakah* (religious alms) tax, and a land settlement in accordance with the classical conception of *kharaji* land, whereby the land is considered a collective property and the cultivators pay revenues to the state based on the value of their harvest. This would "eliminate the feudalism and absentee landlordism" which is deeply trenchant in Pakistan, while providing another tax stream. The elimination of inequality is also mentioned, with everyone to be made accountable before the law without exception and the election of the caliph by direct franchise. These features of the proposed caliphate would need to be promoted within Pakistan, hence the launch of a specific "movement for Khilafat in Pakistan" to convince the masses of its necessity,[31] alongside the renaming of the Tanzeem's regular publication *Neda* as *Neda Khilafat*, in order to impress the term upon the minds of its readers.

Dr. Ahmad continued his relationship with Hizb ut-Tahrir, and was invited to deliver a speech in 1994 at a conference in London entitled "The Khilafah Conference." On his return to Lahore, he gave a speech outlining his views on the group where he made a number of minor criticisms of the Hizb, such as the adoption of a name for the movement not drawn from Islamic terminology. Another more relevant point was his criticism of the Hizb for not working toward Khilafah in the West—many members were Western converts to Islam and therefore in a prime position to promote the idea to audiences of their own racial and ethnic background.[32] This comment may also have been an indirect criticism of the Hizb for not pursuing the establishment of the caliphate in Pakistan at that time, something that Dr. Ahmad believed was achievable and in fact more realistic since "the conditions are much more congenial for the establishment of Khilafah in Pakistan than in many of the other Muslim countries."[33]

Given that the Hizb is a much larger organization with greater global reach and a history of activism pursuant to establishing the caliphate in the Middle East, particularly at the time of their establishment, it is perhaps unsurprising that the Tanzeem have taken clear measures to explain the differences between the two, especially as both now believe that the "Islamic State should be established and the System of Khilafah should be revived."[34] Though there existed other groups in the region closer to Pakistan who were also calling specifically for the establishment of a caliphate, such as Khilafat Majlis—a group set up in 1989 in Bangladesh by Maulana Abdul Ghaffar—due to the size, influence and local nature of their politics, they do not appear to be addressed at all by Dr. Ahmad. There are two substantial differences that the Tanzeem have emphasized in marking a clear distinction between themselves and the Hizb: their articulation of what a future caliphate would look like and the methodology by which it may be reached.

While the statement to the Karachi Press Club at the launch of the Tehreek movement made it clear that the adoption of the call to a caliphate was genuine and not mere rhetoric, Dr. Ahmad's thinking at that time had not moved beyond a few general principles for the foundation of the state. While the Hizb had written of the caliphate as a unique system whose executive structure is derived from Islamic sources, the Tanzeem adopted the view of the Jama'at and Muslim Brotherhood that Muslims should take advantage of new political institutions which had evolved over the past few centuries, primarily in the West, since, as articulated by Iqbal, "the republican form of government" is "thoroughly consistent with the spirit of Islam."[35] The key issue was one of sovereignty, with both popular sovereignty as practiced by democracies and individual sovereignty as practiced by monarchies and dictatorships considered antithetical to the Islamic ideal of sovereignty belonging to God. As long as political institutions placed this foundation at their base they would be considered compatible with Islam. The American republican model in particular was considered to be "the highest stage of political evolution," from which they could "learn a lot," with a federal and presidential form of government thought to be the most appropriate for implementation in Pakistan.[36] Where Dr. Ahmad differed with the Brotherhood and found agreement with the Hizb was in the permissibility of a multi-party system, to be adopted as long as each party did not promote anything considered outside the realms of Islamic law.

As far as methodology was concerned, while Dr. Ahmad's understanding of the Hizb was that it sought support from the military in order to establish an Islamic state, his own experience working as an advisor to the government of Zia ul-Haq in the early 1980s convinced him that coming into power through a coup was undesirable as it did not leave any scope for advancement, since the public may not be supportive (what is meant by public here is the influential elites such as the landowning classes or the growing middle class). Therefore the revolution needed to establish an Islamic state would have to be one with popular rather than military support. This was thought to be particularly viable in Pakistan, while in the opinion of Dr. Ahmad, the Hizb may have adopted such a method in Arab countries due to their persecution and lack of channels to express themselves openly in order to garner wider support.[37] After 1991, Dr. Ahmad produced his own six stage *ijtihad* to bring about revolutionary change and establish the caliphate, which begins with propagation of his ideology (in this case through the establishment of Qur'an academies) and the organization of a revolutionary group (Tanzeem-e-Islami) which would then train their members and prepare them for passive and active resistance before finally engaging in armed conflict. The necessity of armed conflict was deduced from his reading of the life of the Prophet Mohammad, but he believed that this should be replaced in contemporary times with non-violent resistance due to the futility of trying to fight the established militaries at the disposal of most modern states. This movement was to be called "nahi anil-munkar"—"the Islamic imperative to eradicate everything that is evil, wrong, unjust or immoral"[38] through propagation and eventually civil disobedience.

In such a program, the revolutionary movement requires a leader capable of organizing the masses. Dr. Ahmad held that the "only approach that was used to organise the masses" throughout Islamic history had been the *bay'a* or pledge of allegiance. Utilizing the narration of the Prophet Mohammad, "whoever dies without the pledge of allegiance upon his neck, dies the death of *jahiliyya*," also used by Hizb ut-Tahrir to emphasize the obligation to establish the caliphate in order to give the caliph the aforementioned pledge, the Tanzeem claimed that in the absence of the caliph the pledge must be given to the leader of the party which works to establish the caliphate in an organized manner.[39] This led to criticism of the movement on the grounds that in orthodox Islamic teachings the pledge of allegiance is only to be given to the single overall ruler of Muslims, and goes beyond the structural discipline and leadership found in the other movements which inspired much of the Tanzeem's work and ideas.

In reality, the Tanzeem had adopted the global outlook and explicit goal of Hizb ut-Tahrir, but combined with the original methodology employed by the Jama'at along with their more general vision of what an Islamic state should be, and believing that the torch for Islamic revivalism lay firmly in Pakistan and not in Arab lands. Though Dr. Ahmad gave up leadership of the movement in 2002 due to health issues, it was passed on to his son who appears to have not fundamentally altered the direction of the Tanzeem. It is as yet too early to predict the effect of the death of Dr. Ahmad in 2010, though it is unlikely that his son will manage to greatly extend its appeal given the movement's reliance on his father for ideological and practical direction.

The Jama'ah-tul-Muslimeen and their Quraishi Caliph

In the early 1990s, the period that saw Dr. Israr Ahmad announcing the establishment of the Tehreek-e-Khilafat in Karachi, another medical doctor took a different pledge of allegiance from Muslims. While Dr. Ahmad was taking the *bay'a* as the leader of a group working to establish the caliphate, Dr. Mohammad al-Rifaa'e was anointed as the caliph himself. Originally from Jordan and tracing his lineage directly to the Quraishi tribe of the Prophet, it is claimed that Dr. al-Rifaa'e left for Afghanistan in the 1980s to participate in the jihad against the Soviet Union. Upon his return to Jordan he participated in several protests against the First Gulf War in 1990 and was expelled by the Muslim Brotherhood over their disapproval of his "radical" opinions before being arrested and held in detention by the Jordanian regime.[40] As a result of the infighting that took place in Afghanistan after the fall of Kabul, and constant harassment from the Jordanian regime, Dr. al-Rifaa'e sought asylum in the United Kingdom in 1991.

After settling in England, a number of people referred to as "a group of *Muhaajireen* and *Ansar*"—a reference to the emigrants and supporters who initially gave their pledge of allegiance to the Prophet Moham-mad—gathered together "to support Islam." This was through the "re-establishment of unity [...] under the authority of one Imam," giving their pledge to Dr. al-Rifaa'e.[41] According to the group's own narrative of the event, Dr. al-Rifaa'e initially refused their proposal but was sub-sequently convinced to accept their pledge to him "after a great deal of deliberation and dialogue." It is also claimed that the majority of those who had given the pledge of allegiance to him came from abroad, with his followership based in approximately forty different countries.[42]

This group of followers refer to themselves by the name "Jama'ah-tul-Muslimeen," literally meaning "the group of Muslims." This name was derived from various Prophetic narrations which refer to this grouping, with one giving the instruction that during an era of evil the believer must "stick to the main body of Muslims (*Jama'a al-muslimin*) and their leader."[43] Classical Islamic scholarship has traditionally understood this expression as a reference to the united political entity of Muslims under the leadership of the caliph or local Sultan,[44] but it has been used by numerous contemporary movements to position themselves as the central Muslim community and to ask individuals to come forward and pledge their allegiance to their leader.

One such group that has used this name in the last fifty years is the Jamaat-ul-Muslimeen of Pakistan. This group was established in the 1960s by Masood Ahmed and is currently headed by Mohammad Ishtiaq based in Karachi. It promotes a return to *ijtihad* from the original sources of the Qur'an and *Sunna* (traditions of the Prophet), but unlike other more mainstream movements it considers reliance on any part of traditional Islamic jurisprudence as articulated by the major orthodox Sunni schools of thought as an innovation, making it an extreme strand of contemporary *Salafi*[45] thinking. At the same time it also holds that the command to adhere to the pledge of allegiance is applicable to any leader, even without a government or authority,[46] and that such a leader has been given this pledge by his followers in order to facilitate "the expansion of Islam to all corners of the globe," and it is now binding on the rest of the Muslim community to follow. Anyone who refuses to give the pledge or removes themselves from the group is argued to have fallen into disbelief and heresy,[47] justifying this position by reference to the narration which states that the one who dies without a pledge of allegiance upon his neck dies an un-Islamic death.[48]

In terms of the fundamental idea and core justification constitutive of their concept of the pledge of allegiance, the UK-based Jama'ah appears virtually identical to the Pakistani Jamaat. This could be because Dr. al-Rifaa'e had previously spent enough time in the region to have come across and been influenced by the arguments of the Pakistani Jamaat, quite likely given that they both represent strands of Salafism, with perhaps the only major exception being that the Jama'ah is not as explicit in their excommunication of Muslims who remain outside the "authority" of their pledge. Both groups are concerned with promoting a pure Islam, and vigorously attack what they see as innovation in matters of belief and religion, instead promoting the return to a direct interpretation of the Qur'an rather than reliance upon any of the traditional Islamic schools of thought.[49]

The difference between the two is that the Pakistani Jamaat primarily focuses on pointing out and criticizing the practice of *taqlid* (when a Muslim defers his opinion in any matter to an alternative authority either due to inability to practice *ijtihad* or out of deference to the greater knowledge of the one they choose to follow). This practice is widespread across the Muslim world and is particularly prevalent in the Indian subcontinent since the prerequisite knowledge of the language and texts of Islam required to properly undertake *ijtihad* means that it is often considered outside the remit of most people, particularly those who have little or no knowledge of Arabic. In the Indian subcontinent over the last half century there have been many debates between the "deobandi" scholars who consider it necessary to stick to one school of thought, since its original scholars possessed a greater degree of knowledge than contemporary scholars, and the "ahlel-hadis" who believe that such a practice is unnecessary and that Islamic opinions should be derived directly from the Qur'an and *Sunna*. The Jamaat follows the second strand of thinking, asserting that taking the words of an Islamic scholar as final and infallible is tantamount to polytheism as it puts the words of mortal men on an equal level with the words of God and His Prophet;[50] anyone who follows a particular school of thought has fallen into the trap of sectarianism. The role of the Jamaat and its leader are to provide a unified, non-sectarian Muslim community which draws its beliefs directly from the Qur'an and *Sunna* rather than relying on an intermediary traditional juristic opinion.

While the Jamaat is concerned with the disunity that follows prescription to different schools of thought, the UK-based Jama'ah is focused on resolving a disunity more political in nature, borne out of the experience of seeing the victors of the conflict against the Soviet Union turn their guns upon each other due to membership of different groups, with multiple leaders representing various tribal and sectarian interests. Having seen the destruction of what was initially seen as a basis on which an Islamic state might be established in Afghanistan, brought down by a lack of a unified command prior to the victory over the communist regime of Dr. Najibullah, the group believes that "the cause of unity in Islam is not the existence of force and power" and instead "unity is a command in itself." Therefore the "command to unity" is a separate but prerequisite condition for establishing an Islamic State.[51]

This unity is a command from God for the Muslim *Umma* to "act as one body" with all its parts "under the command of one control centre," the caliphate. This authority is a necessity at all times since without it all Islamic rules relating to social interaction, such as marriage and employment, would become suspended. The line of argument which holds that power and authority are necessary prerequisites for the establishment of such a caliph or caliphate is considered to be a modernist interpretation which compared Islamic leadership to the leadership of a nation-state. Where a nation-state ceases to exist, so too does its leadership, whereas Islamic leadership is "not applied due to the existence of a state that tries to enforce it" but rather is a command in its own right.[52]

According to internal sources, Dr. al-Rifaa'e's supporters imposed the fulfillment of that command upon him, and so he was accordingly proclaimed as the "legitimate head of all Muslims" since taking the pledge in the early 1990s, with a duty now incumbent upon "every sincere Muslim" to follow in pledging their allegiance to him and submit themselves to his command.[53] An alternative view is given by Egyptian veteran of the jihad in Afghanistan Mustafa Hamed[54] in his online book which chronicles the experience of the Arab contingent of the *mujahidin* in Afghanistan, where he states that a small group of Arabs gave their *bay'a* to one of their own who had proposed the idea and offered himself as caliph (identified simply as someone who had British citizenship or residency). The group then demanded that everyone else recognize him as their caliph and proceeded to wage a campaign of kidnapping and fighting against anyone who opposed them. The caliph also supposedly issued several strange rulings including permission to deal in cannabis and the prohibition of paper money, but his followers were eventually run out of Afghanistan by the Taliban (who had refused to give their allegiance to the caliph).[55] It is not clear which of these two narrations is true, but it is possible that the events as mentioned by Hamed have been exaggerated since there is no clear source and they seem to be based on a mix of personal experience and hearsay.

By claiming the position of caliph or leader of the global Muslim *Umma* for themselves, the Jama'ah not only ignored the claim of the Pakistani Jamaat—perhaps understandable given that the Jamaat did not lay claim to the position of caliph—but they also seemed unaware of the claims of Camaleddin Kaplin, who proclaimed the title for himself while residing in Germany after he split from the Turkish group "Milli Gorus" in 1983 and established his own group "Hilafet Devleti" or "caliphate state."[56] Had the two groups been more aware of one another, the conclusion may not have been pleasant. Incumbent caliph Metin Kaplan had been convicted for incitement to murder after the leader of a splinter group proclaimed himself caliph, supposedly resulting in a fatwa from Kaplan based upon the words of the Prophet "when a second caliph challenges the first, kill the second of them,"[57] for which he served four years in jail (Kaplan is now also serving a jail sentence in Turkey, having been found guilty of involvement in an alleged plot to fly aeroplanes into the mausoleum of Mustafa Kemal).

However, while the similarities between the two movements extend beyond their respective claims to the caliphate—in their mutual emphasis on puritanical views, consequently labeling most other Muslims as traitors, for example—the Hilafet Devleti is more a reaction of the Turkish Diaspora in Germany in order to establish a link to their country of origin and is focused more on politics in the homeland.[58] By contrast, the Jama'ah is more cosmopolitan and globally grounded, without a shared country of origin at the basis of their identity. Much of their discourse relates either to the general state of Muslims globally or the position of Muslims in the UK where their caliph resides.

The most prominent issue addressed is voting in the British parliamentary elections, something directly related to their call for the establishment of a system of governance based on Islamic sources alone. While the Jama'ah holds the relatively common view that democracy is not compatible with Islam since it contradicts the sovereignty of God, their position goes further in that anyone who votes for a non-Islamic entity is automatically rendered an apostate—a position detailed in a piece of work released just after the 2005 elections which referred to the Respect party, who had strongly canvassed the Muslim vote in the Bethnal Green constituency.[59] Other issues include "unveiling" what they consider to be the "British Establishment's hatred of Islam" by discussing the position of the government and media with respect to the choice of Muslim women to wear the veil, linking it to a series of Orientalist attacks intended to discredit ideas such as polygamy, jihad and the caliphate itself.[60] However, the majority of their literature either decries the disunity of Muslims, urging them to fulfill their obligation and pledge allegiance to their caliph, or explains and justifies the group's particular understanding of what the caliph and caliphate is.

While on paper Dr. al-Rifaa'e's role as the caliph or *amir al-mu'minin* (leader of the believers) is to "spearhead the charge to demolish all man-made laws" which contradict Islamic *shari'a* by abandoning all relationships with un-Islamic individuals, bodies and organizations,[61] in reality his authority is restricted to his small group of followers. According to the Jama'ah, the pledge they give is not simply a single obligatory act but is in fact "the doorway to many obligations" and the direction given to "the one who was previously without objectives and direction." Joining them "is not like joining a group" which one may subsequently lose interest in "and then leave and join another" since abandoning them is akin to abandoning the Islamic system. So, while those "ignorant of the laws of Allah" may consider the pledge as an isolated act, for the members of the group it is "the way out of the darkness" and an intercession for themselves in front of God. At the same time, they are commanded to "cling" to their leadership "even if the Imam is oppressive," or "if there is selfishness and unfair preferences."[62] In other words, the Jama'ah is akin to a cult movement which demands complete submission from its members who form a distinct community, not by living in a particular location, but through obedience to their caliph and his appointed representatives, who have the authority to resolve their issues and command them in their affairs, even though as a non-state entity they have no real coercive capacity in such issues.

As a consequence, much of the group's literature is defensive in nature, justifying its position and putting forward arguments against their opponents and alternative viewpoints while giving comfort to its members by proclaiming them as a minority in possession of the truth.[63] This position is necessary as the group has inverted the common understanding that in order to establish a caliphate, authority over its intended territory is required and instead call for the establishment of the caliphate in order to then seek such authority.[64] The Jama'ah criticizes groups working for the caliphate, by which they appear to primarily mean Hizb ut-Tahrir judging by the details they provide, as adopting methodologies that contradict their objective since they seek the support of the army to establish a caliphate, while the Jama'ah considers existing armies to be disbelievers due to their support for incumbent un-Islamic regimes in place across the Muslim world. The common understanding that the caliphate cannot be established without power is viewed by the Jama'ah as a "grave error" and "diseased thinking which is preventing the revival of Islam," whereas "if all the groups were united behind one man then this would change everything."[65] A lot of their discourse is confrontational, arguing against the ideas espoused by other groups, and their tendency to erect barricades around themselves is often seen where they challenge others for proof that they were "not allowed [...] to be united in this present condition of weakness in which unity is most needed"[66] as they sought to justify their unorthodox ideas.

Though the Jama'ah's membership appeared to be growing in the years immediately following 9/11, the detention of their leader by the British security services in 2006, held until he was granted bail in 2008 owing to his deteriorating health, raised questions about their viability.[67] Given that their caliph was not only powerless and stateless, but was also being held in detention, some of the group's members were confused as to what their status was. In response to this the group wrote a piece entitled "The Continuation of *Imaarah* [Leadership] in the Case of a Captive Imam," which stated that "people should not spread panic when an Imam is captured nor should they despair," and that rather than telling people that "the *Imaamah* has ceased," they must instead follow whichever leaders the caliph had previously conferred authority on. The piece indicates that there was understandable internal turmoil at the time, and instructs followers that they are obliged to refer all their matters to such delegated authorities, ensuring that the group's leadership maintain their position of dominance over those who had pledged allegiance to their Imam.[68] To bolster their position from an Islamic point of view, reference is made to classical texts which detail the conditions under which the captive Imam may continue to be obeyed, while ignoring the fact that the same texts also articulate the orthodox understanding of the caliph as the head of the Islamic state and authority in power. The fact that the group continues to follow the same leadership since Dr. al-Rifaa'e's release, despite his reportedly poor physical and mental health, further supports an analysis that identified cult-like features, with junior leaders having free rein to exercise whatever authority they believe they have without constraint, a wry parallel to the image of the impotent caliph who provides religious justification for the authority of the sultan below him.

While the Jama'ah has many similarities to the Jamaat of Pakistan and the Hilafet Devleti of Germany, it is also unique in its own right. It is a group firmly based in the diaspora, led by an Arab refugee originally at the behest of veterans of the Afghanistan conflict, with individual members as far afield as Pakistan and Bangladesh (though as a movement they appear to be limited to Southeast England), which posits itself as the global leader of Muslims worldwide. Its influences are an eclectic mix of Salafi influenced beliefs, of a movement seeking to establish an Islamic state and the experience of its founding members, who saw the collapse of what they had fought for in Afghanistan, brought about by the disparate nature of the resistance which become more marked after the expulsion of the Soviets and the fall of the communist-backed regime, leaving a power vacuum in which groups that had previously been allies competed for authority. The caliphs of London, Cologne and Karachi are all reactions to the lack of a credible Islamic authority around which these disparate communities can unite, exacerbated by the lack of legitimacy of the nation-state in Muslim lands and feelings of exclusion as minorities living as part of a Muslim diaspora.

Sheikh Abdalqadir as-Sufi and the Gold Dinar Community

The growing rate of conversion to Islam in Europe and the United States means that many Muslims living in the West are no longer diaspora in the ethnic sense of the word. From among them, individuals and movements have emerged who proclaim their loyalty to a global Muslim *Umma,* and yet their roots and lineage lie firmly in places like the American Midwest, middle England or Scotland. The most prominent of these is the global movement known as the Murabitun, led by Sheikh Abdalqadir as-Sufi, a Scotsman from Ayr born as Ian Dallas in 1930. Their ultimate aim is the destruction of the global capitalist banking system and the re-establishment of the caliphate, to be achieved through the creation of Islamic trading communities around the world, which would undermine the existing world order and naturally bring about the emergence of Islamic rule. They claim to have more than twenty established communities as far afield as England, Mexico, South Africa, Indonesia and Russia,[69] with an estimated 10,000 followers worldwide,[70] and have minted their own gold dinar currency as part of the "World Islamic Mint" organization, most recently introduced in Indonesia[71] and Malaysia.[72] As Nils Bubandt rightly points out, the Murabitun represents another example that defies attempts at categorization by academics such as Olivier Roy, whose view of Western movements who lay claim to radical protest of an international nature is limited to either secular forms of sub-politics or Islamist terror.[73] One wonders what such analysts would make of a group whose membership are often whiter in complexion and more proficient in Arabic, Islamic theology and political philosophy than themselves, given their own view of modernity and secularism as a level of enlightenment that Muslims have not yet evolved to while Western converts to Islam are merely rebels looking for a cause which has nothing to do with theology.[74]

Originally from a land-owning clan in Ayr, Scotland, Ian Dallas embraced Islam while in Morocco in 1967, and subsequently achieved success and recognition as an author and playwright while based in London. His circle of acquaintances included musicians such as Eric Clapton and George Harrison, American playwright and left-wing political activist Lillian Hellman and Scottish psychiatrist R.D. Laing.[75] After his conversion, he became a follower of Sufi scholar Sheikh Muhammad ibn al-Habib, who was a leader of the Darqawi *Tariqa*[76] (a position now held by Abdalqadir himself) before returning to the UK, where he decided to create an Islamic group with the intention of spreading a communal rather than personal Islamic model. This initially small group of converts included figures such as the Bewleys who have become established authorities in Islamic circles for the translation work they did at the behest of their Sheikh Abdalqadir.[77]

The first community, created in 1976, was set up near Norwich with the initial goal of being a self-sufficient farming village existing in isolation from the British state, which owing to difficulties in sustaining themselves eventually moved into Norwich itself. Another community was established in Arizona in the United States in the late 1970s, with others set up in Cordoba and Granada in Spain. The spread of these communities from the heartland of the West to places as far afield as Mexico and Russia, often established with indigenous converts, also demonstrates an evolution of the movement into an ambitious project for a global Islamic revival.[78] These communities serve a dual purpose as a symbolic rejection of their previous way of life and as generative of the initial grounds for an Islamic revival to spread, and may be considered somewhat similar to certain aspects of some anti-globalization movements such as eco-socialism which seeks the establishment of self-sufficient communities through a "commons" system. Additionally, in recent years Abdalqadir has also been involved in setting up of the Dallas College in Cape Town, South Africa, where he now resides. The institution is an effort to create what the movement calls a "post-*madrasah*" education system, capable of equipping Muslims for "leadership in the modern world," covering subjects such as political philosophy and Shakespearian rhetoric, with plans to also establish a secondary school as well.[79]

Abdalqadir's early studies in North Africa led him to believe that the best method by which to return to the original teachings of Islam would be through the adoption of Imam Malik's school of thought. The Maliki school of thought was dominant during the period of Islamic Andalusia and continues to hold influence in North and West Africa, along with its founder, Imam Malik, a resident of the first Islamic city-state of Medina, who adopted the customs of its residents as a source of jurisprudence. Abdalqadir commissioned his followers to translate some of the key texts of the Maliki school such as *al-Muwatta* into English, and his rereading of sections dealing with economic and commercial transactions in the early Islamic community, contrasting them with contemporary economic issues, led some of his senior followers to give him the title of the reviver of the Islamic religion in the modern era[80] whose methodology will lead to the restoration of Islamic rule.

The Murabitun declare the caliphate to be an issue "of primordial importance" and an individual obligation "necessary for the completion of many obligatory acts" of the religion, such as jihad and the collection of the *Zakah* tax.[81] They believe that the cause of the decline and eventual destruction of the caliphate was the adoption of paper money by the Ottoman State and its involvement in interest-based transactions. In his book entitled *The Return of the Khalifate*, Abdalqadir identifies the beginning of this decline to the reform period of Sultan Mahmut II from 1839, when according to him, all that remained of Islamic law were taxes on non-Muslims and cattle. By 1842, paper money had been introduced and the relationship between the debt economy and social engineering meant that loans were being tied to state reforms. The ruin of the Ottoman State was caused by the banking institutions, "which bled the Ottoman's dry of finance."[82] In the end, the caliphate did not fall "to an enemy sword," nor to "historical depassement by a higher civilization," but rather to "unsurpassable, mathematically unmeetable usury-debt." Consequently, political reform could not save them from mounting interest on their debts, and as a result "the Islamic society that was the Osmani reality" gave way to "feudalism and bourgeois Capitalism."[83] The deposition of Sultan Abdul-Hamid II was "in truth the end of the Khalifate" since after him "the Osmani ruler was reduced to the condition of a constitutional monarch."[84]

Since the introduction of paper currency and the banking system are seen as the chief reasons for the decline and eventual destruction of the caliphate, capitalism is posited as the root problem in the world today. Abdalqadir detaches this ideology from the nations that uphold it, with his ire instead focused on a nebulous global banking entity. Though placing blame on freemasonry and other secretive movements is commonplace, for the Murabitun this is also a result of the repositioning of Islamic revivalism as emanating from the West and back into the Arab world, rather than of Arab origin, with Islam not in conflict with the United States per se, since "the USA is today the most active zone of entries into Islam in the whole world," but rather at war with disbelief and therefore "at war with Capitalism, its instruments, its institutions and its leadership."[85] Consequently, "it is the bankers themselves who must be seen as the enemy of the Muslim community,"[86] while the state has been subjugated to external monetary forces and therefore has no real connection to its citizens, who are simply debtors. This posture allows the Western converts who make up the bulk of the intellectual leadership of the group to focus on propagation of their call within their home countries.

The foremost ideologue of the group, Umar Vadillo, responsible for articulating most of the detailed theological works explaining the alternative Islamic currency, states that Islam is the only force capable of resisting a rapidly developing world state with "the coming battle" being "the Muslims versus the banks."[87] The Murabitun are the "most advanced front-line against Capitalism,"[88] with their minting of the "Islamic Gold Dinar" in Granada in 1992 heralded as the beginning of the end of the new world order. As it was the introduction of paper currency and interest-based transactions which led to the destruction of the caliphate, its re-establishment should be achieved by the reintroduction of the *shari'a* currency of Gold dinars and withdrawal from contemporary economic structures, favoring independent trading communities which circumvent the banking economy.

The Gold Dinar is considered critical for Islamic revival since, according to their *ijtihad*, it is the only permissible currency in which the *Zakah* tax can be paid. It "cannot be collected unless in the Islamic Gold dinar," and according to Abdalqadir's reading of the Qur'anic verses regarding the tax, it "must be taken (not given) under authority," which consequently makes the establishment of a leadership necessary. Accordingly, "the minting of the Islamic dinar by a Muslim leader" and its collection "by power" is considered to be "the foundational event for the return of the Islamic Khalifate."[89] The return of the caliphate is thus achieved by the establishment and growth of a grassroots movement which undermines the global capitalist system by separating itself from it, as well as leading to the end of the modern state which had been "born from the fusion of government and banking,"[90] with governance reduced to "nothing more than a political front for banking,"[91] and the return of "personal rule" in its place.

The caliphate is considered to be the highest form of authority and is the opposite of the modern "fiscal state," with power concentrated in the hands of a monarch-like caliph figure, an idea promoted by Abdalqadir, who thinks that "leadership and the capacity to lead is genetically inherited." The caliphate is therefore based on "personal rule," and yet is the opposite of dictatorship," since the caliph is to be "surrounded by a collegiate group who command and fulfill command."[92] Since "it is not an autocracy," it could never be like the "centralized [modern] state," and power is devolved at the local level to provincial leaders and governors.[93] In his book *The Muslim Prince*, the image Abdalqadir paints of the caliph he hopes for is that of a benevolent monarch or the Orientalist portrait of the Sultan's court, for whom it would be "unthinkable" to "visit a town or a village without a feast being laid out for the local people,"[94] and whose wives wield enormous power.

This affection for monarchy extends to contemporary monarchs as well, so while the Egyptian, Libyan and Syrian regimes are all labeled as "thug dynasties" with the "inheriting sons" being "ten times worse than their father," Saudi Arabia's King Abdullah is "excellent" (though ill advised by the Saudi religious establishment, which the Murabitun consider to be heretical), while the Moroccan regime is the "one surviving Muslim state,"[95] with King Muhammad VI served by the Sufi scholars from the mosque in which Abdalqadir first embraced Islam. It could be argued that Abdalqadir favors monarchy because of his theological position, but his position extends also to the British monarchy, with the restoration of a powerful monarch in place of a failed parliament seen as the prelude to the spread of Islam in the UK.[96] The abolition of constitutionalism is paramount, as the "abstract instrument of the Constitution" invests power "in a structural system which was both totalitarian and voided of any moral imperatives," with "humanism as its ideology and consumerism as its bitter reality," while the norm "through all history in every place" had been "government by a person,"[97] the monarch, or preferably the Muslim Prince.

The group considers their work towards re-establishing the caliphate as the most pressing issue facing Muslims today, to the point that "the ultimate answer to the person who enquires about the content of pork in the gelatine of a biscuit" is that he needs a caliph[98] (in order to resolve the dispute and ensure that the goods in the market are acceptable according to Islamic law). They contrast this "ultimate goal that unifies all Muslims" with the programs of other movements, claiming that their vision is not concerned with "the romance of the past," but rather "with a clear-cut programme of unity based on a common currency: the Islamic dinar," to be achieved through the "emergence" of rulers (as a result of the emergence of their communities who naturally require leaders) rather than by "mass election."[99] Hassan al-Banna and the Muslim Brotherhood are criticized for believing in a caliph that was "elected by an Islamic League of Nations" and would be merely a "constitutional monarch," while their "pan-Islamism" was a "United States of Islam, a union despite frontiers."[100] Scholars emerging in the last fifty years under the banner of "reform" were engaging in the "Islamization of knowledge," which was in effect the "Islamization of Capitalism," resulting in a shift of "focus away from our Islamic model."[101] As for fellow Sufis, one prominent head of a famous *tariqa*, Sheikh Nazim, is compared to "Christian preachers" who make people "submissive" by basically claiming that the return of the caliphate will be linked to the end of times and the emergence of an Imam sent by God[102] (statements which subsequently set off a round of online insults and rebuttals between the groups).[103]

This attack on apologetics is not exclusive to the Murabitun among other Islamic movements, though there is some credence to the words of Abdalhaqq Bewley who held that because his sheikh Abdalqadir, (and therefore by extension any other member of Murabitun who are Western converts), had "emerged right from the heart of enemy territory [the West]," it enabled him "to abandon the defensive mode adopted by so many Muslim scholars and, without mincing words, to take the battle right to the enemy." However, the background of the head of the Darqawi *tariqa* also prompts views at odds with what is considered mainstream Muslim opinion. Unlike the other movements, who all place importance on the issue of Palestine, he considers them to be a "self-degraded people" living in "virulent anarchy," who only distract Muslims "from the vital and massive issues facing the '*Umma*'"—"the liberation of the sub-continent Muslims and the preservation of Uyghur culture and people from the pagan cruelty of China."[104] Instead of resisting Israel, the Palestinians should have surrendered, which in Abdalqadir's opinion would have been the Islamic approach at the time, and through intermarriage the Palestinians would subsequently demographically defeat the occupiers (a tactic he also encourages Muslims in Britain to follow). Indeed, given their elevation of economic issues above all else, they consider that Dubai, not Palestine, is the real disaster of the Arab world.[105]

The Murabitun represent a unique and interesting combination of ideas which deserve more detailed discussion in their own right—a mixture of traditional Islamic positions, Western influenced philosophy and ideas drawn from classical texts of political theory, and a longing for a return to the politics of the past, projected from a Western rather than Middle Eastern standpoint. The fact that many of them are educated white Europeans makes their critique of capitalism and democracy uncompromising, and their advocacy of Islam is without apology. At the same time they exhibit a number of contradictions, such as their claim to return to an authentic, pre-madhabic Islam while forcefully adopting the Maliki school. They oppose constitutionalism as it is, in their view, un-Islamic, and criticize al-Banna's vision of the caliph as a constitutional monarch while adopting monarchism and hereditary rule as the alternative. The group's methodology is separatist in its attempts to set up authentic Islamic communities based around the concept of "Mosque and Market," as well as being virulently anti-assimilatory, and yet they also call for political engagement, advising Muslims in Britain to vote for and work with the Conservative party in the 2010 general elections, attributing "energy, concern and high moral purpose" as well as "eloquence and openness"[106] to its leader David Cameron (a position subsequently withdrawn as a result of his position vis-à-vis Pakistan and Kashmir).[107] There is little doubt as to the zeal of their leader and the group's commitment to their cause, as the presence of small Murabitun communities around the world bears testimony to. However, their sectarian position and unusual, perhaps contradictory, politics, along with the question of the long-term viability of these small trading zones using gold currency means that as a collective they remain largely unknown and often eyed with suspicion by other communities, though it is also clear that a number of them are respected and appreciated for their scholarship and contribution to Islamic knowledge in the West.

The Quest for Lost Authority

All three of the groups examined here agree on the necessity of the caliphate and establishment of an Islamic polity that would implement Islam while serving as the unitary point of leadership for the Muslim *Umma*, and each of them shares an adoption of this call in the absence of any legitimate Islamic political authority in the Arab world. They are also all adept in the use of modern media and the internet each using it in different ways to achieve different objectives. While Dr. Ahmad projected himself and his movement globally through TV appearances on satellite channels, the Jama'ah use the Internet to guide and instruct their small and dispersed following in theological matters. Abdalqadir utilizes his online presence for the dual purpose of political commentary and to dispense advice to the elites and monarchies of the Middle East and beyond.

At the same time, there are other more significant differences between them. On the issue of *ijtihad*, opinions range from the Murabitun's wholesale adoption of the Maliki school at the expense of the legitimacy of others to the Jama'ah's decision to ignore them all and pursue a return to the Qur'an and *Sunna* directly. When it comes to interaction with society, members of the Jama'ah separate themselves from political authority by swearing a pledge to their caliph, but remain part of wider society, while the Murabitun create their own Islamic trade communities in a true act of separation. Yet Abdalqadir encourages Muslims to engage in the British political system, an act of disbelief according to the Jama'ah and a course of action that the Tanzeem consider apologetic and assimilative, just as the Murabitun view the Tanzeem's acceptance of constitutionalism. While Dr. Ahmad argues that the caliphate could adopt a republican structure of government, the Murabitun believe it is a power without a state structure comparable to that of the modern fiscal state. The Jama'ah does not consider power a necessary condition for the establishment of the caliphate.

At the same time the groups also vary from a creedal perspective, with the Salafi-inspired Jama'ah considering the acts and beliefs of Sufi orders, such as that of the Darqawi, as modern innovations, while Abdalqadir pronounces Saudi-inspired Salafi Wahabi doctrine as falling outside of Islam altogether. However, these differences do not prevent the exchange of ideas and positions on the issue of the caliphate, with the Jama'ah extensively quoting "Shaykh Abdul Qadir al Murabit['s]" statements about how the "caliphate is not only fundamental to Islam, it is the necessary foundation of its power."[108] The exchange, debate and verification of ideas between these groups is clear, with the spread of Hizb ut-Tahrir to America sparking the creation of Tehreek-e-Khilafat in Pakistan, and the ideas of an older Pakistani group influencing others, who then elected a caliph in the UK whose subjects reference a Sufi leader who validates his own understanding by comparing it to that of the Muslim Brotherhood. What ties them together is their belief that the caliphate is not just an ideal but an Islamic obligation, without which Islam has no extant reality.

For Dr. Ahmad, the adoption of the call to the caliphate marked his belief that leadership and hope for Muslims worldwide now lay in the Indian subcontinent rather than with the Arabs. Dr. al-Rifaa'e's election as caliph came in the wake of the fracturing of the Afghan resistance and the loss of leadership among the Arabs who had participated. The Murabitun see the caliph through the prism of their rejection of the encroaching "World State" by a return to personal, provincial and community rule, authentic free trade and the restoration of Islam in place of the religion of capitalism. Each of them reflects a struggle against different elements of the modern state. For different reasons, each of these groups lack connection to the nation-state, either due to their location in the diaspora as opposed to the homeland, the artificial and arbitrary justification for the state itself or disaffection with modernity and the nature of the state, and each posits itself as an authority in the absence of a unifying central anchor for Sunni Islam and the vacuum of religious and political authority in the heart of the Muslim Middle East. The symbolic pledge of allegiance given to Dr. Ahmad, the pledge given to Dr. al-Rifaa'e as caliph and the devotion of the followers to their Sheikh in the Murabitun, also given as a *bay'a*, are each different manifestations of a perceived need for the unifying symbol of the caliphate and an executive authority which represents Islam, also acting as an anchor for the disparate factions which live under it.

7

COMMON GOALS, DIVERGENT
METHODOLOGIES

*The Muslims are like a single man; if his eye has a complaint, all of him complains,
and if his head has a complaint, all of him complains.*

The Prophet Mohammad[1]

At the time of the abolition of the caliphate in 1924, the only public
movement consistently promoting it was the Khilafat movement, based
outside of the borders of the caliphate as it had existed, and established
to advocate its continuation in its final days in the aftermath of the First
World War. Prior to its abolition, the caliphate was not necessarily imagined by the general populace to be in any danger of elimination. While
in existence, the state advocated its maintenance, as shown by the pan-
Islam policy introduced under Sultan Abdul Hamid II following the
state's attempt at adopting Ottomanism to strengthen civil affiliation
within its territories, in the face of external encroachments and internal
nationalist and ethnic dissent. Movements in the Muslim world in the
same period were more commonly directed against colonialism, with a
series of uprisings taking place across the region based around two key
principles, namely that the primary cause for weakness in front of European expansion was religious laxity and therefore only by a return to
true Islam would the situation be reversed in totality, and a physical

resistance (jihad) against colonial rule—both with the final goal of establishing a purely Islamic state.[2]

The removal of the caliphate was a blow of great psychological as well as political significance, removing the symbol of Islamic unity in the world and evoking a great variety of responses. The fact that hundreds of groups were established in the two decades following 1924 with the aim of reviving Islam and implementing the *shari'a* implicitly suggests widespread attempts to compensate for this loss of political leadership, even if this goal was not explicitly mentioned or even recognized by its proponents. The Muslim Brotherhood, as led by Hassan al-Banna, sought to reconstruct an Islamic society in the absence of an Islamic state, and through a process of first reconstituting the Muslim individual, followed by the family, society, and state, the caliphate would eventually be re-established, built upon solid foundations that were missing at the time of its defeat and abolition. Following the creation of the State of Israel and the dispossession of Muslims in the region in 1948, Hizb ut-Tahrir was formed amid the emergence of strong Arab nationalist trends in the Middle East, which put the re-establishment of the caliphate at the head of its program both symbolically and practically. They believed that without reinstating the political representation of Islam, Muslims would continue to suffer from an inability to defend Islamic interests and lands from foreign encroachment, whether ideological or military, and would be unable to undertake any comprehensive reformation of society living under un-Islamic rules. In the final decade of the twentieth century other groups emerged, such as Tanzeem-e-Islami's Tehreek-e-Khilafat in Pakistan and the nebulous al-Qaeda, initially from within Afghanistan. The West has also given birth to a number of movements calling for the re-establishment of the caliphate, varying from largely immigrant-based groups, such as Hilafet Devleti and Jama'ah-tul-Muslimeen, to indigenous convert-based movements, such as the Murabitun.

While analysis of the Middle East during the 1960s from outside might have led to the conclusion that the involvement of Islamic movements in Middle Eastern politics looked to be finished in the wake of the harsh crackdown on the Brotherhood in Egypt[3] by Gamal Abdul-Nasser, coupled with the apparent rise of pan-Arabism, the period that followed the 1967 Arab-Israeli war actually saw a resurgence and growth of such movements. The humiliating defeat of the Egyptian military was taken as a negative judgment of the capability of pan-Arab nationalism and unity to uphold the interests and honor of the region. The subsequent success of the Iranian revolution injected confidence into the belief that an Islamic polity could replace secular regimes, irrespective of the sectarian aspect of ideological justifications for the rule of the Shia clerical class, as espoused in the doctrine of *walayat-e-faqih*. With Saudi Arabia's involvement in the Gulf War of 1990, the most prominent example of a polity which drew legitimacy from Sunni Islam lay exposed as inviting a non-Muslim army into hallowed lands to fight against another Muslim nation, opening the door to increasing disillusionment. The failure of alternative ideologies, whether Arab nationalism or complete Westernization as advocated by the Shah of Iran, has meant that the artificially established and imposed nation-states of the region faced severe legitimacy deficits—helping to explain the increasing popularity of Islamic politics. However, it does not necessarily explain the content of the ideas and trends that have vied to fill this resulting political void, with all the aforementioned movements attempting in various ways to reconstruct a global or transnational authority based on an Islamic foundation.

The plurality of movements, aims and methodologies suggests the need for a comparative summation at this point before any final conclusion can be made drawing out the agreements, similarities, nuances and differences between them. The aspects considered in this study are examined in order to make analytical comparisons between the various *ijtihad* that are fundamental to each movement, the manner of membership and the differing conceptions of the caliphate within their programs and discourse. Much of the material has been discussed separately in earlier chapters, and it is brought together here to assist in highlighting underlying trends in their attempts to reconstitute what the movements consider a legitimate political expression of the spiritual unity of the Muslim world.

Disputed Ijtihad and Understanding Reality

The problem of resolving the political decline and impotence of the Muslim *Umma* has seen several solutions, ranging from grassroots moral reform to global armed struggle against a far enemy to the undermining of the global financial system through the adoption of alternative currencies. Such disparity between the respective *ijtihad* of each movement may be understood as evidence of different interpretations of Islam since the process of *ijtihad* is considered legitimate according to its ultimate reference to and reliance on authentic teaching from primary Islamic sources. At the same time, the starting point for any proposed solution is an understanding of the reality of the problem. The process of *ijtihad* is no different, since the derivation of an Islamic solution to any issue depends first on identifying the issue at hand. The stronger this understanding of the situation, coupled with knowledge of Islamic sources and the process by which law may be derived from them, the stronger the resulting *ijtihad* will be, with the reverse also true.

The Brotherhood under al-Banna believed that the root cause of the humiliation and decline of Muslims was their moral weakness and misunderstanding of Islam, and that individual reform would lead to the reform of society as a whole. This revived society would then expel colonial influence from the country, with armed force if necessary, at which point the independent state would be able to fully implement Islam in the correct manner and resolve practical societal problems. While the British were still in effective control of the country, al-Banna considered the ruling elite sufficiently legitimate as to be considered on the side of Islam. He viewed the structure and constitution of the government as compatible with Islam, and the nation-state as a legitimate vehicle for the expression of political will, as long as the people did not lose their Islamic identity, and that when independence was achieved there would have to be a process which would purify the executive power of the state from those who did not practice the rules of Islam. Al-Banna's vision was the establishment of an Islamic government once the British had left, to eventually become joined with neighboring countries who had gone through the same process to create an Arab unity, which would then spread to unite with all other Islamic countries to form an Islamic league of nations who would duly re-establish the lost caliphate, their ultimate goal.

Hizb ut-Tahrir linked the decline of the Muslim *Umma* to their reduced intellectual state, arguing that the establishment of the caliphate was an immediate step necessary to reverse that decline rather than an ultimate goal to be achieved once other problems had been resolved. This approach is explained by their view that the moral decline and perversion of the individual cannot be reversed by individual improvement, but rather that the emergence of openly corrupt practices was a result of the absence of the *shari'a*. Established during a period of decolonization, the apparent autonomy of some of the governments was considered inconsequential, since they were all based on secular principles. All of the existing political systems in the Muslim lands were considered illegitimate, and the morality of the rulers was not thought of as relevant since the government itself was systemically incompatible with Islam. The nation-state fundamentally contradicted Islamic views of unity and the basis of affiliation to the state, and therefore the solution was not to work within the system and to purify it from corrupt individuals from inside, but rather to remove the corrupted system in its entirety and establish the Islamic caliphate in its place. Such a radical solution required the details to be clearly laid out, as it was thought that the failure of other efforts to re-establish Islamic governance was explained by their inability to present themselves as a clear political alternative, leaving people confused as to exactly what they meant, knowing only that it was supposedly desirable and better than secular rule.

After the establishment of American army bases across Saudi Arabia and other parts of the Gulf, the perceived physical occupation of the Middle East overrode any cultural or political dimensions attached to the decline of the Muslim *Umma* in the mind of Osama bin Laden. Following the defeat of the Soviet Union in Afghanistan there was a belief that Muslims had the capacity to successfully resist foreign encroachment if they focused their efforts and were sufficiently motivated to do so, with the imagery of the caliphate intended to unite and motivate geographically disparate forces in a global *jihadi* struggle. In his understanding, a decline in individual morality among the general public was not the root issue, but rather a decline in morality among the ruling classes. Whereas al-Banna had positioned the ruling elite of his time as victims of Western colonization, the new reality, according to al-Qaeda, was that local regimes were complicit in Western colonization and were working as local agents for the foreign invaders. In keeping with this understanding the rulers were considered to be infidels and therefore rebellion against them was a permitted act, reflecting an understanding that the problem of governance was intrinsically linked to the ruling elite and their lack of religiosity. The globalization of this struggle was prompted by their belief that it is the support of America, militarily and otherwise, that props up incumbent regimes who lack real legitimacy derived from the support of their own people after years of "independence."

The Murabitun also view the problem in terms of an existing global hegemony that must be undermined, but in their case it is the economic system of global capitalism rather than the imperial framework of America that is the central problem. Since, in their view, it was the products of the global capitalist economic system—interest-based loans and paper currency—that brought down the caliphate, the reintroduction of the gold dinar and abandonment of the banking system would lead to its re-establishment. The majority of current rulers have become submerged in this global system as victims, with the Moroccan monarchy the most worthy of their support, though the nation-state model itself is considered illegitimate. Their proposed solution is a form of economic separatism—the creation of a parallel economic system. Through the growth of this system, which relies upon the formation of Islamic communities, each with their own leader, the caliphate would emerge and thus Islamic governance would be established.

Dr. Israr Ahmad formed Tehreek-e-Khilafat to establish the global caliphate, taking Pakistan as its foundation. He considered the problem of the state to be systemic, describing electoral politics as a methodology by which rulers are selected to run the system and therefore an invalid method for bringing about the revolutionary change needed to establish an Islamic system in place of the Pakistani government. The central movement, Tanzeem-e-Islami, focused on grassroots activities with individual religious and moral reform as their primary goal, believing that the corruption of Muslim society by materialism and secularism had led to the spiritual decline of the population. The goal of achieving the caliphate is their foremost aim without the need for any intermediary steps to be reached through other systems of governance, in a manner similar to the Hizb, but their methodology is individual moral reform as originally proposed by the Brotherhood and Jamaat-i-Islami.

With the continued absence of a central Islamic political authority to symbolize the normatively claimed unity of the Muslim *Umma* and the lack of any credible alternative to fill its space, various cult-like movements have also arisen, each claiming that their leader should be recognized as the caliph both inside and outside of traditional Islamic territories. Those which have emerged in the Muslim diaspora, whether

Hilafet Devleti or Jama'ah-tul-Muslimeen, are attempts to reunify as a precondition of establishing political authority, a reversal of the positions taken by the other movements studied.

Although the groups generally recognize that the failure to achieve the complete application of Islam through the establishment of an Islamic polity is the chief reason for the weakness of the Muslim *Umma*, they each have different understandings of why this Islamic polity is yet to be realized. The movements view the problems as systemic, and ultimately seek the same goal, but they differ in their account of the nature of society and how it changes. Differences in their diagnosis of the barrier to establishing the caliphate vary from the lack of morals in society to foreign occupation, intellectual decline leading to the following of alternative ideologies, and the economic hegemony of the capitalist banking system. Their accounts of the process through which the caliphate is to be re-established also differ, ranging from the gradual reformation of the current institutional setup to radical revolutionary change to undermining external support, whether through violent resistance or separation.

One unique aspect that stands out is that the only group which attaches any legitimacy to the nation-state model is the Muslim Brotherhood, and as a result they are also the only group that permits working within some of the current systems where the opportunity to achieve their aims arises. This difference has also lent itself to a form of inconsistency from the Brotherhood and its affiliates outside of Egypt, with branches of the group in places such as Syria and Jordan taking radically different approaches with respect to their local governments, leading to accusations of pragmatism and compromise from opponents, while being praised for the very same characteristics by their supporters. As a consequence of operating as part of national governance structures, the group has often found itself clashing with other actors as differing national interests and agendas contradict one another.[4]

It is worth noting the differences in approach between the Brotherhood while under al-Banna and during the post-Banna period, in which the same *ijtihad* was followed while the reality of direct foreign occupation, at which al-Banna had targeted the movement, was no longer present. It is therefore debatable as to whether he would have continued along the same path as the one pursued today given the statements he made towards the end of his life, which suggested that working with the existing regime was not unconditional and everlasting. It is also possible that the group would have pursued a more consistent and uniform set of aims under al-Banna due to the charismatic nature of his leadership, whereas it can be argued that as time passes the international element of the organization has become less and less relevant.[5] The other movements all tend to be more consistent in the application of their ideas across national boundaries for the reason that they do not recognize or participate within the framework of the nation-state, seeing it as illegitimate, and therefore the differences between the regions in which they operate are usually more related to style than methodology.

The rejection of participation within existing structures is often seen as a rejection of the process of elections, equated to a rejection of democracy, a debatable assertion given that the reason that groups like the Tanzeem and the Hizb do not participate in elections is not the electoral process but rather the democratic foundation of legislation which is based upon popular sovereignty rather than the sovereignty of God. In other words, they differentiate between the process of elections and the purpose of those elections, believing that working within the system confers a degree of legitimacy upon it and therefore, rather than being able to change the system from within, the movement's goals may become compromised. The direction of the Brotherhood and other movements inspired by them often bears out this analysis, with members of the Egyptian Brotherhood even going as far as to deny that the caliphate was an aim at all, contradicting their leaders assertion that it was at the head of their program (even if only symbolically at the time). This could be the result of pragmatism and gradual reform, which is seemingly transforming them into part of the status quo rather than a real and radical alternative. However, as a movement lacking an ideological core, it should be noted that there are multiple strands of thinking in the Muslim Brotherhood today, and it is by no means certain that such thinking represents the point of view of the bulk of their membership, as evidenced by the mixed messages which have emanated from different quarters of the group in the aftermath of the Egyptian uprising in 2011.

This pragmatic approach should not disguise the fact that none of the movements studied, including the Brotherhood, view the nation-state as ideal or accept it by choice, but rather see it as an alien construct based on artificially imposed borders and divisions, and all proclaim their aim of unifying Muslim lands, whether in cooperation with the nation-state or through its removal. Though the other movements studied all explicitly reject the nation-state as illegitimate and decry participation in the prevailing political systems, this does not necessitate internal violence against the personnel of the state since, aside from al-Qaeda, their methodologies are non-violent, radical and revolutionary. Even the position of al-Qaeda's leaders has evolved as a result of their view of the futility of trying to effect change in any way other than overthrowing what they see as imperial powers, who ultimately deny the people of the region agency in choosing both polity and politicians.

Conceptions of the Caliphate, Mobilization and Legitimacy

There is agreement between all the groups that the caliphate is to be the singular political leadership for the Muslim *Umma* worldwide, and that it is the responsibility of the caliph to implement the *shari'a*. This echoes the overwhelming theological consensus in orthodox Islamic scholarship that the ideal polity is one in which Muslims have a single leader whose legitimacy is dependent on his application of Islamic law, a view firmly reasserted in the wake of the Ali Abdul-Raziq dispute which occurred in Egypt shortly after the abolition of the Ottoman caliphate. In other words, there is a consensus between these movements that reflects the consensus in normative Islam that it is obligatory to have a single ruler, and that the *shari'a* has to be applied. Beyond these two fundamental tenets there are differences, ranging from Dr. Ahmad's adoption of the "theo-democracy" theory of Abul A'la Maududi to the visions of a hereditary position as envisaged by the Murabitun. The key issues are the concept of sovereignty, the role of the ruler and where authority lies in selecting him, the role of consultation (*shura*) and the structure of government.

Al-Banna's vision of the re-establishment of the caliphate was that it would come on the back of several national Islamic states, united in a league, and appointing a single leader to rule over them. The role and powers of this overall leader are not explained, but given that it was seen as a symbol of Islamic unity it can safely be assumed that he would nominally represent the Muslim *Umma* abroad while negotiating and resolving differences which occurred within the Islamic league. This vision was probably heavily informed by the ideas of Rashid Rida, who was one of al-Banna's major influences. Rather than detailing the speci-

ficities of the caliphate, al-Banna was more concerned with the immediate form of governance with which the Brotherhood was confronted.
He did not favor the radical overthrow of these structures as this was
against his principles of gradualism and his conviction that the movement should begin by removing foreign influence. Rather, he favored a
move towards constitutional government with a representative parliamentary system compatible with Islam. The Brotherhood was not
concerned with the form of government, but rather that its content
(chiefly its legislation) would be Islamic. It was thus necessary that
society produce individuals who could utilize existing state institutions
in the correct manner, and for these individuals to garner popular support to fill those positions as required, ensuring Islamic governance, all
of which was dependent on being politically independent. Therefore the
concern for and framing of the caliphate in their discourse was more of
a utopian ideal than an explicit and practical political goal at the time,
with the construction of a global Islamic polity to be built from bonded
national units. Consequently, membership of the Brotherhood was based
on a shared moral outlook and a general program of culturing, so as to
be able to attract as wide a support base as possible for the idea that Islam
had an essential role in the state and its legislation, hence their membership is based largely on affiliation, with a wide range of opinions on
critical issues such as methodology existing within the movement. While
this is a good strategy of opposition in order to gain widespread support,
it remains to be seen how the Brotherhood's leadership will negotiate
these different strands as they move into positions of rule in the future.

This stands in contrast with the views of Hizb ut-Tahrir, who take a
legalistic rather than utopian view of the caliphate, constructing a
constitution and structure for it which is largely in line with the positions espoused in orthodox literature, which is claimed to be based upon
the Prophetic model and practice of the first four caliphs. Such a position rejects the point of view that the form of government is irrelevant
and only the content matters, connecting the two together and attempting to derive the structure of government from the same sources as the
law. Therefore the slogan of the Brotherhood, that the Qur'an *is* the
constitution, is rejected, and rather the constitution must be derived
from Islamic sources such as the Qur'an, and is the product of *ijtihad*
rather than something open to discretion. Consequently, existing national polities, whether monarchies or republican presidencies, are rejected,

as their basis is un-Islamic and participation in such political systems would be futile since their foundations are fundamentally flawed. Rather than a mass membership, the group aims at a more concentrated culturing process for its core membership, who act as a vanguard movement in expressing the interests of the *Umma* and pushing the masses to establish the caliphate through a radical and revolutionary moment, either by coup-d'état or revolution. With its developed literature and ideology, detailed to rebuild public confidence in the uniqueness and capability of Islamic governance, membership is based upon conviction and adoption of the party's *ijtihad* on the caliphate and related issues. It is this membership which calls the public to adopt its diagnosis and prognosis of the situation, positioning the absence of the caliphate and the necessity of its re-establishment in the center of their discourse.

Dr. Ahmad's ideas on the caliphate fall somewhere between those of the Brotherhood and the Hizb. While he believes in the necessity of implementing the caliphate directly, he posits that no generation of Muslims after the earliest generations are of a high enough moral and Islamic caliber to implement a system based on the Prophetic model and that of the first generation of rulers. This problem necessitates the adoption of modern structures of government, such as the federal structure used in America, but infusing them with the values and principles of early Islamic governance. It is of pivotal importance that the caliphate is based upon the complete rejection of human sovereignty, but in all areas not covered by Islamic stipulations popular choice should be enacted through the mechanism of an elected parliament. The caliph was also to be elected rather than imposed or the product of hereditary rule, giving rise to Maududi's terms "theo-democracy" and "popular vicegerency." Although Dr. Ahmad embraced the call for a caliphate as the single form of legitimate polity, he remained committed to the Brotherhood's idea of the mass reform of individuals as a prerequisite for any revolution, and called upon others to pledge their allegiance to him as the leader of a united party, which would work to first purge the individuals within it from un-Islamic practices before entering society to establish good and forbid evil.

As mentioned in the chapter on al-Qaeda, few details have emerged detailing the form of the caliphate the group seeks, beyond deriving the normative elements of legislation from Islamic sources and a united rule for all Muslims. It may be that they felt ill-equipped to articulate such a vision, or that it was unnecessary as the details could either be found in the classical texts or in the literature of other movements. The only details we have are that they differentiated between smaller "Islamic states" or "Emirates" which would be founded on the back of liberation struggles in countries such as Afghanistan, and would subsequently be used as a base to unite with other such disparate polities until emerging as an entity large and legitimate enough to claim the mantle of the caliphate for all Muslims. The caliphate is not therefore seen as a solution to the problems facing Muslims, but rather as a motivating factor which justifies the spread of a global struggle against occupation to seek its establishment. Consequently, agreement on the image and model of the caliphate is not a prerequisite of membership, but rather by participating in the resistance itself, someone can become a part of the global jihad. This is why the articulation of grievances and the expression of religious legitimacy to be conferred upon those physically fighting are much more important in the framing of their discourse.

The view of the caliphate in the vision of the Murabitun is probably somewhat closer to the ideas of al-Qaeda than those of the Brotherhood or the Hizb in that they consider rule to be the personal function of a monarch rather than an institution. They accuse the Brotherhood of attempting to Islamize every modern institution in their efforts to make Islam and modernity compatible, in agreement with the Hizb that the Islamic ruling system is unique and based upon its own sources. However, while the Hizb has articulated a vision of the caliphate using a constitution as the basis for the state, the Murabitun consider this an innovation, though they hold that the type of state would be a form of nomocracy with the *shari'a* as its basis. The role of the caliph is considered two-fold—as the final arbiter in the collection of the *Zakah* and the promotion of jihad, while governance is delegated to the level of the Emirates and local leaders backed by the power of the Sultan. Therefore the establishment of local communities, each with their own leader collecting the *Zakah* and managing the affairs of the community through the use of a gold and silver based currency, is a prerequisite for the establishment of the caliphate. Their belief that the global capitalist system and paper currency are the major ills confronting the world today drives their will to seek alternative modes of trade and markets. The small Islamic communities set up by the Murabitun aim to achieve this, with admittance to these communities attained by accepting the authority of the *shari'a* and swearing a pledge of allegiance to the head of the Order.

To the movements who have given their allegiance to a caliph, the caliphate is simply the individual leader of Muslims rather than their practical ruler. It is possibly for this reason that such fringe movements seem to be more prevalent in the West, since the idea of Muslims ruling in a European or American context as a diaspora appears extremely unlikely. Hence the individual caliph is the unifying symbol, despite their existence as a minority in an environment where ruling by the *shari'a* cannot be practically implemented.

There are two underlying factors which are agreed upon by all of the groups calling for a caliphate—namely that the Muslim *Umma* should be united politically under a single ruler, and that this single ruler has to rule them in accordance with Islam. All are also in agreement that the ruler derives his legitimacy from his application of the rule of law over society, and should be removed if he deviates from this. They also all agree that the caliph is ideally chosen through consent, and should not be imposed on the people, though the Murabitun seem somewhat equivocal on the matter and at times lean towards hereditary rule in their discourse. The role of *shura* is discussed, often in terms of an expression of democracy or democratic values, by the Tanzeem and the Muslim Brotherhood, which could be considered as a form of apologia, whereas the Hizb and Murabitun see the issue of *shura* in terms of non-binding advice to the ruler, though there are exceptions and nuances to this. While the Tanzeem and Brotherhood also adopt modern institutions as vehicles to implement the *shari'a*, the other movements all consider the caliphate as a unique form of governance, and criticize efforts to Islamize existing alien constructs of government.[6] None of these advocates consider the caliph to be infallible or unaccountable, indicative of the parallel lack of a utopian vision of the state, though they all invariably believe that it will act as a panacea for the economic and political afflictions of the Muslim world.

The Call to the Caliphate

With respect to Islamic theory of government, for which there are normative positions that were reasserted by scholars at the time of the abolition of the Ottoman caliphate, these positions have to a varying extent set the parameters of subsequent discussion and theorizing on the subject. Separate to this is the call to the caliphate, which has been either utilized or ignored as appropriate according to the various *ijtihad* of the movements, from a motivating justification for global resistance to a radical alternative to existing systems to a global symbol uniting disparate Islamic states.

Prior to the abolition of the Ottoman caliphate it was seen as the final independent Sunni power, the highest representative of Islamic unity and authority for at least the last three centuries, if not since the conquest of Constantinople in the fifteenth century, which fulfilled a prophecy linking back to the Prophet Mohammad eight centuries earlier. While it remained the world's foremost Islamic power during the period of colonization, its decline and imperiled position led to the creation of the Khilafat movement in India to advocate for its continued existence while more local support came from the reformer Rashid Rida. These efforts to keep the last independent representative of Sunni Islamic unity and political authority alive in the face of the overwhelming force of colonialism left hope for its reform and revitalization as the foremost representative of the *Umma*.

The formal abolition of the caliphate in 1924 removed the final vestiges of the institution which had been stripped of its official temporal power two years earlier, though it had in any case been a severely curtailed force since the deposition of Sultan Abdul Hamid II. There were two challenges to the caliphate theory at the time. The first questioned whether it was in fact an Islamic institution and if Islam even required a political manifestation, instead confined to the personal realm much as other religions were imagined in the Western post-enlightenment period. The second stemmed from dominant Western ideal of secular governance.

The first challenge was resolved as a result of the conflict between Ali Abdul-Raziq and the rest of the scholarly community, with the strident reassertion of the normative theory of caliphate roundly agreed as far removed from the poor example set by the Ottomans and other previous dynastic states. This difference between practice and theory further separated the idea of the caliphate from the practical political solutions proffered at the time. Though the theory was reasserted and confirmed, the only competitors for the claim to become caliph would have ended with the position either simply becoming the crowing coronation for a national monarch or a spiritual epithet equivalent in meaning to an

Islamized pope-like figure. The period of formal Empires and a universal polity were seemingly over. However, the Kurdish rebellion of Sheikh Said raised two potential issues that highlighted the problems of the legacy of the nation-state—the first being that any nation-state formed on the basis of ethnicity or tribe would end up excluding significant parts of the population, who would have no reason to give their allegiance to the state, and the second being that memories of the caliphate, even in its final weakened form, were still thought of as an alternative model holding the allegiance of Muslims.

In the short period after the stabilization of the modern Turkish state, the caliphate represented a failed and manipulated polity responsible for the signing of the Treaty of Sèvres, an albatross standing in the face of independence and progress which was duly removed by Mustafa Kemal. It was perhaps too soon after its failure to immediately reimagine the caliphate as priority, and the efforts for its re-establishment by others gave the impression that it was to be symbolic, rather than the kind of practical solution that some were looking for the state to implement. Since in the past the Ottoman state maintained the form of the caliphate but diluted its Islamic content, activists may have been primarily concerned with reintroducing the content, and believed that the form necessary was not that which may have Islamic precedence, but rather that which was most practical in modern times. Reference to the caliphate was either envisaged as something distant so as not to distract from the immediate situation or as a formal institutional position perched on top of the national political structures of the day. In other words, at this time the caliphate was not seen as a positive alternative, with those who were advocating the appointment of a caliph generally envisaging this as a symbolic position.

The process of decolonization in the immediate post-Second World War period opened political opportunities within the Arab and wider Muslim world, with the rise of Arab nationalism and pan-Arabism in place of the national ideologies of the divided regional states. While some of the monarchies of the region tried to hold onto the national regimes bequeathed to them by the departing West, they were threatened by the independent republics led by Gamal Abdul-Nasser's Egypt. With the "Wilsonian moment" of the 1920s ultimately leaving the aspirations of the colonized nations of Africa and Asia unfulfilled, anti-imperial movements looked for alternative inspirations. The establishment of the State of Israel in 1948 was seen as a further example of the weakness and impotence of the divided Arab nations. While most of the alternatives posited at this time took their inspiration from the Soviet Union and styled themselves as socialists and communists, it is not unsurprising that among the Muslim community there were those who looked back and examined Islamic history and normative positions, trying to revive the caliphate theory as an alternative unifying symbol in place of an Arab one. This would seem more likely to emerge from within the Arab world given that the history of the spread of the Arabs as a people is intrinsically linked to Islam, as is the Arabic language.

However, this call was relegated to the sidelines as secular pan-Arabism became the dominant framework in the struggle for independence and unity in the 1950s and 1960s. But after a series of setbacks, culminating in defeat in the 1967 Arab-Israeli War, this ideology lost its luster. If disunity was blamed for defeat in 1948, then secularism was blamed for the defeat suffered in 1967. However, the most significant rebellion against a secular regime occurred in Shia Iran and not in a Sunni country, with the clerical establishment forming an Iranian religious authority to rule the country after the Shah's overthrow. While groups in Egypt attempted to overthrow Anwar Sadat as a response to his Camp David peace deal with Israel, the attempt failed to remove the regime and establish an Islamic state in its place, instead prompting a small-scale internal conflict that continued for almost two decades.

The call for religious politics at this time was growing, and the complicity of the Saudi regime in American actions against Iraq in 1991 severely damaged their claim to legitimacy as the foremost Islamic state representative of Sunni Islam. In any case, most of the governments in the region were increasingly seen as unrepresentative, divisive and only able to maintain power through the use of oppression and by external support from Western backers who would at best turn a blind eye to indiscretion (while at worst encouraging or being involved in it) for the sake of securing resources and geopolitical interests. Increased disillusionment with capitalism has become a recurring feature,[7] with communism no longer seen as an alternative, and so consequently the search for alternatives continues to lead an ever greater number of Muslims to look back into their religion and history for answers to the contemporary political malaise in their lands, with some finding that solution in the theory of the caliphate.

Temporal distance from the failure of the Ottoman caliphate has allowed a greater number of people to consider the caliphate model without the natural restrictions incurred by living in the shade of the failure of its most recent historical precedent. Events in the region over the last century have made the achievements of the Ottomans relatively more appealing, as most reasonable polities would appear when compared to Pakistan, Egypt, Uzbekistan, Tunisia and other regimes. With increased religiosity across Muslim countries, it is not unnatural that the call for the caliphate is now embraced by a diverse range of Muslims since it is so prominent in normative Islamic political theory. As a result of increased ethnic conflict in Muslim countries, alternative forms of allegiance to the state are more attractive. At the same time, the weakening of the nation-state and the rise of the idea that power projection requires large political and military entities, which appears to be prompting the formation of different blocs and unions, have further rehabilitated the concept of a regional power which would swallow many of the states in the Muslim world. The perceived failures of other ideologies and systems have provided an opportunity for the idea of the caliphate as a system rather than just a symbol to be more widely considered. However, bridging the gap between the practical reality of the nation-state and the more universal nature of the caliphate is still a point of contention between the different groups that call for it.

The diffusion of ideas across national boundaries has been a prominent feature of Islamic trends, with students from all over the world heading to centers of Islamic study in Egypt and Saudi Arabia. However, although the Middle East may be seen as the core of the Muslim world by virtue of either having the most prominent universities such as al-Azhar in Egypt or being home to revered sites such as Mecca and Medina in Saudi Arabia, this transfer of ideas is not unidirectional. With the Khilafat movement's Abul Kalam Azad inspiring Rashid Rida, the adoption of the Abul Hasan al-Nadwi's explanation of *jahiliyya* by Sayyid Qutb, the Palestinian diaspora transferring the ideas of Hizb ut-Tahrir into Asia and the Caucasus, the meeting between the leader of Pakistan-based Tanzeem-e-Islami with a member of the Hizb in America, and the exchange of ideas between convert Sufi Sheikhs and Salafi adherents, there can be little doubt as to the global nature of the Muslim *Umma*, and the transfer of universal ideas based upon shared Islamic ideals within it.

It is not surprising in a world where artificially drawn borders are challenged in multiple ways that the exchange of ideas includes one which posits a vision of a polity based on other organizational paradigms. That the current model exists in a specific civilizational and religious setting makes it all the more accessible, especially when all other alternatives are thought to have failed. While some have used the caliphate to legitimate existing polities and their engagement with them by claiming they are a stepping stone to the establishment of the caliphate, this has become less effective as local regimes have increasingly become more distanced from their populations, and suffer from a lack of popular support and authority, meaning that the primary utilization of the call to the caliphate has become one linked to realizing political self-determination and radical change, overturning the status quo. As collective sentiment in the Middle East and wider Muslim world against foreign interference, whether military or otherwise, grows, and the existing regimes fail to protect their own population's interests and security, let alone that of their co-religionists in neighboring countries, discontent will continue to propel a desire for alternatives that are considered to be more representative of their beliefs and values. This discontent drove the uprisings across the Middle East at the end of 2010, with people unified in their belief that the status quo was unacceptable and that the oppression they were subjected to by their governments had to end. Though in the aftermath of the uprisings a more open political system will emerge, it is not clear what political direction this will take over time. It is argued that the regimes have largely remained in place with a shuffling of the personalities involved, but whatever the case, what cannot be denied is that a new atmosphere of active political discussion has arrived in the region. With this, it is inevitable that the discussion of the caliphate will continue and likely emerge more forcefully in the public sphere. The continued absence of a legitimate central Islamic political authority which would represent Islamic interests in international relations has led some to adopt it as a motivating call to globalize resistance against perceived Western injustices and continued imperialism, with the absent religious authority shifted to those involved in resistance rather than those in the established regimes.

8

THE END OF A HISTORY

On résiste à l'invasion des armées; on ne résiste pas à l'invasion des idées.

Victor Hugo

There are many factors that have driven Muslim populations in the Middle East and beyond to seek alternatives to their current political order. These include the occupation of lands considered to be of religious significance such as Palestine, the oppression of Muslim populations in areas believed to be historically Islamic such as in Kashmir or the Caucasus region, poverty across wide swathes of the Muslim community despite a wealth of both natural and man-made resources, the perceived subservience of the state to foreign agendas, and living under oppressive governments who have imposed themselves on the people without concern for their interests and values, whether republics like Egypt, pseudo-democracies like Pakistan, or monarchies like those of Morocco or Jordan. These are thought of as shared grievances due to the collective Muslim identity represented in the idea of the *Umma*, even though the nation-state has been the only form of polity in the region for several generations. With the failure of the nation-state to resolve the problems faced by the *Umma*, the caliphate is proffered as an alternative. Both the idea of the *Umma* and its political representation in the caliphate are derived from Islamic sources—something that the structural factors cannot explain.

At the same time, it could also be argued that the multiplicity of groups with their own idiosyncratic methods and goals proves that there is no single Islam or Islamic ideal of politics but rather a multitude of "little Islams" and interpretations. The sometimes fractious relationships and discourse between individuals from these movements can be seen as further evidence of disunity and fundamental disagreement, for example the numerous tracts written by al-Qaeda directed against the Muslim Brotherhood, or the fact that a Jordanian member of parliament and Brotherhood supporter voted with the government to expel a Hizb ut-Tahrir member from the Jordanian assembly, and so on.

The alternative thesis is that there is a space for difference within Islam so long as it exists within agreed parameters. Such a thesis tells us that the approach of both the essentialists, who consider Muslims to be a single monolithic bloc without difference, and the contingencists, who view Islam as a nominal culture but ultimately irrelevant due to its multiplicity of interpretations, are inaccurate in explaining Islamic movements, motivations and actions, a task which instead requires a framework that interprets their ideas and actions with reference to their driving force—normative Islam. Though it is true that there are areas of difference and interpretation, this cannot be used as evidence to ignore some of the essential shared elements. In Islamic jurisprudence there is scope for difference, with certain fundamental issues agreed upon and not open to interpretation, while other issues have that flexibility afforded to them by the nature of the Islamic sources themselves.

The fact that there are variations in Islamic understandings of politics does not detract from the presence of core aspects, just as people can talk about democracy but also differentiate between its variants and forms without undercutting the democratic ideal. Indeed, the caliphate is based on the idea of the unity of the Muslim *Umma* under a single leader, and the belief that the basis of this rule should be Islamic. There is a type of social contract between the ruler and the *Umma*, whereby he is appointed as their representative, and so is ultimately responsible for the implementation and arbitration of the *shari'a*, and the management of the public affairs of the population. These fundamental positions are enough to claim a unity of purpose for those who advocate the caliphate's re-establishment, with differences in the institutions falling within the caliphate a matter of *ijtihad*. There is also no dictate in normative Islam or in the literature of these contemporary movements that suggests that the word "caliphate" is exclusively the name for an Islamic political system, with alternative labeling permitted as long as the core features remain the same.

The extent to which popular agreement on these two core issues exists is open to debate, and any discussion about the role of the caliphate and its position in Muslim political discourse needs to be aware of the context of the dominant discourse which enforces the hegemony of liberal democracy as the yardstick for measuring political legitimacy, something plainly visible in the political discourse of the media and in public space. The popular uprising which culminated in the removal of Hosni Mubarak as Egyptian President on 11 February, 2011 is a good example of how this discourse is managed and perpetuated. Millions of protestors who took to the streets were quickly labeled as "pro-democracy" activists on Western and international television channels, and were adopted by some of the younger middle- and upper-class activists who had helped to organize the initial protests, later joined by a wider slice of Egyptian society. In such a discourse, the legitimacy of the position of Islam and Islamic politics is judged according to how far it is willing to work within the confines of a secular and democratic system, with commentators and analysts all questioning this specific issue well before Mubarak's departure. Consequently, the call to a system which does not accept the legitimacy of post-Versailles national boundaries is certainly not to be given credence.

However, the caliphate is now openly discussed in Egypt and beyond. In Yemen, at the height of protests against then president Ali Abdullah Saleh, the leading opposition figure, Sheikh Abdul Majid al-Zindani, informed the people that the re-establishment of the caliphate was approaching.[1] In Syria, local scholar Sheikh Yusuf al-Eid told crowds of demonstrators in the city of Daraa that the return of the caliphate was inevitable.[2] The popular Saudi scholar Mohammad Arifi proclaimed that the Arab spring was a sign of the nearing of the return of the caliphate.[3] These are just a few voices among a number of other prominent Islamic personalities across the Middle East and North Africa who have openly talked about the re-establishment of the caliphate, almost invariably referring to the narration which ends with the promise "and then there will be caliphate (once again) upon the Prophetic method."[4] This open discussion about the caliphate has compelled movements such as the Egyptian Muslim Brotherhood and the Tunisian an-Nahda to simultaneously use the slogan of the caliphate to satisfy certain popular demands, while explaining it away within their program of gradualism and co-operation with secular politicians to appease opposition to Islamic rule, whether domestic or international.

Evidence from numerous polls taken in the last few years indicate that majorities or at a minimum substantial minorities in Muslim countries in Africa, the Middle East and Asia favor political unification on an Islamic basis with the full application of *shari'a* law by the government. At the same time democracy and freedom are normally praised, while Western values and secularism are rejected. Upon further investigation it becomes clear that while, for example, freedom of speech is praised, the belief that someone who insults Islam should be punished is heavily favored, including the implementation of capital punishment for such offences in line with the majority view of the normative position found in Islamic scholarship. While people often agree that democracy is the best option, it is far from clear whether they understand democracy in the same way as the pollsters, linking back to a point made in the introduction: the problem with using democracy as the basic reference point for analysis. Respondents who live under regimes where elections count for very little and popular choice is not represented in government are asked to choose between statements such as "Democracy is preferable to any other kind of government" and "In some circumstances, a non-democratic government can be preferable," possibly having been told all their lives that democracy means the election of government according to the people's choice and not considering the finer details of what is meant by popular sovereignty.[5]

Bruce Rutherford has written that the works of contemporary Islamic political theorists such as the prominent Qatar-based Egyptian scholar, Yusuf al-Qaradawi, widely acknowledged as one of the more popular scholarly figures in the Middle East due to his involvement and interaction with contemporary political issues across satellite television in the region, define Islamic constitutionalism in a manner that shares many characteristics with classical liberalism and democracy, as demonstrated by their belief in the rule of law, constraints on state power and public participation in politics. Rutherford's work is perhaps one of the most thoughtful and provocative articles written on the subject of comparison between contemporary Islamic political theory and democracy, and he concludes that if democracy is considered as a set of institutions that constrain the state, enforce law and allow for public political participation, then the two are compatible. On the other hand, if democracy is understood as a set of values, notably individual liberty and popular sovereignty, then the conclusion would be much more "ambiguous."[6] This is reflected in the work of Qaradawi, who claims that Muslims can adopt the tools and institutions of democracy without embracing its philosophy,[7] a typical position in the original ideology of the Muslim Brotherhood and reflected also by the Tanzeem-e-Islami.

While these types of comparison are potentially enlightening, and help to introduce Islamic ideas of government to Western audiences in a language they can understand, a perusal of Qaradawi's work reveals problems with the adoption of a redefined democratic discourse, with discussion between him and others effectively descending into arguments over terminology rather than substance, each side using terms we might identify with democracy, such as pluralism, but meaning entirely different things by them.[8] There is nothing new or even specific to intra-Muslim debates in this, but submitting to or enforcing a hegemonic discourse that assumes the universality of a "democracy," which is in any event contested, with anything else labeled as "authoritarian" will hardly help in understanding what each side is positing as everyone rushes to claim the "democratic" mantle.

It is therefore important that the democratic paradigm either be dismissed in analysis of Islamic politics or understood in a much more nuanced manner, which would ultimately remove any meaning for the term itself. At most it should be used as a comparative tool and not a yardstick for acceptability. If public sentiment for Islamic rule continues to grow, and the call for greater unity increases, there is likely to be a parallel increase in the frequency of discussions centered around the caliphate, its re-establishment and the form it should take. This will be particularly apparent should there be an opening up of public space to discuss politics without restriction in the region. Analysis of these discussions should be undertaken through a lens that appreciates the sources they are based on and without preconditions of what they accept as compatible with the democratic ideal, which is in any case highly disputed and non-existent in a practical sense.

Another concern is the media coverage and political discourse around the caliphate emanating from the West since the end of the Cold War, but also after the Iranian revolution and then again after 9/11. Islam and politics have long been seen as an undesirable mix, with the *shariʿa* vilified, sometimes as part of a wider campaign of the ridicule of Muslims and their values. There is an attempt to link aspirations for an Islamic unity and polity to the actions of those who are proclaimed as "terrorists" in the Western media, with the caliphate considered as an "extremist" goal. This can be thought of as part of a propaganda campaign engineered to distract their own populations from the fact that interference in foreign lands, whether by economic sanction, war, support for illegitimate regimes and a perceived partiality to Israel above the rights of the Palestinians, are all causal factors for retaliation, either by those directly affected or those who consider themselves as part of this collective identity.

It should be noted at this stage that history has shown that the caliphate, whether in its Ottoman form or previously, had all manner of relations with external states and polities. These ranged from peaceful co-existence and military support to hostile relations and open warfare, much the same as intra-polity relations throughout history. In any case, the application of International Relations theories like Realism may see the realignment of many of those speaking out against the idea of a unified Islamic state to accommodate it, if it emerges for the sake of their own interests on realization of the resources that may fall under its control. However, the continued demonization of a polity considered as part of normative Islam will likely only be detrimental for relations with the populations of Muslim countries in the future, where there is already substantial support for greater application of Islamic law and values in governance along with increased unity, irrespective of whether the masses are actively agitating for the re-establishment of the caliphate or not. In the past this has been of little concern to Western policymakers given their historical propensity for discounting popular sentiment in the Middle East in favor of supporting unrepresentative governments in the region, while pursuing a range of what can only be considered counterproductive policies vis-à-vis regional diplomacy, whether with respect to the question of Israel or Iran. But as the wheels of history turn, such viewpoints may soon look outdated and ill-judged, especially if the return of the caliphate is indeed an inevitability.

The reality is that the hegemony of Western governments and their values is being disputed more openly as time passes. As rising powers—Russia, China and India—begin to assert themselves both regionally and internationally, pressure to adopt the political values and philosophy of

Western governance will become less important, as competition in the provision of diplomatic and financial support increases. This is particularly the case as the aforementioned values and philosophy lie largely discredited even in the heart of the West itself as the result of Western actions over the last century with regards to the rest of the world, whether symbolized by prisoners in Guantanamo Bay at the start of the twenty-first century or those in Malta at the start of the twentieth,[9] along with a litany of foreign policy mishaps, crude *realpolitik* and human rights abuses in the hundred years in between, which are too many to list and too widely acknowledged to make it necessary to do so. The only remaining major attraction of the West was its economic confidence and the "free market" model it readily imposed upon others, now also exposed as a hollow philosophy in light of the massive government bailouts of the private sector in 2008, and openly questioned from within Western society itself for its failure to establish a model awarding fair economic dividends across society.

Consequently, attempts to establish a form of Islamic polity which would be considered legitimate by its citizens should be accepted as alternatives worthy of examination in their own right, without a policy, deliberate or otherwise, of framing the debate to deny them validity or impose external conditions. While the triumphant claims of "the end of history" and the beginning of the so-called "New World Order" were derided at the time in some quarters and have subsequently been exposed as erroneous, it may be that the end of a *Western* history is in sight, where the dominant narratives, universals and hegemonic discourses which have stemmed from the West throughout the twentieth and twenty-first centuries, are not only challenged, but eventually overturned. As the peoples of the Middle East and beyond find their voice and are able to articulate their demands for good governance publicly, it would be foolish to try to sideline those who propose Islamic solutions. This is especially so given their growing constituency and the likelihood that, in the more open discursive environment emerging in the aftermath of the "Arab Spring," the popularity of their ideas will likely continue to rise as they have greater freedom to articulate the authenticity of their vision of government, derived from Islamic sources rather than a discredited Western formula. This book is a contribution to these efforts: analyzing the discourses, ideas and methods of individuals and groups within their appropriate context, and situating those movements in a greater, alternative history.

APPENDIX

The following is a small selection of translated quotes from the verdicts of the leading scholars from Al-Azhar on the book "Islam and Governance (Al-Islam wa Usul al-Hukm)."

Ali Abdul-Raziq

"The council of senior scholars, in a disciplinary meeting on Wednesday, 22 Muharram the year 1344 (August 12 1925), under the chairmanship of the distinguished Professor Sheikh Mohammed Abu Fadl, the Grand Sheikh of the al-Azhar in the presence of twenty-four scholars from the senior scholars, who are the following distinguished professors:

[lists names of professors]

discussed the charges against Sheikh Ali Abdul Raziq, a member of the University of Al-Azhar and a *Shari'a* judge in the Primary *Shari'a* Court of Mansoorah, that are included in his book ("Islam and Governance"), and were announced on Wednesday 8th of Muharram 1344 (29 July 1925)."

The Facts

"The book called ("Islam and Governance") was published under the name of Sheikh Ali Abdul-Raziq who is one of the scholars of al-Azhar University; so petitions were presented to the scholars of al-Azhar University; signed by a large number of scholars on the dates of 23 Dhil Qa'adah, and the 1st and 8th Dhil Hijjah 1343 (15, 23 and 30 June,

217

1925). The petitions included that the book in question contains things contrary to the *din* and to the texts of the Qur'an and the *Sunna* of the Prophet and the consensus of the *Umma*.

The charges include:

1. That he made the Islamic *Shari'a* law purely spiritual, unrelated with governing and implementation in the matters of this life.
2. That he claims that the *din* does not prevent understanding that the jihad of the Prophet was for kingship (*mulk*) not for the *din*, nor for making the call (*da'wa*) to the world.
3. That he claims that the system of ruling in the era of the Prophet was the subject of uncertainty, ambiguity, turbulence or shortcomings and so is perplexing.
4. That he claims that the mission of the Prophet was to deliver the law abstract of governance and implementation.
5. The denial of the consensus of the Companions on the obligation of establishing an Imam and that it is imperative for the *Umma* to have someone who establishes their religious and worldly affairs.
6. The denial that the judiciary is a *shari'a* vocation.
7. That he claims that the government of Abu Bakr and the caliphs after him, may Allah be pleased with them were secular (*La diniya*)."

"As, for the denial of a consensus of the Companions on the obligation of establishing an Imam and that it is imperative for the *Umma* to have someone who establishes their religious and worldly affairs […]

Sheikh Ali Abdul Raziq admits in his defence that he denies the consensus on the necessity of appointing an Imam in the sense mentioned by scholars, he said of himself: he stands on the side of a not insignificant group of the people of the Qiblah (he means some of the *Kharijites* and Al-Asam). This defence does not prove his innocence of going against the consensus of the Muslims, and it is enough for him that in his *bid'a* (innovation) he is the row of the *Kharijites* not the rows of the masses of Muslims. Does his standing on the side of *Kharijites*, who violated the consensus after its convention, justify for him departure from the consensus of the Muslims? In *al-Mawaqif* and its explanation it is said: "The *tawatur* of the consensus of the Muslims during the first period after the death of the Prophet over the prohibition of there being a time without a caliph and an Imam; even Abu Bakr said—may Allah be pleased with him—in his famous speech at the time of his death: Muhammad has died, so it is necessary for this *din* that there be one who executes it, so everyone hurried to accept him, without anyone saying: "There is no need for that," rather they agreed on him and said: we will look into this issue, then rushed to *Bani Sa'idah*, and left for its sake the most important of things, which is to bury the Messenger of Allah. Their differences regarding who should take the post do not disprove their agreement in the matter. The people did not stop establishing an Imam to be followed in every era until our time today."

"As for his claim that the government of Abu Bakr and the caliphs after him, may Allah be pleased with them were secular (*La diniya/* unreligious), he said on page 90: "it is natural and reasonable to me, to the level of being obvious, that there should not be after the Prophet a religious leadership. What one can imagine the existence of is a new type of leadership, unrelated to the message nor based on the *din*, so it is therefore a secular type."

This boldness is secular. What is natural and reasonable for Muslims to the point of obviousness is that the leadership of Abu Bakr—may Allah be pleased with him—was religious. The Muslims predecessors and their followers knew that, generation after generation. His leadership was on the basis "it is necessary for this *din* that there be one who executes it." A consensus of the Companions—may Allah be pleased with them all—was established on that, as mentioned.

Sheikh Ali's defence that what he meant from "the leadership of Abu Bakr was secular" is that it does not relate back to revelation nor to the message is regrettably a laughable position, as no one imagines that Abu Bakr—may Allah be pleased with him—was a prophet receiving revelation, such that Sheikh Ali should defend against this illusion.

The masses of Companions, from the emigrants and al-Ansar, pledged allegiance to Abu Bakr—may Allah be pleased with him—on that he establishes the matter of the *din* in this *Umma* after the Prophet Muhammad, so he established the matter well, and like him, the rest of the rightly guided caliphs.

What Sheikh Ali described Abu Bakr with—may Allah be pleased with him—that his government was secular has not been put forward by anyone of the Muslims.

But the one who can degrade the status of Prophethood can find it easy to degrade the status of Abu Bakr and his brothers, the rightly guided caliphs, may Allah be pleased with them all."

"Sheikh Ali says on page 103: "nothing in the *din* prevents Muslims from competing with the other nations in all the knowledge of society and politics, and to demolish the ancient system, which they resigned to and debased them, and to build their own principles of their ruling and system of their government upon the most modern of what is produced by human minds, and the most secure of what the experience of nations leads to, as it is the best governance.""

It is well known that the foundation of governance and the sources of legislation for Muslims are the Book of Allah, the Messenger of Allah and the consensus of the Muslims, and there are none better than the Muslims. Sheikh Ali requested that what was built on these foundations of their system of government (out-of-date) be demolished."

"As it is apparent from the foregoing that the accusations against Sheikh Ali Adbul Raziq remain, and is thus not suited to be described as a scholar (*'Alim*) in accordance with article (101) of Act No. 10 of 1911, which reads: "If one of the scholars, whatever their occupation or profession, issue that which does not fit the description of being a scholar, then he is to be judged by the Sheikh of the University of al-Azhar and the unanimous agreement of nineteen of the council of senior scholars, as provided for in Part VII of this Act, with removal from the community of scholars. No appeal is to be accepted about this judgement. It follows on from the judgement mentioned, that the name of the convicted person be erased from the records of the University of al-Azhar and other institutions, that they be expelled from all posts, that their payroll is cut, and that they are not suitable to be employed for any public job, whether religious or non-religious."

"Based on these reasons:

We, the Sheikh of the University of al-Azhar along with the unanimous agreement of twenty-four scholars from the Council of Senior Scholars, judged Sheikh Ali Abdul Raziq, a member of the University of al-Azhar and a *shari'a* judge in the Primary *shari'a* Court of Mansoora and the author of the book (Islam and governance) be expelled from the community of scholars.

The Office of General Administration of the Religious Institutions issued this judgement on Wednesday 22 Muharram 1344 (August 12 1925).

Signed: the Sheikh of the University of al-Azhar"

NOTES

1. INTERPRETING IDEAS: AN INTRODUCTION

1. Noah Feldman, *The Fall and Rise of the Islamic State* (Princeton: Princeton University Press, 2008), p. 19.
2. Staff Writer, "Israel to come under Sharia law, says Israeli Arab Cleric," *Israel Today*, October 21, 2007.
3. Lucy Williamson, "Stadium crowd pushed for Islamist Dream," BBC News Website, August 12, 2007. http://news.bbc.co.uk/1/hi/world/south_asia/6943070.stm.
4. Osama bin Laden, "Nucleus of the Caliphate," http://www.memri.org.
5. Abdul Majid al-Zindani, "Sheikh Zindani in Yemen Calls for 'Khilafah Rashidah'" http://www.youtube.com/watch?v=pcBMJl0ESyY.
6. Yusuf al-Eid, "Sheikh Yusuf Al-Eid Yubashir Bi Auda Al-Khilafa Fi Suriya," http://www.youtube.com/watch?v=IEld6EZ_qfY.
7. Umar bin Abdul Aziz, "Khutbah on Khilafah: Sh Abdul Aziz in Egypt," http://www.youtube.com/watch?v=ZgQoVyjbz0A.
8. Tarek Amara, "Tunisia Islamist Causes Outcry with 'Caliphate' Talk," *Reuters*, November 15, 2011. http://ca.reuters.com/article/topNews/idCATRE7AE1ZD20111115.
9. WorldPublicOpinion.org, "Muslim Public Opinion on US Policy, Attacks on Civilians and al-Qaeda" (Maryland: The Center for International and Security Studies at Maryland, 2007), p. 15.
10. Lisa Miller and Matthew Phillips, "Caliwho?," *Newsweek*, October 12, 2006.
11. Dick Cheney, "Interview with Tim Russert—10/9/2006," http://www.whitehouse.gov/news/releases/2006/09/20060910.html.
12. Peter Fedynsky, "Rumsfeld Says Military Effort Alone Will Not Bring Success in Iraq—11/12/2006," *Voice of America*, http://www.voanews.com.

13. Andrew Anthony, "Richard Dannatt: 'If the Tories win, I will not be a defence minister'," *The Guardian*, December 20, 2009; Richard Dannatt, *The Today Programme*, BBC Radio, May 17, 2010.

14. Vikram Dodd, "Anti-terror code 'would alienate most Muslims,'" *The Guardian*, February 17, 2009.

15. "Libya: Up to a Million Refugees Could Pour into Europe," *The Telegraph*, February 21, 2011. http://www.telegraph.co.uk/news/worldnews/africaandindianocean/libya/8339225/Libya-up-to-a-million-refugees-could-pour-into-Europe.html.

16. Peter Schorsch, "Alan West Says 'Arab Spring' About Restoration of Islamic Caliphate," *SaintPetersBlog*, http://saintpetersblog.com/2011/08/alan-west-says-arab-spring-about-restoration-of-islamic-caliphate/.

17. Jack Mirkinson, "Glenn Beck Stands by Egypt Caliphate Conspiracy Theory: 'I'm Not Wrong'," *Huffington Post*. http://www.huffingtonpost.com/2011/02/04/glenn-beck-egypt-caliphate-conspiracy-theory_n_818564.html.

18. BBC Monitoring Service, "Text of report by Iranian Students News Agency (ISNA) website," November 13, 2006.

19. Patrick Goodenough, "OIC Fulfills Function of Caliphate, Embodies 'Islamic Solidarity,' Says OIC Chief Monday, May 10, 2010." http://www.cnsnews.com/news/article/65537.

20. Rashid al-Ghannouchi, "Rashid Al-Ghannouchi: Al-Khilafa Amal Wa Tamuh Kullu Muslimin." http://www.youtube.com/watch?v=SEkOP2ZflOM.

21. Mohammad Ayad, "Al-Ikhwan Wa Mawqifahum Min Al-Khilafa." http://www.youtube.com/watch?v=SEkOP2ZflOM.

22. Mohammad Ismail and Mahmoud Hijaj, "Badie: Al-Khilafa Al-Rashida Wa Ihya Dawla-Tul-Islam Wal-Shari'a Hadaf Al-Ikhwan." http://www.youm7.com/News.asp?NewsID=565958.

23. Further details of these reactions will be mentioned in the next chapter. For a good overview refer to: Mona F. Hassan, *Loss of Caliphate: The Trauma and Aftermath of 1258 and 1924* (PhD, Princeton University, 2009).

24. Elie Kedourie, *The Chatham House Version and Other Middle Eastern Studies* (London: University Press of New England, 1984), p. 182.

25. Mohammad 'Amara, *Al-Islam wa Usul al-hukm—Darasa wa watha'iq* (Beirut: Al-Mu'asasa al-'Arabiyya li-l-Darasat wa-l-nashr, 1972), p. 22.

26. Kedourie (1984), p. 195.

27. Sean Oliver-Dee, *The Caliphate Question: The British Government and Islamic Governance* (Lanham: Lexington Books, 2009).

28. Mark Jonathan Wegner, "Islamic Government: The Medieval Sunni Islamic Theory of the Caliphate and the Debate Over the Revival of the Caliphate in Egypt, 1924—1926" (PhD, University of Chicago, 2001).

29. Souad Tagelsir Ali, "'Ali 'Abd Al-Raziq's 'al-Islam wa Usul al-Hukm': A Modern, Liberal Development of Muslim Thought" (PhD, The University of Utah, 2004).

30. Hassan (2009).

31. James Piscatori, "Imagining Pan-Islam: Religious Activism and Political Utopias," Proceedings of the British Academy, 131 (2004), p. 425.

32. Fred Halliday, "The Politics of 'Islam'—A Second Look," British Journal of Political Science, 25 (3), 1995, pp. 400–1.

33. Peter R. Demant, Islam vs. Islamism: The Dilemma of the Muslim World (Westport: Praeger, 2006), pp. 181–200.

34. Michael E. Salla, "Political Islam and the West: A New Cold War or Convergence?," Third World Quarterly, 18 (4), 1997, p. 730.

35. Elizabeth Shakman Hurd, "Political Islam and Foreign Policy in Europe and the United States," Foreign Policy Analysis, 3, 2007.

36. David Brumberg, "Rhetoric and Strategy: Islamic Movements and Democracy in the Middle East," in Martin Kramer (ed.), The Islamism Debate (New York: Syracuse University Press, 1997), p. 15.

37. John L. Esposito, Unholy War (Oxford: Oxford University Press, 2002), p. 54.

38. Salla (1997), p. 737.

39. David Brumberg, "Rhetoric and Strategy: Islamic Movements and Democracy in the Middle East," in Kramer (1997), p. 15.

40. Bassam Tibi, "The Fundamentalist Challenge to the Secular Order in the Middle East," The Fletcher Forum of World Affairs, 23 (1), 1999, p. 200.

41. Bobby S. Sayyid, A Fundamental Fear: Eurocentrism and the Emergence of Islamism (London: Zed Books, 1997), pp. 37–9.

42. François Burgat and France. Ministère de la Culture, Face to Face with Political Islam, (London: I.B Tauris, 2003), p. 6.

43. François Burgat and John L. Esposito, Modernizing Islam: Religion in the Public Sphere in the Middle East and Europe (London: C. C. Hurst & Co. & Co., 2003).

44. Ira M. Lapidus, "Islamic Revival and Modernity: The Contemporary Movements and the Historical Paradigms," Journal of the Economic and Social History of the Orient, 40 (4), 1997, p. 448.

45. John L. Esposito, The Islamic Threat: Myth or Reality (Oxford: Oxford University Press, 1999), p. 47.

46. Ibid., p. 225.

47. Ibid., p. 268.

48. Nazih Ayubi, Political Islam: Religion and Politics in the Arab World (London: Routledge, 1991), p. 218.

49. Fred Halliday, Islam and The Myth of Confrontation (London: I.B.Tauris, 2003), p. 114.

50. Ibid., p. 157.

51. Abul Husain 'Asakir-ud-Din Muslim, *Sahih Muslim* (Beirut: Dar al-fikr, 1998). Among the narrations which could be referenced here are: 1718: that any action undertaken based on anything other than Islam is rejected; 1853: that if two caliphs are given allegiance, to kill the second of them; 1855: a ruler should not be fought as long as he establishes prayer.

52. Olivier Roy, *Globalised Islam: The Search for a New Umma* (London: C. Hurst & Co., 2002), p. 10.

53. Ibid., p. 49.

54. ibn Nuhhas, *mushari'a al-Aswaq* (Beirut: Dar al-basha'ir al-islamiyya, 2002), p. 101.

55. Roy, (2002), p. 179

56. Abul Hasan Ali al-Mawardi, *al-Ahkam al-Sultaniyya* (Beirut: Dar Al-Kotob Al-ilmiya, undated), p. 5; Mohammad bin al-Hussain al-Faraa, *al-Ahkam al-Sultaniyya* (Beirut: Dar Al-Kotob Al-ilmiya, 1983), p. 19; Abdul Malik bin Abdullah al-Juwaini, *al-Ghiyathi* (Beirut: Dar Al-Kotob Al-ilmiya, 2003), p. 15.

57. Roy, (2002), p. 1.

58. Ibid., p. 40.

59. Fawaz A. Gerges, *The Far Enemy: Why Jihad Went Global* (New York: Cambridge University Press, 2005).

60. Elizabeth Shakman Hurd, "Political Islam and Foreign Policy in Europe and the United States," *Foreign Policy Analysis*, 3, 2007, p. 350.

61. Michael E. Salla, "Political Islam and the West: A New Cold War or Convergence?," *Third World Quarterly*, 18 (4), 1997, pp. 737–8.

62. Dalia Mogahed, "Special Report: Muslim World—Islam and Democracy" (Washington DC: The Gallup Center for Muslim Studies, 2006); WorldPublicOpinion.org, "Defamation of Religion" (Maryland: The Center for International and Security Studies at Maryland, 2009); WorldPublicOpinion.org, "Muslim Public Opinion on Us Policy, Attacks on Civilians and Al-Qaeda," (Maryland: The Center for International and Security Studies at Maryland, 2007).

63. Yusuf al-Qaradawi, *Min Fiqh Al-Dawla Fi al-Islam* (Cairo: Dar al-Sharouq, 1997), p. 150.

64. The contemporary *Salafi* movement, also described as *Wahabi*, is largely led by scholars in Saudi Arabia, and its adherents believe that the first three generations of Muslims demonstrated the best example of Islamic practice. However, this does not really differentiate between the *Salafi* trend and other schools of thought—which would also claim to follow the example of the early generations of Islam—but they are more clearly identified by their focus on personal practices and worship, and their stance against what

they consider to be deviations from the original forms of worship by the followers of the more spiritualistic Sufi trend within Islam.

65. Qur'an (5:44), (5:50), (4:65), (4:59), (42:10).

66. Ali Juma Muhammad, *Al-Hukm Al-Shar'i 'Ind Al-Usuliyin* (Cairo: Dar al-Salam, 2002), pp. 121–4.

67. The major exception to this is the opinion of some of the Shia Twelvers sect, who consider their Imams to be infallible.

68. Ahmad bin Hanbal, Musnad Al-Imam Ahmad Bin Hanbal (Beirut: Muassisa al-Risala, 1999), vol. 30, p. 355, narration 18406.

69. Abul Husain 'Asakir-ud-Din Muslim, *Sahih Muslim* (Beirut: Dar al-fikr, 1998), vol. 6, p. 191, narration 1853.

70. Mohammad Shaybani, *Al-Sayar Al-Kabir* (Beirut: Dar Al-Kotob Al-ilmiyah, 1997), vol. 5, p. 327.

71. Abul Hasan Ali al-Mawardi, *Al-Ahkam Al-Sultaniyya* (Beirut: Dar Al-Kotob Al-ilmiya), p. 5.

72. Mohammad bin al-Hussain al-Fara, *Al-Ahkam Al-Sultaniyya* (Beirut: Dar Al-Kotob Al-ilmiya, 1983), p. 271.

73. Abdul Qadir al-Baghdadi, *Usul Al-Deen* (Istanbul: Matba al-Dawla, 1928).

74. Ali bin Ahmad bin Said bin Hazm al-Dhahari, *Al-Fasl Fi al-Malal Wal-Ahwa Wa-l-Nahl* (Cairo: Maktaba al-Khanji, 1994), vol. 4, p. 72.

75. Abdul Rahman bin Ahmed al-Egee, *Al-Mawaqif Fi 'Ilm Al-Kalam* (Beirut: 'Alim al-Kutub, 1988), p. 395.

76. Abu Abdullah Al-Qurtubi, *Al-Jami' li-Ahkam Al-Qur'an* (Beirut: Dar Al-Kotob Al-ilmiya, 2000), vol. 1, p. 182.

77. Asma Afsaruddin, "The 'Islamic State': Genealogy, Facts, and Myths," *Journal of Church and State*, 48, (1), 2006, p. 171.

78. The *Mu'tazila* sect, which flourished between the eighth and tenth centuries, took the Islamic creed and *Shari'a* as their ultimate reference point but believed that the wisdom behind the *Shari'a* could be rationally explained and held numerous beliefs considered outside of traditional Sunni orthodoxy, linked to issues such as the Creation of Quran and predestination.

79. The *Khawarij* were an early sect of Islam which emerged during the conflict between Ali and Mu'awiyya who held several beliefs contrary to the orthodox position, such as that anyone who commits a major sin is destined for eternal hellfire.

80. Abul Hasan Abdul Jabbar, *Al-Mugni Fi Abwab al-Tawheed Wal-'Adl*, Abdul-Halim Mahmud and Sulayman Dunya (eds.), vol. 20 (Cairo), p. 48.

81. Ibid., p. 243.

82. Mona Hassan, "Modern Interpretations and Misinterpretations of a Medieval Scholar: Apprehending the Political Thought of Ibn Taymiyyah," in Shahab Ahmed and Yossef Rapoport (eds.), *Ibn Taymiyyah and His Times* (Oxford: Oxford University Press, 2010), pp. 338–66.

83. These four groups encompass most of the differing opinions on aspects of Islamic theology, with the *ahl al-sunna* generally used to refer to the considered orthodox majority.

84. Ali bin Ahmad bin Said bin Hazm al-Dhahari, *Al-Fasl Fil-Malal Wal-Ahwa Wal-Nahl* (Cairo: Maktaba al-Khanji, 1994), vol. 4, p. 72.

85. Abdulrahman al-Juzayri, *Al-Fiqh 'Ala al-Mathahib Al-Arba'a* (Cairo: Al-Maktaba al-Tawqifiyya, undated), vol. 5, p. 392.

86. Sayyid (1997), p. 56.

87. Gail Minault, *The Khilafat Movement: Religious Symbolism and Political Mobilization in India*, Studies in Oriental Culture, 16 (New York: Columbia University Press, 1981), p. 4; Sayyid (1997), pp. 48–56.

88. Wegner (2001), p. 121.

89. Sir Thomas W. Arnold, *The Caliphate* (Delhi: Adam Publishers, 1992), p. 182.

90. Mohammad 'Amara, *Ma'raka al-Islam wa Usul al-Hukm* (Cairo: Dar al-Sharook, 1997).

91. Mohammad Diya' al-Deen al-Rayyis, *Al-Islam wa-L-Khilafa Fi al-Asr Al-Hadith* (Cairo: Dar al-Turath, 1976).

92. Wegner (2001).

93. Armando Salvatore, *Islam and the Political Discourse of Modernity* (International Politics of the Middle East) (Reading: Ithaca Press, 1997).

94. Kedourie (1984).

95. Mona F. Hassan, "Loss of Caliphate: The Trauma and Aftermath of 1258 and 1924" (PhD, Princeton University, 2009).

96. Azmi Özcan, *Pan-Islamism: Indian Muslims, the Ottomans and Britain, 1877–1924* (The Ottoman Empire and its Heritage: Politics, Society and Economy), vol. 12 (Leiden & New York: Brill, 1997).

97. Minault (1981), p. 57.

98. Suha Taji-Farouki, *A Fundamental Quest: Hizb al-Tahrir and the Search for the Islamic Caliphate* (London: Grey Seal, 1996).

99. Ibid., p. x.

100. Ibid., p. 65.

101. Emmanuel Karagiannis, *Political Islam in Central Asia* (London: Routledge, 2009), p. 56.

102. Mahmoud Osman Haddad, "Arab Religious Nationalism in the Colonial Era: Rereading Rashid Rida's Ideas on the Caliphate," *Journal of the American Oriental Society*, 117 (2), 1997, p. 277.

103. Mahmoud Osman Haddad, "Rashid Rida and the Theory of the Caliphate: Medieval Themes and Modern Concerns," (PhD, Columbia University, 1989), p. 129.

104. Kemal H. Karpat, *The Politicization of Islam: Reconstructing Identity, State,*

Faith, and Community in the Late Ottoman State (Oxford: Oxford University Press, 2001); Jacob M. Landau, *The Politics of Pan-Islam Ideology and Organization* (Oxford: Clarendon, 1989).

105. Kedourie (1984).
106. Özcan (1997); Minault (1981).
107. Cemil Aydin, *The Politics of Anti-Westernism in Asia* (New York: Columbia University Press, 2007).
108. For variations of these explanations refer to: Roy, (2002); Gerges (2005); Piscatori (2004).
109. Sayyid (1997), pp. 19–22.
110. Ibid., p. 158.
111. Duncan S. A. Bell, "The Cambridge School and World Politics," http://www.theglobalsite.ac.uk/press/103bell.htm.
112. James Tully, Quentin Skinner et al., *Meaning and Context: Quentin Skinner and his Critics* (Princeton: Princeton University Press, 1988), p. 55.
113. Ibid., p. 41–42.
114. Abdul Allah bin Yusuf al-Juda'i, *Tayseer 'ilm usul al-fiqh* (Beirut: Mu'assa al-Rayyan, 2006), p. 12.
115. Ibid., p. 341.

2. THE END OF AN ERA: THE CALIPHATE BETWEEN EJECTION, REFORM AND REVIVAL

1. Kemal Mustapha, *A Speech Delivered by Ghazi Mustapha Kemal, President of the Turkish Republic, October 1927*, (Leipzig: K.F. Koehler, 1929), p. 378.
2. Ibid., p. 363.
3. Ibid., p. 574.
4. Rashid Rida, "Khutba Ghazi Mustafa Kemal Basha," *al-Manar*, 23 (10), 1922.
5. Gail Minault, *The Khilafat Movement: Religious Symbolism and Political Mobilization in India*, Studies in Oriental Culture 16 (New York: Columbia University Press, 1981), pp. 202–3.
6. Mustapha (1929), pp. 684–5.
7. Ibid., p. 378.
8. Bobby S. Sayyid, *A Fundamental Fear: Eurocentrism and the Emergence of Islamism* (London: Zed Books, 1997), p. 56.
9. Mahmoud Osman Haddad, "Rashid Rida and the Theory of the Caliphate: Medieval Themes and Modern Concerns" (PhD, Columbia University, 1989), p. 83.
10. Azmi Özcan, *Pan-Islamism: Indian Muslims, the Ottomans and Britain,*

1877–1924 (The Ottoman Empire and its Heritage: Politics, Society and Economy), v. 12 (Leiden & New York: Brill, 1997), p. 34.

11. Ibid., p. 77.

12. Ibid., p. 29.

13. Haddad (1989), pp. 83–4.

14. Özcan (1997), pp. 23–4, 30.

15. Among others, the Syrian head of the Rafa'i Sufi order Sheikh AbulHuda al-Sayyadi; Sheikh Mohammad Zafir—the head of the Shadhili-Madani order in Libya; Sheikh Ahmed bin Sumayt—an Islamic judge in Zanzibar. For further details see: B Abu-Manneh, "Sultan Abdulhamid and Shaikh Abulhuda Al-Sayyadi," *Middle Eastern Studies in Intelligence* 15 (2), 1979; Martin S. Kramer and Merkaz Dayan, *Islam Assembled: The Advent of the Muslim Congresses* (New York: Columbia University Press, 1985), pp. 6–7; Özcan (1997), p. 53.

16. Minault (1981), p. 75.

17. Haddad (1989), p. 193.

18. Minault (1981), p. 64.

19. Ibid., p. 176.

20. "Dispatch 4657 dated August 27,1923 from District Governer of Jerusalem-Jaffa to the Chief secretary titled Recognition of New caliph," in *The Caliphate Question, IOR/L/PS/10/895/* (London: India Office, British Library, 1920).

21. "Syrian Consultate, Beyrout, August 1 1923," in *Egyptian Consulate General Correspondance 1915–1926 FO/141/587/2* (London: Foreign Office, National Archives, 1923).

22. Abul Kalam Azad, "al-Khilafa al-Islamiyya—1," *al-Manar*, 23 (1), 1922.

23. Qur'an (24:55).

24. Abul Kalam Azad, "al-Khilafa al-Islamiyya—1," *al-Manar*, 23 (1), 1922.

25. Abul Kalam Azad, "al-Khilafa al-Islamiyya—3," *al-Manar*, 23 (3), 1922.

26. Abul Kalam Azad, "al-Khilafa al-Islamiyya—1," *al-Manar*, 23 (1), 1922.

27. Abul Kalam Azad, "al-Khilafa al-Islamiyya—3," *al-Manar*, 23 (3), 1922.

28. Ibid.

29. Claudia Anna Gazzini, *Jihad in Exile: Ahmad al-Sharif al-Sanusi 1918–1933* (PhD, Princeton University, 2004), p. 79.

30. Minault (1981), p. 202.

31. Tarek al-Bishry, "al-Malik wa-l-Khilafa al-Islamiyya," *Al-Katib*, 13 (142), 1973, p. 45.

32. Al-Sayed Yusuf, *Rashid Reda wa-l-'auda illa minhaj al-salaf* (Cairo: Miyriyt li-l-Nashr wa-l-Ma'lumat, 2000), p. 86.

33. "Memorandum on Angora and the caliphate, to High Commissioner Egypt dated November 9, 1922," in *Egyptian Consulate General Correspondance,*

1915–1926 FO/141/587/2 (London: Foreign Office, National Archives, 1922).

34. Rashid Rida, "Khutba Ghazi Mustafa Kemal Basha," *al-Manar*, 23 (10), 1922.

35. Rashid Rida, "Zafar al-Turk bi-l-Yunan," *al-Manar*, 23 (9), 1922.

36. Rashid Rida, *Al-Khilafa 'aw al-Imama al-'uthma* (Cairo: *Al-zahara li-l-'ilam al-arab*, 1988), pp. 10–11.

37. Ibid., pp. 70–2.

38. Ibid., pp. 72–3.

39. Ibid., pp. 74–7.

40. Ibid.

41. Ibid., p. 93.

42. Ibid., pp. 103–5.

43. Ibid., p. 83.

44. Rashid Rida, "al-Ahkam al-Shara'iyya al-Muta'laqa bi-l-Khilafa al-Isla-miyya—6," *al-Manar*, 24 (5), 1923.

45. Rashid Rida, "al-Shura fi Bilad al-Shams," *al-Manar*, 9 (7), 1906.

46. Rashid Rida (1988), p. 82.

47. Ibid., p. 78.

48. Ibid.

49. Rashid Rida, "al-Ahkam al-Shara'iyya al-Muta'laqa bi-l-Khilafa al-Isla-miyya—6," *al-Manar*, 24 (5), 1923.

50. Mahmoud Osman Haddad, "Arab Religious Nationalism in the Colonial Era: Rereading Rashid Rida's Ideas on the Caliphate," *Journal of the American Oriental Society*, 117 (2), 1997, p. 277.

51. Abdul al-Ghani Bek, *al-Khilafa wa Sulta al-Umma* (Cairo: Dar al-Nahr, 1924), p. 120.

52. Rashid Rida, "Khutba Ghazi Mustafa Kemal Basha," *al-Manar*, 23 (10), 1922.

53. Bek (1924), p. 100.

54. Ibid., pp. 118.

55. Rashid Rida, "Intiqad al-Manar li Kitab Khilafat wa Hakimiyyat Milliyya," *al-Manar*, 24 (7), 1923.

56. Rashid Rida, "al-Ahkam al-Shara'iyya al-Muta'laqa bi al-Khilafa al-Isla-miyya—5," *al-Manar*, 24 (4), 1923.

57. Rida,(1988), p. 77.

58. Mustapha (1929), p. 572.

59. Ibid., p. 583.

60. "Public Letters from the Aga Khan," in *The Caliphate Question, IOR/L/PS/10/895/*, (London: India Office, British Library, 1920), p. 50.

61. Mustapha (1929), p. 584.

62. Mona F. Hassan, "Loss of Caliphate: The Trauma and Aftermath of 1258 and 1924" (PhD, Princeton University, 2009), p. 243.

63. Martin van Bruinessen, "Popular Islam, Kurdish Nationalism and Rural Revolt: The Rebellion of Shaikh Said in Turkey (1925)," in Martin van Bruinessen (ed.), *Mullas, Sufis and Heretics: The Role of Religion in Kurdish Society: Collected Articles* (Istanbul: The Isis Press, 2000), p. 2.

64. Paul White, "Ethnic Differentiation among the Kurds: Kurmancî, Kizil-bash and Zaza," *Journal of Arabic, Islamic & Middle Eastern Studies*, 2 (2), 1995.

65. F.O. 371/10218/E2823, March 21, 1924.

66. Mona F. Hassan, "Loss of Caliphate: The Trauma and Aftermath of 1258 and 1924" (PhD, Princeton University, 2009), pp. 70–5.

67. "Extracts from the *Pioneer Mail* dated March 14, 1924," in *The Caliphate Question, IOR/L/PS/10/1111* (London: India Office, British Library, 1924), pp. 298–301.

68. "Kabul's Despatch 54," in *The Caliphate Question, IOR/L/PS/10/1111*, (London: India Office, British Library, 1924), pp. 99–101.

69. Mohammad Diya' al-Deen al-Rayyis, *Al-Islam wa-L-Khilafa Fi al-Asr Al-Hadith* (Cairo: Dar al-Turath, 1976), p. 63.

70. Tarek al-Bishry, "Al-Malik Wa-L-Khilafa Al-Islamiyya," *Al-Katib* 13 (142), 1973, p. 46.

71. Rashid Rida, "Inqilab al-deen al-siyasi fi-l-jumhuriyya al-Turkiyya," *al-Manar*, 25 (4), 1924.

72. Tarek al-Bishry, "Al-Malik Wa-L-Khilafa Al-Islamiyya," *Al-Katib* 13 (142), 1973, p. 47.

73. Rashid Rida, "al-Khilafa wa-l-mu'tamar al-Islami," *al-Manar*, 25 (5), 1924.

74. "Nejd Affairs—extracts from Bombay Chronicles June 23, 1924," in *The Caliphate Question: Deposition of Caliph Abdul Mejid by the Angora Assembly, IOR/L/PS/10/1111* (London: India Office, British Library, 1924), pp. 34–5.

75. al-Rayyis (1976), p. 66.

76. Mohammad Husain Haikal, *Muthakkirat Fi al-Siyassa Al-Misriya* (Cairo: Maktaba al-Nahda al-Masriyya, 1951), p. 231.

77. Tarek al-Bishry, "Al-Malik Wa-L-Khilafa Al-Islamiyya," *Al-Katib* 13 (142), 1973, p. 55.

78. al-Rayyis (1976), p. 127.

79. Ali Abdul-Raziq, "*Al-Islam wa Usul al-hukm*," in Mohammad 'Amara (ed.), *Al-Islam wa Usul al-hukm—Darasa wa watha'iq* (Beirut: Al-Mua'sasa al-Arabiyya li-l-Darasat wa-l-nashr*, 1972), p. 182.

80. Ibid., pp. 117–20.

81. Ibid., p. 145.

82. Ibid., p. 163.

83. Ibid., pp. 174–5.

84. Ibid., p. 136.

85. Ibid., p. 182.

86. Mohammad 'Amara, *Ma'raka al-Islam wa Usul al-Hukm* (Cairo: Dar al-Sharook, 1997), p. 171.

87. Rashid Rida, "al-Islam wa Usul al-Hukm," *al-Manar*, 26 (2), 1925.

88. Ibid.

89. The Council of Senior Scholars, "The ruling of the Council of Senior Scholars regarding the book 'Islam and the fundamentals of ruling'—12/8/1925," in 'Amara (1997), p. 126.

90. Ali Abdul-Raziq, "Opinion regarding the ruling of the Council of Senior Scholars 3/9/1925," Ibid.

91. 'Amara (1972), pp. 23–4.

92. 'Amara (1997), p. 150.

93. Mohammad Al-Tahir ibn 'Ashur, *Naqd 'ilmy li Kitab al-Islam wa usul al-hukm* (Cairo: Maktaba al-Salafiyya, 1925), p. 5.

94. Ibid., p. 11.

95. Ibid., pp. 35–6.

96. Mohammad Bakhit al-Mutee'i, *Haqiqa al-Islam wa Usul al-Hukm* (Cairo: Al-Matba'a al-Salifiyya, 1925), p. 4.

97. Ibid., p. 24.

98. Mohammad al-Khidr Hussain, "Naqd Kitab al-Islam wa Usul al-Hukm," in Mohammad 'Amara (ed.), *Ma'raka al-Islam wa Usul al-Hukm* (Cairo: Dar al-Sharook, 1925), p. 225.

99. Ibid., p. 233.

100. Ibid., p. 258.

101. Ibid., p. 290.

102. Ibid., p. 239.

103. 'Amara (1997), p. 172.

104. For further reading and details on this issue see Martin Kramer and Merkaz Dayan, *Islam Assembled: The Advent of the Muslim Congresses* (New York: Columbia University Press, 1985).

105. "Note regarding The Caliphate to High Commissioner Egypt, March 7 1924," in Egyptian Consulate General Correspondance 1915–1926, FO/141/587/2 (London: Foreign Office, National Archives, 1924).

106. Azmi Özcan (1997), p. 73.

107. Kramer and Dayan (1985), p. 12.

108. Martin van Bruinessen, "Muslims of the Dutch East Indies and the Caliphate Question," *Studia Islamika*, 2 (3), 1995, p. 125.

109. Hassan (2009), p. 247.

110. Claudia Anna Gazzini, "Jihad in Exile: Ahmed Al-Sharif Al-Sanusi 1918–1933" (PhD, Princeton University, 2004), p. 85.

111. Kramer and Dayan (1985), p. 90.

112. Mark Jonathan Wegner, "Islamic Government: The Medieval Sunni Islamic Theory of the Caliphate and the Debate Over the Revival of the Caliphate in Egypt, 1924—1926" (PhD, The University of Chicago, 2001), p. 239.

113. Yusuf (2000), p. 86.

114. Mustapha (1929), p. 592.

115. Minault (1981), pp. 204–5.

116. Wegner (2001), p. 262.

117. al-Mutee'i (1925), p. 58.

3. GLOBAL UNITY THROUGH A NATION STATE: BANNA, THE MUSLIM BROTHERHOOD AND AUTHORITY UNDER OCCUPATION

1. Hassan al-Banna, "Bain al-ams wa-l-yawm," in *Majmu'a al-Risa'il li-l-Imam al-Shahid Hassan Al-Banna* (Cairo: Dar al-tawzee', 1992), p. 110.

2. Hassan al-Banna, *Muthakarat Al-Da'wa Wa-L-Da'iyya* (Beirut: Dar al-Shihab, 1966), pp. 60–1.

3. Qur'an 2:286

4. al-Banna, (1966), p. 61.

5. Ibid., p. 87.

6. Christina Phelps Harris, *Nationalism and Revolution in Egypt* (The Hague: Mouton & Co., 1964), p. 139.

7. Hassan al-Banna, "Risalat al-mu'tamar al-khamis," in al-Banna (1992), p. 144.

8. Tariq al-Bishri, *Al-Harakat Al-Siyasiyya Fi Misr 1945–1952* (Cairo: al-hai'iyyat al-masriyya al-'aama li al-kitab, 1972), p. 55.

9. Hoda Gamal Abdel Nasser, *Britain and the Egyptian Nationalist Movement 1936–1952* (Reading: Ithaca Press, 1994), p. 57.

10. Dr. Zakariya Sulaiman Buyumi, *Al-Ikhwan Al-Muslimin wa-l-Jama'at al-Islamiyya fi-l-Hiyat al-Siyasiyya al-Masriyya* (Cairo: Maktaba Wahba, 1979), p. 59.

11. Ishaq Musa Husaini, *The Moslem Brethren: The Greatest of Modern Islamic Movements* (Beirut: Khayat's College Book Cooperative, 1956), p. 17.

12. Richard Paul Mitchell, *The Society of the Muslim Brothers*, Middle Eastern Monographs—9 (Oxford: Oxford University Press, 1969), pp. 244–5.

13. Ahmad S Moussalli, *Moderate and Radical Islamic Fundamentalism: The*

Quest for Modernity, Legitimacy, and the Islamic State (Gainesville: University Press of Florida, 1999), pp. 117–8.

14. Anwar al-Jundi, *Hasan al-Banna* (Beirut: Dar al-Qa'a, 1978).

15. Hamid Enayat, *Modern Islamic Political Thought* (London: I.B.Tauris, 2005), p. 52.

16. al-Banna, (1966), p. 31.

17. Buyumi (1979), p. 49.

18. Rashid Rida, "Khutba Ghazi Mustafa Kemal Basha," *al-Manar*, 23 (10), 1922.

19. al-Banna, (1966), p. 57.

20. al-Jundi (1978), p. 36.

21. al-Banna (1966), p. 64.

22. Mahmoud AbdulHaleem, *Al-ikhwan al-Muslimun: Ahdath sana'at al-tarikh Part 1* (Alexandria: Dar al-Da'wa, 1981/a), p. 63.

23. Brynjar Lia, *The Society of the Muslim Brothers in Egypt: The Rise of an Islamic Mass Movement, 1928–1942* (Reading: Ithaca Press, 2006), p. 27.

24. AbdulHaleem (1981/a), p. 66.

25. al-Banna (1966), p. 128.

26. Ibid., p. 87.

27. Ibid., p. 169.

28. Ibrahim al-Bayoumi Ghanim, *al-fikr al-siyasi li-l-Imam Hasan al-Banna* (Cairo: Dar al-tawzee' wa-l-nashr al-Islamiyya, 1992), p. 335.

29. Hassan al-Banna, "Da'watuna," in al-Banna (1992), p. 18.

30. Ghanim (1992), p. 203.

31. Hassan al-Banna, "Hal nahnu Qawmun 'amaliyyun," in al-Banna (1992), p. 84.

32. Hassan al-Banna, "Risalat al-mu'tamar al-khamis," in al-Banna (1992), p. 136.

33. Hassan al-Banna, "Illa ay shay nado' al-Nas," in al-Banna (1992), p. 107.

34. Hassan al-Banna, *Tarbiyya al-nasha* (1927), p. 3. www.hassanalbanna.org.

35. al-Banna (1966), pp. 168–9.

36. Buyoomi (1979), p. 42.

37. Hassan al-Banna, "Bain al-ams wa-l-yawm," in al-Banna (1992), p. 97.

38. Hassan al-Banna, "Da'watuna," in al-Banna (1992), p. 19.

39. al-Banna (1966), p. 105.

40. al-Banna (1966), p. 146.

41. AbdulHaleem (1981/a), p. 148.

42. al-Banna (1966), p. 228–9.

43. Lia (2006), p. 215.

44. Sean Oliver-Dee, *The Caliphate Question: The British Government and Islamic Governance* (Lanham: Lexington Books, 2009), p. 146.

45. Hassan al-Banna, "Risalat al-mu'tamar al-khamis," in al-Banna (1992), p. 144.

46. Ibid., p. 138–9.

47. Hassan al-Banna, "Nitham al-hukm," in al-Banna (1992), p. 322.

48. Ghanim (1992), p. 335.

49. al-Banna (1966), p. 282.

50. Qur'an.

51. AbdulHaleem (1981/a), pp. 378–9.

52. Hassan al-Banna, "Nahu al-Nur," in al-Banna (1992), p. 295.

53. Ibid.

54. Ibid., p. 288.

55. Ibid., p. 289.

56. Hassan al-Banna, "Illa-l-Shabab," in al-Banna (1992), p. 177.

57. Hassan al-Banna, "Bain al-ams wa-l-yawm," in al-Banna (1992), p. 101.

58. Ghanim (1992), p. 286.

59. Hassan al-Banna, "Da'watuna fi tur al-jadid," in al-Banna (1992), pp. 230–1.

60. Hassan al-Banna, "Risalat al-mu'tamar al-khamis," in al-Banna (1992), pp. 142–44.

61. Hassan al-Banna, "Nahu al-Nur," in al-Banna (1992), p. 290.

62. Hassan al-Banna, "Risalat al-mu'tamar al-khamis," in al-Banna (1992), p. 137.

63. AbdulHaleem (1981/a), p. 313.

64. Ibid., pp. 173–5.

65. Mahmoud al-Sabbagh, *Haqiqa al-Tanthim al-Khas* (Cairo: Dar al-'Itisam, 1989), p. 173.

66. Qur'an, 5:44.

67. AbdulHaleem (1981/a), p. 203.

68. Lia (2006), p. 256.

69. Taufiq Yusuf al-Waa'i, *Al-Fikr Al-Siyasi Al-Mu'aser 'Ind Al-Ikhwan Al-Muslimin* (Kuwait: Maktaba al-Manar al-Islamiyya, 2001), p. 139.

70. AbdulHaleem (1981/a), p. 258.

71. Hassan al-Banna, "Bain al-ams wa-l-yawm," in al-Banna (1992), p. 110.

72. Ghanim (1992), pp. 418–9.

73. Hassan al-Banna, "Risalat al-Jihad," in al-Banna (1992), p. 437.

74. Hassan al-Banna, "Illa ay shay nado' al-Nas," in al-Banna (1992), pp. 44–6.

75. Love of life and fear of Death.

76. Hassan al-Banna, "Min Fiqh al-Da'wa," in *Fiqh al-Waqi'* (Mansoora: Dar al-Kalima, 1999), p. 100.

77. Hassan al-Banna, "Risalat al-mu'tamar al-khamis," in al-Banna (1992), pp. 135–6.

78. Hassan al-Banna, "Bain al-ams wa-l-yawm," in al-Banna (1992), p. 110.

79. Hassan al-Banna, "Fi Ijtima' Ru'asa al-Manataq wa-l-Shab," in al-Banna (1992), pp. 249–70.

80. AbdulHaleem (1981/a), p. 409.

81. al-Sabbagh (1989), p. 174.

82. Ghanim (1992), p. 266.

83. al-Waa'i (2001), p. 233.

84. Mitchell (1969), p. 58.

85. AbdulHaleem (1981/b), p. 81.

86. Hassan al-Banna, "Qadayatuna" (1949). http://www.daawa-info.net/books1.php?parts=132&au=%CD%D3%E4%20%C7%E1%C8%E4%C7.

87. Nasser (1994), p. 174.

88. AbdulHaleem (1981/b), p. 449.

89. Husaini (1956), p. 75–83.

90. Mohammad Ghazali, *Min huna na'lam* (Cairo: Nadatu Masr, 2005), pp. 45–52.

91. Barbara Zollner, "Hasan Isma'il al-Hudaybi's role in the Muslim Brotherhood. A contextual analysis of 'Preachers not Judges'" (PhD, University of London, 2004), p. 36.

92. AbdulHaleem (1981/b), p. 473.

93. Ibid., p. 479.

94. Nasser (1994), pp. 311–2.

95. Qur'an, 2:30.

96. Sayyid Qutb, *Ma'alam Fi-l-Tariq. Kuwait: IIFSD* (Undated), p. 7.

97. Ibid., vol. 6, p. 3387.

98. Ibid., vol. 4, p. 2087.

99. Ibid., vol. 4, p. 2477.

100. Ibid., vol. 5, p. 3019.

101. Sayyid Qutb, *Ma'alam Fi-l-Tariq. Kuwait: IIFSD* (Undated), pp. 150–1.

102. Abul Hasan al-Nadwi, *Matha khasara al-'Alam binhitat al-Muslimin*, p. 3. http://www.saaid.net.

103. Takfir—broadly to excommunicate, or declare someone claiming to be a Muslim as outside of Islam.

104. Sayed Khatab, "Al-Hudaybi's influence on the Development of Islamist Movements in Egypt," *The Muslim World*, 91, Fall 2001, p. 467.

105. Giles Kepel, *The Roots of Radical Islam* (London: Saqi, 2005), p. 61.

106. Zainab al-Ghazali, *Return of the Pharaoh*, trans. Mokrane Guezzou (Leicester: The Islamic Foundation, 1994), p. 40.

107. Hasan al-Hudaybi, *Du'at la Qudat*, p. 199. (Electronic version).

108. Barbara Zollner, "Hasan Isma'il Al-Hudaybi's Role in the Muslim Brothe-

rhood: A Contextual Analysis of 'Preachers Not Judges'," (PhD, University of London, 2004), p. 100.

109. Hasan al-Hudaybi, *Du'at La Qudat*, p. 165.

110. Sayyid Qutb, *Milestones* (Birmingham: Maktabah Booksellers and Publishers, 2006), p. 35.

111. Hesham al-Awadi, *In Pursuit of Legitimacy: The Muslim Brothers and Mubarak 1982–2000*, Library of Modern Middle East Studies—46 (London: I.B. Tauris, 2004), pp. 15–16.

112. Essam el-Errian, "What the Muslim Brotherhood Wants," *New York Times*, February 9, 2011.

113. Said Hijazi and Bassam Ramadan, "Al-Aman Al-Qawmi Had Al-Ahmar." http://goo.gl/4Ira2.

114. Mohammad Ismail and Mahmoud Hijaj, "Badie: Al-Khilafa Al-Rashida Wa Ihya Dawla-Tul-Islam Wal-Shari'a Hadaf Al-Ikhwan." http://www.youm7.com/News.asp?NewsID=565958.

115. Subhi Abdulsalam, "Al-Ikhwan Tataraja' 'Ani-L-Da'wa Li-L-Khilafa." http://goo.gl/xu809.

4. CALIPHATE AS LIBERATION: HIZB UT-TAHRIR—THE PARTY OF LIBERATION IN THE POST-COLONIAL ERA

1. Taqiudeen al-Nabahani, *Al-Nitham Al-Iqtisadi Fi al-Islam* (Beirut: Dar al-Umma, 1990).

2. Eugene L. Rogan and Avi Shlaim, *The War for Palestine: Rewriting the History of 1948*, Cambridge Middle East studies—15 (Cambridge: Cambridge University Press, 2001), p. 81.

3. A. I. Dawisha, *Arab Nationalism in the Twentieth Century: From Triumph to Despair* (Princeton: Princeton University Press, 2003), p. 3.

4. Ilan Pappé, *Britain and the Arab-Israeli Conflict 1948–51* (Basingstoke: Macmillan, in association with St Antony's College, Oxford, 1988), p. ix.

5. Ibid., p. 11.

6. Auni al-Ubaidi, *Hizb ut-Tahrir al-Islami* (Amman: Dar al-liwa li-l-Sahafa wa-l-Nashr, 1993), p. 15.

7. Ibrahim al-Nabahani, "Interview with Ibrahim al-Nabahani." khilafah.dk/audiodate/20091124_ibrahim_sheikh_taqqiuddinnabahani.asx.

8. Sheikh Taleb Awadallah, *The Beloveds of Allah—Emergence of Light from Al-Aqsa Mosque—Launch of Hizb ut-Tahrir's March* (2006), p. 83. (Electronic version).

9. Hizb ut-Tahrir, "Bayan min Hizb ut-Tahrir al-Muqaddam li-l-Hukuma al-'Ordaniyya 1/6/1953," (1953).

10. Suha Taji-Farouki, *A Fundamental Quest: Hizb al-Tahrir and the Search for the Islamic Caliphate* (London: Grey Seal, 1996), p. 6.

11. Ibid., p. 9.

12. al-Ubaidi (1993), p. 21.

13. Uriel Dann, *King Hussein and the Challenge of Arab Radicalism: Jordan, 1955–1967* (New York: Oxford University Press/Moshe Dayan Center for Middle Eastern and African Studies, 1989), p. 17.

14. Lucy Williamson, "Stadium crowd pushed for Islamist Dream," *BBC News Website*, August 12, 2007. http://news.bbc.co.uk/1/hi/world/south_asia/6943070.stm.

15. Emmanuel Karagiannis, *Political Islam in Central Asia* (London: Routledge, 2009), p. 56.

16. Husain Haqqani, "Understanding HT ideology," in Zeyno Baran (ed.) *The Challenge of Hizb ut-Tahrir* (Ankara: Nixon Center, 2004), p. 34.

17. Muhiddin Kabiri, "HT and the Islamic Revival Party of Tajikistan," in Baran (2004), p. 77.

18. Sadek Hamid, "Islamic Political Radicalism in Britain: The Case of Hizb ut-Tahrir," in Tahir Abbas (ed.), *Islamic Political Radicalism: A European Perspective* (Edinburgh: Edinburgh University Press, 2007), p. 157.

19. Jean-Francois Mayer, "Hizb ut-Tahrir—The Next Al-Qaida, Really?," *PSIO Occasional Paper* (2004), p. 11.

20. Ibid., p. 24.

21. Emmanuel Karagiannis, "Hizb ut-Tahrir al-Islami: Evaluating the Threat Posed by a Radical Islamic Group That Remains Nonviolent," *Terrorism and Political Violence*, 18 (2), 2006, p. 316.

22. John Horton, "Hizb ut-Tahrir: Nihilism or Realism," *Journal of Middle Eastern Geopolitics*, 2 (3), 2006, p. 80.

23. Karagiannis (2009), p. 104.

24. al-Ubaidi (1993), p. 32.

25. Taji-Farouki (1996), p. x.

26. Awadallah (2006), p. 212.

27. Ibid., p. 22.

28. al-Ubaidi (1993), p. 46.

29. Ibid., p. 47.

30. al-Nabahani, "Interview with Ibrahim al-Nabahani," khilafah.dk/audio-date/20091124_ibrahim_sheikh_taqqiuddinnabahani.asx.

31. al-Ubaidi (1993), p. 43.

32. A graduate of al-Azhar whose father was an adherent of the Qadari Sufi order, he participated in collecting funds for the Libyan resistance as well as serving in the Ottoman forces during the First World War. He also played a role in the Syrian revolt against the French and took up arms against the

British in Palestine until he was killed in 1935. He remains an inspirational figure for Islamic and Palestinian resistance movements.

33. al-Nabahani, "Interview with Ibrahim al-Nabahani," khilafah.dk/audio-date/20091124_ibrahim_sheikh_taqqiuddinnabahani.asx.
34. Hizb ut-Tahrir, *al-Takattul-al Hizbi* (1953/c), p. 30.
35. al-Ubaidi (1993), p. 28.
36. International Crisis Group, "Radical Islam in Central Asia: Responding to Hizb ut-Tahrir," in *Asia Report* (Brussels: International Crisis Group, 2003), p. 3.
37. Karagiannis (2006), p. 316.
38. Hassan al-Banna, *Muthakarat Al-Da'wa Wa-L-Da'iyya* (Beirut: Dar al-Shihab, 1966), p. 169.
39. Richard Paul Mitchell, *The Society of the Muslim Brothers*, Middle Eastern Monographs—9 (Oxford: Oxford University Press, 1969), p. 189.
40. Taji-Farouki (1996), p. 192.
41. al-Ubaidi (1993), p. 17.
42. Christina Phelps Harris, *Nationalism and Revolution in Egypt* (The Hague: Mouton & Co., 1964), p. 139.
43. Hizb ut-Tahrir (1953), p. 24.
44. Hizb ut-Tahrir, *The Methodology of Hizb-ut-Tahrir for Change* (London: Al-Khilafah Publications, 1999), p. 14.
45. al-Nabahani, "Interview with Ibrahim al-Nabahani," khilafah.dk/audio-date/20091124_ibrahim_sheikh_taqqiuddinnabahani.asx.
46. Awadallah (2006), p. 67.
47. al-Ubaidi (1993), p. 10.
48. Ibid., pp. 16–17.
49. Awadallah (2006), p. 68.
50. Ibid., pp. 37–8.
51. al-Ubaidi (1993), p. 83.
52. Amnon Cohen, *Political Parties in the West Bank Under the Jordanian Regime 1949–1967* (London: Cornell University Press, 1982), p. 215.
53. Taji-Farouki (1996), p. 9.
54. Awadallah (2006), pp. 40–4.
55. Dann (1989), p. 170.
56. Awadallah (2006), p. 107.
57. *al-Jazeera*, "al-Islamiyun—Hizb ut-Tahrir," (Qatar, 2009).
58. Cohen (1982), p. 224.
59. Dann (1989), p. 17.
60. Awadallah (2006), p. 59.
61. Ibid., p. 101.
62. Yusuf al-Sabaateen, "Muthakaraat Yusuf al-Sabateen," http://www.alokab.com/forums/index.php?showtopic=23784&st=20.

63. Roger Owen, *Power and Politics in the Making of the Modern Middle East* (London: Routledge, 2000), p. 69.

64. Awadallah (2006), p. 61.

65. Ibid., p. 128.

66. Ricky-Dale Calhoun, "The Musketeer's Cloak: Strategic Deception During The Suez Crisis of 1956," *Studies in Intelligence*, 51 (2), 2007.

67. Miles Copeland, *The Game Player: Confessions of the CIA's Original Political Operative* (London: Aurum, 1989), pp. 161, 167, 181.

68. Hizb ut-Tahrir, *Nitham al-Islam* (1953/b), pp. 71–2.

69. Hizb ut-Tahrir, "Kitab maftuh min Hizb ut-Tahrir ila-l-Malik Hussein," (1969).

70. Taji-Farouki (1996), p. 27.

71. al-Nabahani, "Interview with Ibrahim al-Nabahani," khilafah.dk/audio-date/20091124_ibrahim_sheikh_taqqiuddinnabahani.asx.

72. Hizb ut-Tahrir, "Bayan min Hizb ut-Tahrir," (1982).

73. Hizb ut-Tahrir, *Hatmiyya Sira' al-haDarat* (2002).

74. Hizb ut-Tahrir Britain, "The Global Financial Crisis—The Self Destruction of Global Capitalism and an Introduction to the Alternative Islamic Economic Model," (2009); Ata' bin Khalil Abu al-Rashta, *Economic Crisis: Their Viewpoint and theRreality from the Viewpoint of Islam* (2009).

75. Hizb ut-Tahrir Denmark, "The Environmental Problem—Its Causes & Islam's Solution," (2009).

76. Hizb ut-Tahrir, *Mafahim Hizb ut-Tahrir* (1953/a), p. 60.

77. Hizb ut-Tahrir, a*l-Takattul-al Hizbi* (1953/c), pp. 3–6.

78. Hizb ut-Tahrir, *Nitham al-Islam* (1953/b), pp. 4–5.

79. Hizb ut-Tahrir (1953/a), p. 3.

80. Hizb ut-Tahrir, "al-Dawla al-Islamiyya," (1995), p. 171.

81. Hizb ut-Tahrir (1997), pp. 178–82.

82. Abdul Qadeem al-Zalloom, *Kayfa Hudimat al-Khilafah* (Beirut: Dar al-Umma, 1997), p. 12.

83. Hizb ut-Tahrir (1953/a), pp. 11–2.

84. Hizb ut-Tahrir, "Bayan min Hizb ut-Tahrir al-Muqaddam li-l-Hukuma al-'Ordaniyya 1/6/1953," (1953). [Leaflet].

85. Hizb ut-Tahrir (1953/a), p. 80.

86. Hizb ut-Tahrir (1953/c), p. 19.

87. Hizb ut-Tahrir (1953/a), p. 65.

88. Hizb ut-Tahrir (1954), p. 4.

89. Hizb ut-Tahrir (1953/c), p. 15.

90. al-Zalloom (1996).

91. Hizb ut-Tahrir (1995). [Leaflet].

92. al-Zalloom (1996), pp. 250, 54.

93. Hizb ut-Tahrir (1953). [Leaflet].
94. al-Zalloom (1996), pp. 33–4, 52.
95. Hizb ut-Tahrir (1954), p. 4.
96. Hizb ut-Tahrir, *Muqadimma al-Dustor al-Qism al-Awwal* (Beirut: Dar al-Umma, 2009), p. 109.
97. Muhammad Asad, *The Principles of State and Government in Islam* (Berkeley: University of California Press, 1961), p. 44.
98. Hizb ut-Tahrir (2009).
99. Hizb ut-Tahrir, *Ajhizatu Dawla al-Khilafah* (Beirut: Dar al-Umma, 2005).
100. Hizb ut-Tahrir (1953/a).
101. Hizb ut-Tahrir (2009), pp. 5–6.
102. Hizb ut-Tahrir, "Jawab Su'al 21–1–1970," (1970/b). [Leaflet].
103. Hizb ut-Tahrir (1953/a), p. 51.
104. Cohen (1982), p. 211.
105. Hizb ut-Tahrir (1953/c), p. 27.
106. Hizb ut-Tahrir (1954), p. 4.
107. Ibid., p. 15.
108. Hizb ut-Tahrir (1953). [Leaflet].
109. Hizb ut-Tahrir (1962).
110. Hizb ut-Tahrir (1994), p. 79.
111. Hizb ut-Tahrir (1967/a).
112. Hizb ut-Tahrir (1967/b).
113. Hizb ut-Tahrir (1975).
114. Hizb ut-Tahrir (1978/a).
115. Hizb ut-Tahrir (1970/a).
116. Hizb ut-Tahrir (1979).
117. Hizb ut-Tahrir, "A Message from the Amir of Hizb ut-Tahrir" (2008).
118. Hizb ut-Tahrir (1970/b).
119. Hizb ut-Tahrir (1955).
120. Hizb ut-Tahrir (1964); Hizb ut-Tahrir (1970/c); Hizb ut-Tahrir (1971).
121. Hizb ut-Tahrir (1978/b).
122. Hizb ut-Tahrir Egypt, "al-Khilafah al-Islamiyya Hamiya bilad al-Muslimeen" (2000).
123. Ilene R. Prusher, "Palestinian group sounds like Al Qaeda but forgoes violence," *The Christian Science Monitor*, http://www.csmonitor.com/World/Middle-East/2008/0122/p01s03-wome.html.
124. Hizb ut-Tahrir Indonesia, "Bi Iqamat Al-Khilafah Nunqith Anfusina Wa Nunqith Al-'Alam," (2004).
125. Hizb ut-Tahrir, "Al-Siyasa wal-Siyasa al-Dowliyya," (1974).
126. Patrick Goodenough, "OIC Fulfills Function of caliphate, Embodies 'Islamic SoliDarity,' Says OIC Chief Monday, May 10, 2010," http://www.cnsnews.com/news/article/65537.

127. Hizb ut-Tahrir (1969).

128. Hizb ut-Tahrir (2008).

129. Hizb ut-Tahrir Pakistan, "Declaration to the People of Power," http://
www.hizb-pakistan.com/home/prs/press-note-american-agent-rulers-fai-
led-to-stop-hizb-ut-tahrir.

130. Declan Walsh, "Pakistan Army Officer Held over Suspected Hizb Ut-
Tahrir Links," *The Guardian*, June 21, 2011.

131. Takee100, "Taqrir Al-Ikhbari Al-Suriya 'an Hizb Ut-Tahrir 28–3–2011,"
http://www.youtube.com/watch?v=_y3CNtWnIUw.

5. INSPIRATION FROM THE PAST: OSAMA BIN LADEN AND AL-QAEDA—THE DISCOURSE OF RESISTANCE

1. Peter L. Bergen, *The Osama bin Laden I Know: An Oral History of al Qaeda's Leader* (New York: Free Press, 2006), p. 65.

2. December 4, 1982, speaking from within the defendants' holding cage in
an Egyptian court as part of the series of trials held after the assassination
of Egyptian President Anwar Sadat.

3. R. V. Pillai and Mahendra Kumar, "The Political and Legal Status of Kuwait,"
International & Comparative Law Quarterly, 11, 1962.

4. George Bush Sr., "Toward a New World Order—9/11/1990," http://www.
sweetliberty.org/issues/war/bushsr.htm.

5. Anton La Guardia, "Fanatics around the world dream of the caliph's return,"
Daily Telegraph, August 8, 2005.

6. George Bush, "Address to joint session of congress—20/9/2001," http://
www.whitehouse.gov/news/releases/2001/09/20010920–8.html.

7. George Bush, "Remembering 9/11–9/9/2006." http://www.whitehouse.
gov/news/releases/2006/09/20060909.html.

8. Lisa Miller and Matthew Phillips, "Caliwho?," *Newsweek*, October 12, 2006.

9. Dick Cheney, "Interview with Tim Russert—10/9/2006." http://www.whi-
tehouse.gov/news/releases/2006/09/20060910.html.

10. Peter Fedynsky, "Rumsfeld Says Military Effort Alone Will Not Bring Success in Iraq—11/12/2006," Voice of America. http://www.voanews.com.

11. Charles Clarke, "Lecture at the Heritage Foundation—Published October
21, 2005." http://www.heritage.org/Research/Lecture/Contesting-the-
Threat-of-Terrorism.

12. Osama bin Laden, "Address on 2/7/2006." http://www.memri.org.

13. Bruce O. Riedel, *The Search for al-Qaeda: Its Leadership, Ideology, and Future*
(Washington, D.C.: Brookings Institution Press, 2008).

14. Brassey's (Firm), *Imperial Hubris: Why the West is Losing the War on Terror*
(Washington, DC: Brassey's, 2004), p. 128.

15. Michael Scheuer, *Through Our Enemies' Eyes: Osama bin Laden, Radical Islam, and the Future of America*, Revised ed. (Washington, DC: Potomac Books, Inc., 2006), pp. 46–68.

16. Mohammad-Mahmoud Ould Mohamedou, *Understanding Al Qaeda: The Transformation of War* (London: Pluto, 2006), pp. 45–8.

17. Gene W. Heck, *When Worlds Collide: Exploring the Ideological and Political Foundations of the Clash of Civilization* (Lanham: Rowman & Littlefield, 2007).

18. Lawrence Wright, *The Looming Tower: Al-Qaeda and the Road to 9/11* (New York: Knopf, 2006).

19. Riedel (2008), p. 121.

20. Devin R. Springer, James L. Regens, and David N. Edger, *Islamic Radicalism and Global Jihad* (Washington, DC: Georgetown University Press, 2009), pp. 2, 73.

21. Andrew Hammond, "Islamic Caliphate a Dream, Not Reality—13/12/2006," *Reuters*, http://www.alertnet.org/thenews/newsdesk/L04275477.htm.

22. Robert Fisk, "Why we reject the West," *The Independent*, July 10, 1996.

23. Robert Fisk, "Anti-Soviet warrior puts his army on the road to peace," *The Independent*, December 6, 1993.

24. Aymen al-Zawahiri, "Knights under the Prophets Banner." http://www.aaa3.net/vb/showthread.php?t=1191.

25. Abdullah Azzam, "Defence of Muslim Lands." http://www.religioscope.com/info/doc/jihad/azzam_defence_1_table.htm.

26. Abdus-Salam Faraj, *Jihad: The Absent Obligation* (Birmingham: Maktabah Al Ansaar, 2000), p. 24.

27. Ibid., p. 48.

28. Abdel Bari Atwan, *The Secret History of al-Qa'ida* (London: Saqi, 2006), p. 74.

29. Bergen (2006), p. 65.

30. Richard Bonney, *Jihad: From Qu'ran to Bin Laden* (Basingstoke: Palgrave Macmillan, 2004), p. 158.

31. "Memoranda from Arab Bureau," in *Memoranda IOR/L/PS/18/B221–266* (London: India Office, British Library, 1918), p. 6.

32. Bergen (2006), p. 65.

33. Aymen al-Zawahiri, "Knights under the Prophets Banner." http://www.aaa3.net/vb/showthread.php?t=1191.

34. Osama bin Laden and Bruce B. Lawrence, "Audio Message from Bin Laden to Deobandi Conference April 2001," in *Messages to the World: The Statements of Osama bin Laden* (London & New York: Verso, 2005), pp. 95–9.

35. Tayseer Alouni, "Interview with Osama bin Laden, October 2001." http://archives.cnn.com/2002/WORLD/asiapcf/south/02/05/binladen.transcript.

36. Faraj (2000), p. 20.

37. William Cran, "Jihad—The Man and Ideas Behind Al-Qaeda," (More 4, 2006).

38. Mālik ibn Anas, *al-Muwatta*, Book 45, Number 45.5.18.

39. Robert G. Kaiser and David Ottoway, "Oil for Security Fueled Close Ties," *Washington Post*, February 11, 2002.

40. Osama bin Laden, "Speech on the festival of sacrifice 4/2/2003—document 476." http://www.memri.org.

41. Osana bin Laden, "Letter from Bin Laden to Chief Mufti Bin Baz December 1994," in Laden and Lawrence (2005), pp. 4–14.

42. Osama bin Laden, "New powder keg in the Middle East," *Nida ul Islam*, November 1996.

43. Osama bin Laden, "Message from Bin Laden to the Scholars of the Umma, undated," in Laden and Lawrence (2005), pp. 15–19.

44. Abdel Bari Atwan, "Interview with Bin Laden—Explosions in Riyadh," *Al-Quds Al-Arabi*, November 16, 1996.

45. Osama bin Laden, "Open Letter to King Fahd on the occasion of the recent cabinet reshuffle—July 1995." http://www.answers.com/topic/open-letter-to-king-fahd-from-bin-laden.

46. Eleventh century Andalusia-based Islamic scholar from the literalist tradition.

47. Fourteenth century scholar from the Hanbali tradition. Particularly well known for his position against the Mongols used as inspiration for contemporary movements.

48. Fourteenth century scholar from the *Shafi'i* tradition who was also a student of ibn Taymiyya.

49. Osama bin Laden, "Open Letter to King Fahd on the occasion of the recent cabinet reshuffle—July 1995." http://www.answers.com/topic/open-letter-to-king-fahd-from-bin-laden.

50. Ibid.

51. Ibid.

52. Mamoun Fandy, *Saudi Arabia and the Politics of Dissent* (New York: St. Martin's Press, 1999), pp. 192–3.

53. Osama bin Laden, "Declaration of Jihad against the American occupying the land of the two Holy Places." http://www.pbs.org/newshour/terrorism/international/fatwa_1996.html.

54. Osama bin Laden, "New powder keg in the Middle East," *Nida ul Islam*, November 1996.

55. Osama bin Laden, "Speech broadcast on Al-Jazeera 16/12/2004," (2004).

56. Osama bin Laden, "Declaration of Jihad against the American occupying the land of the two Holy Places." http://www.pbs.org/newshour/terrorism/international/fatwa_1996.html.

57. Ibid.
58. Ibid.
59. Osama bin Laden, "Bin Laden interview with Peter Arnett March 1997," in Laden and Lawrence (2005), pp. 44–57.
60. Osama bin Laden, "Declaration of Jihad against the American occupying the land of the two Holy Places." http://www.pbs.org/newshour/terrorism/international/fatwa_1996.html.
61. Fisk (1996).
62. Osama bin Laden, "Declaration of Jihad against the American occupying the land of the two Holy Places." http://www.pbs.org/newshour/terrorism/international/fatwa_1996.html.
63. World Islamic Front, "Text of the Announcement of the World Islamic Front," *Al-Quds Al-Arabi*, February 23, 1998.
64. Muntasir Zayyat, *The Road to al-Qaeda: The Story of Bin Laden's Right-hand Man*, Critical studies on Islam (London: Pluto Press, 2004), p. 47.
65. Ibid., pp. 64–72.
66. Fawaz A. Gerges, *The Far Enemy: Why Jihad Went Global* (New York: Cambridge University Press, 2005), pp. 122–3.
67. Aymen al-Zawahiri, "Knights under the Prophets Banner." http://www.aaa3.net/vb/showthread.php?t=1191.
68. Bergen (2006), p. 110.
69. FBIS, "*Compilation of Usama Bin Ladin Statements 1994—January 2004.*"
70. Jamal Ismael, "Interview with Bin Laden aired on Al-Jazeera—10/6/1999," *al-Jazeera*. http://www.robertfisk.com/osama_interview_qatari_press_arabic.htm.
71. John Millar, "Interview with Bin Laden May 1998," *PBS*. http://www.pbs.org/wgbh/pages/frontline/shows/binladen/who/interview.html.
72. Atwan (2006), p. 223.
73. Faisal Devji, *Landscapes of the Jihad: Militancy, Morality, Modernity*, Crises in World Politics (London: C. Hurst & Co., 2005), p. 162.
74. Osama bin Laden, "Bin Laden interview with Peter Arnett March 1997," in Laden & Lawrence (2005), pp. 44–57.
75. John Millar, "Interview with Bin Laden May 1998," *PBS*. http://www.pbs.org/wgbh/pages/frontline/shows/binladen/who/interview.html.
76. Geoffrey Alderman, "Can Israeli actions in Gaza be justified on the basis of Jewish scripture?," *The Guardian*, January 12, 2009.
77. Osama bin Laden, "Speech broadcast on Al-Jazeera 21/10/2001," (2001).
78. Tayseer Alouni, "Interview with Osama bin Laden, October 2001." http://archives.cnn.com/2002/WORLD/asiapcf/south/02/05/binladen.transcript.
79. Abu Abdullah Al-Qurtubi, *Al-Jami' li-Ahkam Al-Qur'an* (Beirut: Dar Al-Kotob Al-ilmiya), vol. 5, p. 73.

80. Tayseer Alouni, "Interview with Osama bin Laden, October 2001." http:// archives.cnn.com/2002/WORLD/asiapcf/south/02/05/binladen.transcript.

81. Osama bin Laden, "Bin Laden interview with Peter Arnett March 1997," in Laden and Lawrebce (2005), pp. 44–57.

82. Rahimullah Yusufzai, "Conversation with terror," *Time Magazine*, November 1, 1999.

83. Aymen al-Zawahiri, "Video broadcast on Al-Jazeera 2/9/2005," (2005).

84. David Blankenhorn, "Letter to the American People November 2002," in *The Islam/West Debate: Documents from a Global Debate on Terrorism, U.S. Policy, and the Middle East* (Lanham: Rowman & Littlefield, 2005), pp. 117–25.

85. Ibid.

86. Osama bin Laden, "Bin Laden Audio November 12 2002," in Laden and Lawrence (2005), pp. 173–5.

87. Aymen al-Zawahiri, "Video broadcast on Al-Jazeera 2/9/2005," (2005).

88. Michael Scheuer, "Al-Qaeda Doctrine for International Political Warfare," *Terrorism Focus*, 3 (32), 2006.

89. ibn Rushd Mohammad bin Ahmed, *Bidayat al-Mujtahid wa Nihaya al-Muqtasid* (Cairo: al-Maktaba al-Tawqifiyya, undated), vol. 1, p. 673.

90. Osama bin Laden, "Fax 'to our brothers in Pakistan' 24/9/2001." http:// www.jihadunspun.com.

91. Ibid.

92. Osama bin Laden, "Address on 2/7/2006." http://www.memri.org.

93. Aymen al-Zawahiri, "Speech marking 4 year anniversary of Iraq war 5/7/2007." http://www.switch3.castup.net/cunet/gm.asp?chipmediaID= 822400&ak=null.

94. Ibid.

95. WorldPublicOpinion.org, "Muslim Public Opinion on US Policy, attacks on civilians and al-Qaeda" (Maryland: The Center for International and Security Studies at Maryland, 2007).

96. Osama bin Laden, "Audio broadcast on Al-Jazeera 3/6/2009," (2009).

97. Osama bin Laden, "Audio broadcast on Al-Jazeera 24/1/2010," (2010).

98. FBIS, "Compilation of Usama Bin Ladin Statements 1994—January 2004."

99. Mohamedou (2006), p. 10

100. Geoffrey Robertson, "Why It's Absurd to Claim That Justice Has Been Done." http://www.independent.co.uk/opinion/commentators/geoffrey-robertson-why-its-absurd-to-claim-that-justice-has-been-done-2278041.html.

6. BEYOND THE MIDDLE EAST: THE SUB-CONTINENT, THE DIASPORA, AND THE NEW MUSLIMS

1. Umar Ibrahim Vadillo, *The Esoteric Deviation in Islam* (Cape Town: Madinah Press, 2003), p. 57.

2. WorldPublicOpinion.org, "Muslim Public Opinion on US Policy, Attacks on Civilians and al-Qaeda" (Maryland: The Center for International and Security Studies at Maryland, 2007).

3. I discuss this in more detail, among other related issues, in the following published article: Reza Pankhurst, "Muslim Contestations over Religion and the State in the Middle East," *Political Theology*, 11 (6), 2010, pp. 820–35.

4. Dalia Mogahed, "Special Report: Muslim World—Islam and Democracy," (Washington D.C.: The Gallup Center for Muslim Studies, 2006).

5. Pew Forum on Religion and Public Life, "Tolerance and Tension: Islam and Christianity in Sub-Saharan Africa," (Washington, 2010).

6. Aymen al-Zawahiri, "Speech marking 4 year anniversary of Iraq war 5/7/2007." http://www.switch3.castup.net/cunet/gm.asp? chipmediaID= 822400&ak=null.

7. Elizabeth Lambourn, "Khutba and Muslim Networks in the Indian Ocean—Timurid and Ottoman Engagements," in Kenneth Hall (ed.), *The Growth of Non-Western Cities: Primary and Secondary Urban Networking, C. 900–1900* (Lanham: Rowman & Littlefield Publishing Group, in press), p. 1.

8. Shagufta Ahmad, "Dr.Israr Ahmad's Political Thought and Activities" (Masters, Mc Gill University, 1993), p. 32.

9. Seyyed Vali Reza Nasr, *The Vanguard of the Islamic Revolution: The Jama'at-i-Islami of Pakistan* (Los Angeles: University of California Press, 1994), p. 6.

10. Ibid., p. 8.

11. Ibid., p. 38.

12. Bruce B. Lawrence, *Shattering the Myth: Islam Beyond Violence*, Princeton Studies in Muslim Politics (Princeton: Princeton University Press, 1998), p. 60.

13. Tanzeem e Islami, "Tanzeem e Islami." http://www.tanzeem.org.

14. Israr Ahmad, *The Call of Tanzeem-e-Islami* (Lahore: Markazi Anjuman Khuddam-ul-Qur'an, 1994), p. 6.

15. Ahmad (1993), p. 42.

16. Ibid., p. 57.

17. Israr Ahmad, *Islamic Renaissance—The Real Task Ahead* (Lahore: Markazi Anjuman Khuddam-ul-Qur'an, 1967), pp. 3–5.

18. Ibid., p. 7.

19. Ibid., pp. 8–9.

20. Ahmad (1994), p. 8.

21. Ahmad (1967), p. 12.

22. Ibid., p. 14.

23. Israr Ahmad, *Bai'yah—The Basis for Organization of a Revivalist Party in Islam* (Lahore: Markazi Anjuman Khuddam-ul-Qur'an, 1998), p. 40.

24. Nasr (1994), p. 12.

25. Israr Ahmad, *Rise and Decline of the Muslim Umma* (Lahore: Markazi Anjuman Khuddam-ul-Qur'an, 2002), p. 23.

26. Israr Ahmad, *Three Point Action Agenda for the Muslim Umma* (Lahore: Markazi Anjuman Khuddam-ul-Qur'an, 2001), pp. 38–41.

27. Lawrence (1998), p. 61.

28. Ahmad (1993), p. 3.

29. Ibid., p. 127.

30. Jamal Harwood, July 26 2010.

31. Israr Ahmad, *Khilafah in Pakistan—What, Why and How?* (Lahore: Markazi Anjuman Khuddam-ul-Qur'an, 2001/b), pp. 3–5.

32. Israr Ahmad, "Dr Israr's view on Hizb ut Tahrir (An effort to unite Hizb ut Tahrir and Tanzeem e Islami)," http://www.youtube.com/watch?v=OzTkX-Bjhbg&feature=player_embedded.

33. Tanzeem e Islami, "Tanzeem e Islami." http://www.tanzeem.org.

34. Ibid.

35. Israr Ahmad, *The Constitutional and Legislative Framework of the System of Khilafah in Modern Times* (Lahore: Markazi Anjuman Khuddam-ul-Qur'an, 2001/a), p. 7.

36. Ibid., p. 12.

37. Israr Ahmad, "Dr Israr's view on Hizb ut Tahrir (An effort to unite Hizb ut Tahrir and Tanzeem e Islami)." http://www.youtube.com/watch?v=OzTkX-Bjhbg&feature=player_embedded.

38. Ahmad (1994), p. 19.

39. Ahmad (1998), p. 38.

40. al-Mustaqbal, "I'tiqal al-Islami al-Urdani "Abu Humam" fi Britaaniyya," February 16, 2006.

41. Shaykh Abu Ayub al Barqawi, *A Return to the System of Khilafah*, undated, p. 3. (Accessed online).

42. Unifiedumma.com, "About Us." http://www.unifiedUmma.com/aboutus.htm.

43. Abul Husain 'Asakir-ud-Din Muslim, *Sahih Muslim* (Beirut: Dar al-fikr, 1998), narration 1847.

44. See for example Ahmad bin Ali bin Hajr al-Askalani, *Fath al-Bari* (Riyadh: Dar ibn-Hazm, 1998), narration 7084.

45. Alternatively known as Wahabism, the core concept of modern Salafi

thought is to encourage a return to the sources of Islam and to purify the beliefs and practices from innovative practices.

46. Jamaat-ul-Muslimeen, "Baiyah of an Ameer without any Government." http://www.aljamaat.org/books/jamaatpamphlets/english/baiyah%20 of%20an%20Ameer%20without%20a%20Government/index.html.

47. Jamaat-ul-Muslimeen, "The Distinctive Features of Jamaat-ul-Muslimeen," http://www.aljamaat.org/jamaat-ul-muslimeen/features.htm.

48. 'Asakir-ud-Din Muslim (1998), narration 1848.

49. Shaykh Abu Ayub al Barqawi, *A Return to the System of Khilafah*, undated, p. 6.

50. Jamaat-ul-Muslimeen, "The Invitation To Haq." http://www.aljamaat.org/ jamaat-ul-muslimeen/invitationtohaq/index.html.

51. Unifiedumma.com, "A Call to Unify the Muslims upon the Islamic Method." http://www.unifiedumma.com/sections/articles/data/ACallToUnifyThe-MuslimUmma.htm.

52. Ibid.

53. Shaykh Abu Ayub al Barqawi, *A Return to the System of Khilafah* (undated), p. 6.

54. More famously known as Abul Walid al-Masri, a prominent jihadi strategist, blogger and author who is currently linked to the Taliban, and had a close relationship and frequent communication with several members of al-Qaida, though he asserts to have never been a member himself.

55. Mustafa Hamed, *Saleeb Fi Sama'i Kandahar* (undated), p. 41.

56. Werner Schiffauer, "From Exile to Diaspora: The Development of Transnational Islam in Europe," in 'Az iz Azmah and Effie Fokas (eds.), *Islam in Europe: Diversity, Identity and Influence* (Cambridge: Cambridge University Press, 2007), p. 73.

57. Joan Bakewell, "The Believers who Despise our Ways," *New Statesman*, May 29, 2000.

58. Schiffauer (2007).

59. Abu Abdullah ibn Yousaf, "The World without the Shahada," (undated). http://www.unifiedumma.com/sections/books/books/The_World_Without_The_Shahadah.pdf.

60. Zayd Mustansir, "Unveiling of the British Establishment's Hatred of Islam." http://www.unifiedumma.com/sections/articles/data/Unveiling.html.

61. Barqawi (undated).

62. Jama'ah-tul-Muslimeen, "Does the Baya'ah of Obedience to the Imaam Change the Life of a Muslim?" (undated).

63. Jama'ah-tul-Muslimeen, "Possessing Large Numbers, Agreement with the Majority and Consent of the Masses is Not the Scale to Judge the Truth" (undated).

64. Jama'ah-tul-Muslimeen, "Allah Did Not Give Us Permission to Be Leaderless and Divided At Any Time" (undated).

65. Jama'ah-tul-Muslimeen, "Not Understanding The Shari'h Method Of Unity Is The Key To Failure And Misery" (undated).

66. Jama'ah-tul-Muslimeen, "A Challenge to the Muslim groups, Parties, Scholars and Students Concerning the Illegitimacy of the Division of the Muslim Umma" (undated).

67. BBC, "Second terror suspect wins bail." http://news.bbc.co.uk/1/hi/uk/7392879.stm; al-Mustaqbal, "I'tiqal al-Islami al-Urdani "Abu Humam" fi Britaniyya," February 16, 2006.

68. Jama'ah-tul-Muslimeen, "The Continuation of Imaarah in the Case of a Captive Imaam" (undated).

69. The Murabit Blog, "Biography of the Shaykh." http://murabitblog.wordpress.com/2010/02/13/biography-of-the-shaykh/.

70. Barney Henderson, "Radical Muslim leader has past in swinging London," *Daily Telegraph* February 20, 2010.

71. *al-Arabiyya*, "Muslims shun "worthless" paper money." http://www.alarabiya.net/articles/2010/02/20/100913.html.

72. Abdal Hasid Castineira, "Statement on the Shariah Currency and Legal Tender." http://www.muslimsofnorwich.org.uk/?p=901.

73. Nils Bubandt, "Sacred Money and Islamic Freedom in a Global Sufi Order," *Social Analysis*, 53 (1), 2009, p. 104.

74. "Now only two Western movements of radical protest claim to be "internationalist": the anti-globalization movement and the radical Islamists. To convert to Islam today is a way for a European rebel to find a cause; it has little to do with theology." Olivier Roy, "EuroIslam: The Jihad Within?," *National Interest*, Spring (2003), p. 70.

75. Robert Luongo, "Radical Muslim Leader has Bohemian Past." http://robertluongo.blogspot.com/2010/06/radical-muslim-leader-has-bohemian-past.html.

76. A Sufi Tariqa is a religious order, in which the head of the order is the guide for those who pledge allegiance to him as the head of the order, and is responsible for their spiritual development.

77. The Murabit Blog, "Biography of the Shaykh." http://murabitblog.wordpress.com/2010/02/13/biography-of-the-shaykh/.

78. Nils Bubandt, "Sacred Money and Islamic Freedom in a Global Sufi Order," *Social Analysis*, 53 (1), Spring 2009, p. 106.

79. The Murabit Blog, "Biography of the Shaykh." http://murabitblog.wordpress.com/2010/02/13/biography-of-the-shaykh/.

80. Abdalhaqq Bewley, "The Recovery of True Islamic Fiqh." http://web.archive.org/web/20080119022323/http://ourworld.compuserve.com/homepages/ABewley/saq.html.

81. Abdalqadir as-Sufi, *The Return of the Khalifate* (Cape Town: Madinah Press, 1996), p. 99.

82. Ibid., p. 21.

83. Ibid., p. 34.

84. Ibid., p. 49.

85. Abdalqadir as-Sufi, "The Dumb and the Blind." http://www.shaykhabdalqadir.com/content/articles/Art094_07062009.html.

86. Abdalqadir as-Sufi, *Technique of the Coup de Banque* (Palma de Mallorca: Kutubia Mayurqa, 2000), p. 87.

87. Vadillo (2003), p. 13.

88. Ibid., p. 749.

89. as-Sufi (1996), pp. 92–3.

90. Vadillo (2003), p. 19.

91. as-Sufi (2000), p. 53.

92. Ibid., p. 83.

93. AbdulQadir as-Sufi, *Sultaniyya* (Cape Town: Madinah Press, 2002), p. 118.

94. AbdulQadir as-Sufi, *The Muslim Prince* (Cape Town: Madinah Press, 2009), p. 37.

95. AbdulQadir as-Sufi, "The Last Phase Of Arab Shame." http://www.shaykhabdalqadir.com/content/articles/Art087_01012009.html.

96. AbdulQadir as-Sufi, "The Role of the Muslims of Britain." http://www.shaykhabdalqadir.com/content/articles/Art056_20022006.html.

97. AbdulQadir as-Sufi, "Democracy—The Terrible Truth." http://www.shaykhabdalqadir.com/content/articles/Art025_20112004.html.

98. Vadillo (2003), p. 732.

99. Ibid., p. 740.

100. Ibid., p. 542.

101. Vadillo, "Tijara—The Islamic Trade Bloc," in as-Sufi (2002), p. 80.

102. Vadillo (2003), pp. 66, 448.

103. Gibril F Haddad, "Have you eyes, Murabitun Brethren?" http://www.livingislam.org/o/hyem_e.html.

104. AbdalQadir as-Sufi, "The Last Phase Of Arab Shame." http://www.shaykhabdalqadir.com/content/articles/Art087_01012009.html.

105. AbdalQadir as-Sufi, "Launch of the Islamic World Currency." http://www.shaykhabdalqadir.com/tv/NewWorldIslamicCurrency.html.

106. AbdalQadir as-Sufi, "The Role of the Muslims of Britain." http://www.shaykhabdalqadir.com/content/articles/Art056_20022006.html.

107. AbdalQadir as-Sufi, "The Political Class in Crisis." http://www.shaykhabdalqadir.com/content/articles/Art110_31072010.html.

108. Zayd Mustansir, "The Only Legitimate Political System in Islam is Shari'ah Under One Leader." http://www.unifiedumma.com/sections/articles/data/TheOnlyLegitimatePoliticalSystem.html.

7. COMMON GOALS, DIVERGENT METHODOLOGIES

1. Abul Husain 'Asakir-ud-Din Muslim, *Sahih Muslim* (Beirut: Dar al-fikr, 1998), narration 2586.
2. Rudolph Peters, *Islam and Colonialism: The Doctrine of Jihad in Modern History*, Religion and Society—20 (The Hague: Mouton & Co., 1979), p. 152.
3. See for example Richard Paul Mitchell, *The Society of the Muslim Brothers*, Middle Eastern Monographs—9 (Oxford: University Press, 1969).
4. "The Muslim Brothers—Appease or Oppose?" *The Economist*, October 8, 2009.
5. Nathan J. Brown, "The irrelevance of the international Muslim Brotherhood," *Foreign Policy*. http://mideast.foreignpolicy.com/posts/2010/09/20/the_irrelevance_of_the_international_muslim_brotherhood_0.
6. These positions can also be linked to the principle in Islamic jurisprudence widely claimed in the contemporary era that every action is in origin lawful unless prohibited, something disputed by opponents such as Hizb ut-Tahrir, who believe this is a misunderstanding and instead follow the *Shafi'i* principle that every action requires an Islamic evidence.
7. BBC World Service, "Wide Dissatisfaction with Capitalism—Twenty Years after Fall of Berlin Wall" (PIPA, 2009).

8. THE END OF A HISTORY

1. Abdul Majid al-Zindani, "Sheikh Zindani in Yemen Calls for 'Khilafah Rashidah'." http://www.youtube.com/watch?v=pcBMJl0ESyY.
2. Yusuf al-Eid, "Sheikh Yusuf Al-Eid Yubashir Bi Auda Al-Khilafa Fi Suriya." http://www.youtube.com/watch?v=IEld6EZ_qfY.
3. Mohammad al-Arifi, "Sheikh Muhammad 'Arifi on the Arab Spring and Signs of Khilafah's Return." http://www.youtube.com/watch?v=qjaw-NA1Xno.
4. Ahmad bin Hanbal, *Musnad Al-Imam Ahmad Bin Hanbal* (Beirut: Muassisa al-Risala, 1999), vol. 30, p. 355, narration 18406.
5. Numerous polls and reports can be referred to including: WorldPublicOpinion.org, "Muslim Public Opinion on US Policy, Attacks on Civilians and al-Qaeda" (Maryland: The Center for International and Security Studies at Maryland, 2007); WorldPublicOpinion.org, "Defamation of Religion," (Maryland: The Center for International and Security Studies at Maryland, 2009); Pew Forum on Religion & Public Life, "Tolerance and Tension: Islam and Christianity in Sub-Saharan Africa," (Washington 2010). Dalia Mogahed, "Special Report: Muslim World—Islam and Democracy," (Washington, DC: The Gallup Center for Muslim Studies, 2006); John L. Esposito and Dalia Mogahed, *Who Speaks for Islam? What a Billion Muslims Really*

Think: Based on Gallup's World Poll—The Largest Study of its Kind (New York: Gallup Press, 2007).

6. Bruce K. Rutherford, "What do Egypt's Islamists Want? Moderate Islam and the Rise of Islamic Constitutionalism," *Middle East Journal*, 60 (4), 2006, pp. 730–1.

7. Yusuf al-Qaradawi, *Min Fiqh Al-Dawla Fi al-Islam* (Cairo: Dar al-Sharouq, 1997), p. 150.

8. See for example al-Sayyed Yasin, *al-Khilafa wal-Mu'asira* (Cairo: Tobgy Press, 1999).

9. Political prisoners, such as the some of the leading advocates of the Indian Khilafat movement, were imprisoned by the British Empire on the island of Malta during the early twentieth century.

BIBLIOGRAPHY

Archival References

India Office, British Library, London

"Dispatch 4657 Dated August 27,1923 from District Governer of Jerusalem-Jaffa to the Chief Secretary Titled Recognition of New caliph." In *The Caliphate Question IOR/L/PS/10/895/*. London: India Office, British Library, 1920.

"Extracts from the Pioneer Mail Dated March 14, 1924." In *The Caliphate Question: Deposition of Caliph Abdul Mejid by the Angora Assembly IOR/L/PS/10/1111*. London: India Office, British Library, 1924.

"Kabul's Despatch 54." In *The Caliphate Question: Deposition of Caliph Abdul Mejid by the Angora Assembly IOR/L/PS/10/1111*. London: India Office, British Library, 1924.

"Memoranda from Arab Bureau." In *Memoranda IOR/L/PS/18/B221–266*. London: India Office, British Library, 1918.

"Nejd Affairs—Extracts from Bombay Chronicles June 23, 1924." In *The Caliphate Question: Deposition of Caliph Abdul Mejid by the Angora Assembly IOR/L/PS/10/1111*. London: India Office, British Library, 1924.

"Public Letters from the Aga Khan." In *The Caliphate Question IOR/L/PS/10/895/*. London: India Office, British Library, 1920.

Foreign Office, National Archives, London

"Memorandum on Angora and the Caliphate, to High Commissioner Egypt Dated November 9, 1922." In *Egyptian Consulate General Correspondance 1915–1926 FO/141/587/2*. London: Foreign Office, National Archives, 1922.

"Note Regarding the Caliphate to High Commissioner Egypt, March 7 1924." In *Egyptian Consulate General Correspondance 1915–1926 FO/141/587/2*. London: Foreign Office, National Archives, 1924.

BIBLIOGRAPHY

"Syrian Consultate, Beyrout, August 1 1923 ". In *Egyptian Consulate General Correspondance 1915–1926 FO/141/587/2*. London: Foreign Office, National Archives, 1923.

Audio/Visual

al-Jazeera, "Al-Islamiyun—Hizb Ut-Tahrir," Qatar, 2009.
al-Zawahiri, Aymen, "Video Broadcast on Al-Jazeera 2/9/2005," 2005.
Bin Laden, Osama, "Speech Broadcast on Al-Jazeera 21/10/2001," 2001.
———, "Speech Broadcast on Al-Jazeera 16/12/2004," 2004.
———, "Audio Broadcast on Al-Jazeera 3/6/2009," 2009.
———, "Audio Broadcast on Al-Jazeera 24/1/2010," 2010.
Cran, William, "Jihad—The Man and Ideas Behind Al-Qaeda," More 4, 2006.
Dannatt, Richard, "Radio 4 Today Program May 17," 2010.

Books

'Amara, Mohammad (ed.), *Ma'raka Al-Islam Wa Usul Al-Hukm*, Cairo: Dar al-Sharook, 1925.
———, *Al-Islam Wa Usul Al-Hukm—Darasa Wa Watha'iq*, Beirut: Al-Mu'asasa al-'Arabiyya li-l-darasat wa-l-nashr, 1972.
———, *Ma'raka Al-Islam Wa Usul Al-Hukm*, Cairo: Dar al-Sharook, 1997.
'Ashur, Mohammad Al-Tahir ibn, *Naqd 'Ilmy Li Kitab Al-Islam Wa Usul Al-Hukm*, Cairo: Maktaba al-Salafiyya, 1925.
Abbas, Tahir, *Islamic Political Radicalism: A European Perspective*, Edinburgh: Edinburgh University Press, 2007.
AbdulHaleem, Mahmoud, *Al-Ikhwan Al-Muslimun—Ahdath Sana'at Al-Tarikh Part 1*, Alexandria: Dar al-Da'wa, 1981/a.
———, *Al-Ikhwan Al-Muslimun—Ahdath Sana'at Al-Tarikh Part 2*, Alexandria: Dar al-Da'wa, 1981/b.
Ahmad, Israr, *Islamic Renaissance—the Real Task Ahead*, Lahore: Markazi Anjuman Khuddam-ul-Qur'an, 1967.
———, *Bai'yah—the Basis for Organization of a Revivalist Party in Islam*, Lahore: Markazi Anjuman Khuddam-ul-Qur'an, 1998.
———, *The Call of Tanzeem-E-Islami*, Lahore: Markazi Anjuman Khuddam-ul-Qur'an, 1994.
———, *The Constitutional and Legislative Framework of the System of Khilafah in Modern Times*, Lahore: Markazi Anjuman Khuddam-ul-Qur'an, 2001/a.
———, *Khilafah in Pakistan—What, Why and How?* Lahore: Markazi Anjuman Khuddam-ul-Qur'an, 2001/b.
———, *Three Point Action Agenda for the Muslim Umma*, Lahore: Markazi Anjuman Khuddam-ul-Qur'an, 2001/c.
———, *Rise and Decline of the Muslim Umma*, Lahore: Markazi Anjuman Khuddam-ul-Qur'an, 2002.

Ahmed, Shabab and Yossef Rapoport (eds.), *Ibn Taymiyyah and His Times*, Oxford: Oxford University Press, 2010.

al-Askalani, Ahmad bin Ali bin Hajr, *Fath al-Bari*, Riyadh: dar ibn-Hazm, 1998.

al-Awadi, Hesham, *In Pursuit of Legitimacy: The Muslim Brothers and Mubarak 1982–2000*, Library of Modern Middle East Studies—46, London: Taurus Academic Studies, 2004.

al-Banna, Hassan, *Tarbiyya Al-Nasha*, 1927. (Electronic version accessed June 2008, available at www.hassanalbanna.org).

———, "Qadayatuna," 1949. (Electronic version accessed June 2008, available at http://www.daawa-info.net/books1.php?parts=132&au=%CD%D3% E4%20%C7%E1%C8%E4%C7).

———, *Muthakarat Al-Da'wa Wa-L-Da'iyya*, Beirut: Dar al-Shihab, 1966.

———, *Majmu'a al-Risa'il li-l-Imam al-Shahid Hassan Al-Banna*, Cairo: Dar al-tawzee', 1992.

———, *Fiqh Al-Waqi'*, Mansoora: Dar al-Kalima, 1999.

al-Bishry, Tarek, *Al-Harakat Al-Siyasiyya Fi Misr 1945–1952*, Cairo: al-hai'iyyat al-masriyya al-'aama li al-kitab, 1972.

al-Baghdadi, Abdul Qadir, *Usul Al-Deen*, Istanbul: Matba al-Dawla, 1928.

al-Dhahari, Ali bin Ahmad bin Said bin Hazm, *Al-Fasl Fi al-Malal Wa-l-Ahwa Wa-l-Nahl*, Cairo: Maktaba al-Khanji, 1994.

al-Egee, Abdul Rahman bin Ahmed, *Al-Mawaqif Fi 'Ilm Al-Kalam*, Beirut: 'Alim al-Kutub, 1988.

al-Faraa, Mohammad bin al-Hussain, *Al-Ahkam Al-Sultaniyya*, Beirut: dar al-kutub al-'ilmiyya, 1983.

al-Ghazali, Zainab, *Return of the Pharaoh* (trans. Mokrane Guezzou), Leicester: The Islamic Foundation, 1994.

al-Hilali, Muhammad Taqi-ud-deen, *Interpretation of the Meanings of the Noble Qur'an in the English Language*, Riyadh: Maktaba Dar-us-Salaam, 1997.

al-Hudaybi, Hasan, *Du'at La Qudat*. (Electronic version accessed June 2010, available at http://adel-ebooks.sheekh-3arb.info/library/Other/528.rar).

al-Juda'i, Abdul Allah bin Yusuf, *Tayseer 'Ilm Usul Al-Fiqh*, Beirut: Mu'assa al-Rayyan, 2006.

al-Jundi, Anwar, *Hasan Al-Banna*, Beirut: Dar al-Qa'a, 1978.

al-Juwaini, Abdul Malik bin Abdullah, *Al-Ghiyathi*, Beirut: Dar Al-Kotob Al-ilmiyah, 2003.

al-Juzayri, AbdulRahman, *Al-Fiqh 'Ala al-Mathahib Al-Arba'a*, Cairo: Al-Maktaba al-Tawfiqiyya, undated.

al-Mawardi, Abul Hasan Ali, *Al-Ahkam Al-Sultaniyya*, Beirut: Dar Al-Kotob Al-ilmia, undated.

al-Mutee'i, Mohammad Bakhit, *Haqiqa Al-Islam Wa Usul Al-Hukm*, Cairo: Al-Matba'a al-Salifiyya, 1925.

al-Nabahani, Taqiudeen, *Al-Nitham Al-Iqtisadi Fi al-Islam*, Beirut: Dar al-Umma, 1990.

al-Qaradawi, Yusuf, *Min Fiqh Al-Dawla Fi al-Islam*, Cairo: Dar al-Sharouq, 1997.

al-Qurtubi, Abu Abdullah, *Al-Jami' li-Ahkam Al-Qur'an*, Beirut: Dar Al-Kotob Al-ilmiya, 2000.

al-Rashta, Ata' bin Khalil Abu, *Economic Crisis—Their Viewpoint and the Reality from the Viewpoint of Islam*, 2009. (Printed and distributed in the UK by Hizb ut-Tahrir Britain).

al-Rayyis, Mohammad Diya' Al-Deen, *Al-Islam Wa-L-Khilafa Fi al-Asr Al-Hadith*, Cairo: Dar al-Turath, 1976.

al-Sabbagh, Mahmoud, *Haqiqa Al-Tanthim Al-Khas*, Cairo: Dar al-'Itisam, 1989.

al-Ubaidi, Auni, *Hizb Ut-Tahrir Al-Islami*, Amman: Dar al-liwa li-l-Sahafa wa-l-Nashr, 1993.

al-Waa'i, Taufiq Yusuf, *Al-Fikr Al-Siyasi Al-Mu'aser 'Ind Al-Ikhwan Al-Muslimin*, Kuwait: Maktaba al-Manar al-Islamiyya, 2001.

al-Zalloom, Abdul Qadeem, *Nitham Al-Hukm Fi al-Islam*, Beirut: Dar al-Umma, 1996.

———, *Kayfa Hudimat Al-Khilafah*, Beirut: Dar al-Umma, 1997.

Arnold, Sir Thomas W., *The Caliphate*, Delhi: Adam Publishers, 1992.

as-Sufi, AbdalQadir, *The Return of the Khalifate*, Cape Town: Madinah Press, 1996.

———, *Technique of the Coup De Banque*, Palma de Mallorca: Kutubia Mayurqa, 2000.

———, *Sultaniyya*, Cape Town: Madinah Press, 2002.

———, *The Muslim Prince*, Cape Town: Madinah Press, 2009.

Asad, Muhammad, *The Principles of State and Government in Islam*, Berkeley: University of California Press, 1961.

Atwan, Abdel Bari, *The Secret History of Al-Qa'ida*, London: Saqi, 2006.

Awadallah, Sheikh Taleb, *The Beloveds of Allah—Emergence of Light from Al-Aqsa Mosque—Launch of Hizb Ut-Tahrir's March*, 2006. (Accessed online January 2010, available at http://www.al-dawah.dk/boger/engelske/pdf/HTHistorie.pdf).

Aydin, Cemil, *The Politics of Anti-Westernism in Asia*, New York: Columbia University Press, 2007.

Ayubi, Nazih, *Political Islam: Religion and Politics and in the Arab World*, London: Routledge, 1991.

Azmah, 'Az iz and Effie Fokas (ed.), *Islam in Europe: Diversity, Identity and Influence*, Cambridge: Cambridge University Press, 2007.

Baran, Zeyno (ed.), *The Challenge of Hizb ut-Tahrir*, Ankara: Nixon Center, 2004.

BIBLIOGRAPHY

Barqawi, Shaykh Abu Ayub al, *A Return to the System of Khilafah*, undated. (Accessed online June 2010, available at http://www.unifiedummah.com/sections/books/books/The_Return_To_The_System_Of_Khilafah.pdf).

Bek, Abdul al-Ghani, *Al-Khilafa Wa Sulta Al-Umma*, Cairo: Dar al-Nahr, 1924.

Bergen, Peter L., *The Osama Bin Laden I Know: An Oral History of al Qaeda's Leader*, New York: Free Press, 2006.

Bin Hanbal, Ahmad, *Musnad Al-Imam Ahmad Bin Hanbal* Beirut: Muassisa al-Risala, 1999.

Bin Laden, Osama, Bruce B. Lawrence and James Howarth, *Messages to the World: The Statements of Osama Bin Laden*, London & New York: Verso, 2005.

Blankehorn, David, Abdou Filali-Ansary, Hassan I. Mneimneh and Alex Roberts, *The Islam/West Debate: Documents from a Global Debate on Terrorism, U.S. Policy, and the Middle East*, xi, Lanham, Md.: Rowman & Littlefield, 2005.

Bonney, Richard, *Jihad: From Qu'ran to Bin Laden*, Basingstoke: Palgrave Macmillan, 2004.

Brassey's (Firm), *Imperial Hubris: Why the West Is Losing the War on Terror*, Washington, D.C.: Brassey's, 2004.

Burgat, François, and John L. Esposito, *Modernizing Islam: Religion in the Public Sphere in the Middle East and Europe*, London: Hurst, 2003.

Burgat, François, and France Ministère de la Culture, *Face to Face with Political Islam*, London: I.B Tauris, 2003.

Buyumi, Dr. Zakariya Sulaiman, *Al-Ikhwan Al-Muslimin Wa-l-Jama'at Al-Islamiyya Fi al-Hiyat Al-Siyasiyya Al-Masriyya*, Cairo: Maktaba Wahba, 1979.

Cohen, Amnon, *Political Parties in the West Bank Under the Jordanian Regime 1949–1967*, London: Cornell University Press, 1982.

Copeland, Miles, *The Game Player: Confessions of the CIA's Original Political Operative*, London: Aurum, 1989.

Dann, Uriel, *King Hussein and the Challenge of Arab Radicalism: Jordan, 1955–1967*, Oxford: Oxford University Press/Moshe Dayan Center for Middle Eastern and African Studies, 1989.

Dawisha, A. I., *Arab Nationalism in the Twentieth Century: From Triumph to Despair*, Princeton: Princeton University Press, 2003.

Demant, Peter R., *Islam Vs. Islamism: The Dilemma of the Muslim World*, Westport: Praeger, 2006.

Devji, Faisal, *Landscapes of the Jihad: Militancy, Morality, Modernity* (Crises in World Politics), London: C. Hurst & Co., 2005.

Enayat, Hamid, *Modern Islamic Political Thought*, London: I.B.Tauris, 2005.

Esposito, John L., *The Islamic Threat: Myth or Reality*, Oxford: Oxford University Press, 1999.

———, *Unholy War*, Oxford: Oxford University Press, 2002.

Esposito, John L., and Dalia Mogahed, *Who Speaks for Islam? What a Billion Muslims Really Think: Based on Gallup's World Poll—The Largest Study of Its Kind*, New York: Gallup Press, 2007.

Euben, Roxanne Leslie, *Enemy in the Mirror: Islamic Fundamentalism and the Limits of Modern Rationalism—A Work of Comparative Political Theory*, Princeton: Princeton University Press, 1999.

Fandy, Mamoun, *Saudi Arabia and the Politics of Dissent*, New York: St. Martin's Press, 1999.

Faraj, Abdus-Salam, *Jihad: The Absent Obligation*, Birmingham: Maktabah Al Ansaar, 2000.

Feldman, Noah, *The Fall and Rise of the Islamic State*, Princeton: Princeton University Press, 2008.

Gerges, Fawaz A. *The Far Enemy: Why Jihad Went Global*. New York: Cambridge University Press, 2005.

Ghanim, Ibrahim al-Bayoumi. *Al-Fikr Al-Siyasi Li-L-Imam Hasan Al-Banna*. Cairo: Dar al-tawzee' wa-l-nashr al-Islamiyya, 1992.

Ghazali, Mohammad. *Min Huna Na'lam*. Cairo: Nadatu Masr, 2005.

Haikal, Mohammad Husain, *Muthakkirat Fi al-Siyassa Al-Misriya*, Cairo: Maktaba al-Nahda al-Masriyya, 1951.

Hall, Kenneth (ed.), *The Growth of Non-Western Cities: Primary and Secondary Urban Networking, C. 900–1900*, Lanham: Rowman & Littlefield, in press.

Halliday, Fred. *Islam and the Myth of Confrontation*. London: I.B.Tauris, 2003.

Hamed, Mustafa, *Saleeb Fi Sama'i Kandahar*, undated. (Accessed online June 2010, available at http://bit.ly/V8ymLz).

Harris, Christina Phelps, *Nationalism and Revolution in Egypt*, The Hague: Mouton & Co., 1964.

Heck, Gene W., *When Worlds Collide: Exploring the Ideological and Political Foundations of the Clash of Civilization*, Lanham: Rowman & Littlefield, 2007.

Hizb ut-Tahrir, *Mafahim Hizb Ut-Tahrir* 1953/a.

———, *Nitham Al-Islam* 1953/b.

———, *al-Takattul al-Hizbi* 1953/c.

———, *Nuqta Al-Intilaq Li Hizb Ut-Tahrir*, 1954.

———, *Al-Dawla Al-Islamiyya*, 1997.

———, *The Methodology of Hizb-Ut-Tahrir for Change*, London: Al-Khilafah Publications, 1999.

———, *Hatmiyya Sira' Al-Hadarat*, 2002.

———, *Ajhizatu Dawla al-Khilafah*, Beirut: Dar al-Umma, 2005.

———, *Muqadimma Al-Dustor Al-Qism Al-Awwal*. Beirut: Dar al-Umma, 2009.

Husaini, Ishaq Musa, *The Moslem Brethren: The Greatest of Modern Islamic Movements*, Beirut: Khayat's College Book Cooperative, 1956.

ibn Anas, Mālik, *Al-Muwatta*, Beirut: al-Maktaba al-'ilmiyya, undated.

Jabbar, Abul Hasan Abdul, *Al-Mugni Fi Abwab al-Tawheed Wa-l-'Adl*, Abdul-Halim Mahmud and Sulayman Dunya (eds.), Vol. 20, Cairo: Dar al-Masriyya li-l-Ta'lif wa-l-Nashr, 1965.

Karagiannis, Emmanuel, *Political Islam in Central Asia*, London: Routledge, 2009.

Karpat, Kemal H, *The Politicization of Islam: Reconstructing Identity, State, Faith, and Community in the Late Ottoman State*, Oxford: Oxford University Press, 2001.

Kedourie, Elie, *The Chatham House Version and Other Middle Eastern Studies*, London: University Press of New England, 1984.

Kepel, Giles, *The Roots of Radical Islam*, London: Saqi, 2005.

Kramer, Martin (ed.), *The Islamism Debate*, New York: Syracuse University Press, 1997.

Kramer, Martin S., and Merkaz Dayan, *Islam Assembled: The Advent of the Muslim Congresses*, New York: Columbia University Press, 1985.

Landau, Jacob M., *The Politics of Pan-Islam: Ideology and Organization*, Oxford: Clarendon, 1989.

Lawrence, Bruce B., *Shattering the Myth: Islam Beyond Violence* (Princeton Studies in Muslim Politics), Princeton: Princeton University Press, 1998.

Lia, Brynjar, *The Society of the Muslim Brothers in Egypt: The Rise of an Islamic Mass Movement, 1928–1942*, Reading: Ithaca Press, 2006.

Minault, Gail, *The Khilafat Movement: Religious Symbolism and Political Mobilization in India* (Studies in Oriental Culture—16), New York: Columbia University Press, 1981.

Mitchell, Richard Paul, *The Society of the Muslim Brothers* (Middle Eastern Monographs—9), Oxford: Oxford University Press, 1969.

Mohamedou, Mohammad-Mahmoud Ould, *Understanding Al Qaeda: The Transformation of War*, London: Pluto, 2006.

Mohammad bin Ahmed, ibn Rushd, *Bidayat al-Mujtahid wa Nihaya al-Muqtasid*, Cairo: al-Maktaba al-Tawfiqiyya, undated.

Moussalli, Ahmad S, *Moderate and Radical Islamic Fundamentalism: The Quest for Modernity, Legitimacy, and the Islamic State*, Gainesville: University Press of Florida, 1999.

Muhammad, Ali Juma, *Al-Hukm Al-Shar'i 'Ind Al-Usuliyin*, Cairo: dar al-Salam, 2002.

Muslim, Abul Husain 'Asakir-ud-Dīn, *Sahih Muslim*, Beirut: Dar al-fikr, 1998.

Mustapha, Kemal, *A Speech Delivered by Ghazi Mustapha Kemal, President of the Turkish Republic, October 1927*, Leipzig: K.F. Koehler, 1929.

Nasr, Seyyed Vali Reza, *The Vanguard of the Islamic Revolution: The Jama'at-I-Islami of Pakistan*, Los Angeles: University of California Press, 1994.

Nasser, Hoda Gamal Abdel, *Britain and the Egyptian Nationalist Movement 1936–1952*, Reading: Ithaca Press, 1994.

Nuhhas, ibn, *Mushari'a Al-Aswaq*, Beirut: dar al-basha'ir al-islamiyya, 2002.

Oliver-Dee, Sean, *The Caliphate Question: The British Government and Islamic Governance*, Lanham: Lexington Books, 2009.

Owen, Roger, *Power and Politics in the Making of the Modern Middle East*, London: Routledge, 2000.

Özcan, Azmi, *Pan-Islamism: Indian Muslims, the Ottomans and Britain, 1877–1924* (The Ottoman Empire and its Heritage—v.12), Leiden & New York: Brill, 1997.

Pappé, Ilan, *Britain and the Arab-Israeli Conflict 1948–51*, Basingstoke: Macmillan (in association with St Antony's College, Oxford), 1988.

Peters, Rudolph, *Islam and Colonialism: The Doctrine of Jihad in Modern History* (Religion and Society—20), The Hague: Mouton, 1979.

Qutb, Sayyid, *Fi Dhilal Al-Qur'an*, Cairo: Dar al-Shuruk, 2004.

———, *Ma'alam Fi-l-Tariq*. Kuwait: IIFSD (Undated)

———, *Milestones*, Birmingham: Maktabah Booksellers and Publishers, 2006.

Rida, Rashid, *Al-Khilafa 'Aw Al-Imama Al-'Uthma*, Cairo: *Al-zahara li-l-'ilam al-arab*, 1988.

Riedel, Bruce O., *The Search for Al Qaeda: Its Leadership, Ideology, and Future*, Washington, D.C.: Brookings Institution Press, 2008.

Rogan, Eugene L., and Avi Shlaim, *The War for Palestine: Rewriting the History of 1948* (Cambridge Middle East Studies—15), Cambridge: Cambridge University Press, 2001.

Roy, Olivier, *Globalised Islam: The Search for a New Umma*, London: C. Hurst & Co., 2002.

Salvatore, Armando, *Islam and the Political Discourse of Modernity* (International Politics of the Middle East), Reading: Ithaca Press, 1997.

Sayyid, Bobby S, *A Fundamental Fear: Eurocentrism and the Emergence of Islamism*, London & New York: Zed Books, 1997.

Scheuer, Michael, *Through Our Enemies' Eyes: Osama Bin Laden, Radical Islam, and the Future of America*, (Revised edition), Washington, D.C.: Potomac Books, 2006.

Shaybani, Mohammad, *Al-Sayar Al-Kabir*, Beirut: Dar Al-Kotob Al-ilmiyah, 1997.

Springer, Devin R., James L. Regens, and David N. Edger, *Islamic Radicalism and Global Jihad*, Washington, D.C.: Georgetown University Press, 2009.

Taji-Farouki, Suha, *A Fundamental Quest: Hizb Al-Tahrir and the Search for the Islamic Caliphate* London: Grey Seal, 1996.

Tully, James, Quentin Skinner et al., *Meaning and Context: Quentin Skinner and His Critics*, Princeton: Princeton University Press, 1988.

Vadillo, Umar Ibrahim, *The Esoteric Deviation in Islam*, Cape Town: Madinah Press, 2003.

van Bruinessen, Martin, *Mullas, Sufis and Heretics: The Role of Religion in Kurdish Society—Collected Articles*, Istanbul: The Isis Press, 2000.

Wright, Lawrence, *The Looming Tower: Al-Qaeda and the Road to 9/11*, New York: Knopf, 2006.

Yasin, al-Sayyed, *Al-Khilafa Wal-Mu'asira*, Cairo: Tobgy Press, 1999.

Yusuf, Al-Sayed, *Rashid Rida Wa-L-'Auda Illa Minhaj Al-Salaf*, Cairo: Miyriyt li-l-Nashr wa-l-Ma'lumat, 2000.

Zayyat, Muntasir, *The Road to Al-Qaeda: The Story of Bin Laden's Right-Hand Man* (Critical Studies on Islam), London: Pluto Press, 2004.

Journal Articles

Abu-Manneh, B., "Sultan Abdulhamid and Shaikh Abulhuda Al-Sayyadi," *Middle Eastern Studies in Intelligence*, 15 (2), 1979.

al-Bishry, Tarek, "Al-Malik Wa-L-Khilafa Al-Islamiyya," *Al-Katib*, 13 (142), 1973.

Afsaruddin, Asma, "The "Islamic State": Genealogy, Facts, and Myths," *Journal of Church and State*, 48 (1), 2006.

Azad, Abul Kalam, "Al-Khilafa Al-Islamiyya—1," *al-Manar*, 23 (1), 1922.

———, "Al-Khilafa Al-Islamiyya—3," *al-Manar*, 23 (3), 1922.

Bubandt, Nils, "Sacred Money and Islamic Freedom in a Global Sufi Order," *Social Analysis*, 53 (1), 2009.

Calhoun, Ricky-Dale, "The Musketeer's Cloak: Strategic Deception During the Suez Crisis of 1956," *Studies in Intelligence*, 51 (2), 2007.

Haddad, Mahmoud Osman, "Arab Religious Nationalism in the Colonial Era: Rereading Rashid Rida's Ideas on the Caliphate," *Journal of the American Oriental Society*, 117 (2), 1997.

Halliday, Fred, "The Politics of 'Islam': A Second Look," *British Journal of Political Science*, 25 (3), 1995.

Horton, John, "Hizb Ut-Tahrir: Nihilism or Realism," *Journal of Middle Eastern Geopolitics*, 2 (3), 2006.

Hurd, Elizabeth Shakman, "Political Islam and Foreign Policy in Europe and the United States," *Foreign Policy Analysis*, 3, 2007.

Karagiannis, Emmanuel, "Hizb Ut-Tahrir Al-Islami: Evaluating the Threat Posed by a Radical Islamic Group That Remains Nonviolent," *Terrorism and Political Violence*, 18 (2), 2006.

Khatab, Sayed, "Al-Hudaybi's Influence on the Development of Islamist Movements in Egypt," *The Muslim World*, 91, Fall 2001.

Lapidus, Ira M., "Islamic Revival and Modernity: The Contemporary Movements and the Historical Paradigms," *Journal of the Economic and Social History of the Orient*, 40 (4), 1997.

Mayer, Jean-Francois, "Hizb Ut-Tahrir: The Next Al-Qaida, Really?" *PSIO Occasional Paper*, 2004.

BIBLIOGRAPHY

Pankhurst, Reza, "Muslim Contestations Over Religion and the State in the Middle East," *Political Theology*, 11 (6), 2010.

Pillai, R. V., and Mahendra Kumar. "The Political and Legal Status of Kuwait." *International and Comparative Law Quarterly* 11 (1962): 108–30.

Piscatori, James P. "Imagining Pan-Islam: Religious Activism and Political Utopias." *Proceedings of the British Academy* 131 (2004): 421–42.

Rida, Rashid, "Al-Shura Fi Bilad Al-Shams," *al-Manar*, 9 (7), 1906/a.

———, "Khutba Ghazi Mustafa Kemal Basha," *al-Manar*, 23 (10), 1922/a.

———, "Zafar Al-Turk Bi-L-Yunan," *al-Manar*, 23 (9), 1922/b.

———, "Al-Ahkam Al-Shara'iyya Al-Muta'laqa Bi-L-Khilafa Al-Islamiyya—6," *al-Manar*, 24 (5), 1923/a.

———, "Al-Ahkam Al-Shara'iyya Al-Muta'laqa Bi Al-Khilafa Al-Islamiyya—5," *al-Manar*, 24 (4), 1923/b.

———, "Intiqad Al-Manar Li Kitab Khilafat Wa Hakimiyyat Milliyya," *al-Manar* 24 (7), 1923/c.

———, "Al-Khilafa Wa-L-Mu'tamar Al-Islami," *al-Manar*, 25 (5), 1924/a.

———, "Inqilab Al-Deen Al-Siyasi Fi-l-Jumhuriyya Al-Turkiyya," *al-Manar*, 25 (4), 1924/b.

———, "Al-Islam Wa Usul Al-Hukm," *al-Manar*, 26 (2), 1925.

Roy, Olivier, "Euroislam: The Jihad Within?" *National Interest* Spring, 2003.

Rutherford, Bruce K., "What Do Egypt's Islamists Want? Moderate Islam and the Rise of Islamic Constitutionalism," *Middle East Journal*, 60 (4), 2006.

Salla, Michael E., "Political Islam and the West: A New Cold War or Convergence?" *Third World Quarterly*, 18 (4), 1997.

Scheuer, Michael, "Al-Qaeda Doctrine for International Political Warfare," *Terrorism Focus*, 3 (32), 2006.

Tibi, Bassam, "The Fundamentalist Challenge to the Secular Order in the Middle East," *The Fletcher Forum of World Affairs*, 23 (1), 1999.

Tugal, Cihan, "Islamism in Turkey: Beyond Instrument and Meaning," *Economy and Society*, 31 (1), 2002.

van Bruinessen, Martin, "Muslims of the Dutch East Indies and the Caliphate Question," *Studia Islamika*, 2 (3), 1995.

White, Paul, "Ethnic Differentiation Among the Kurds: Kurmancî, Kizilbash and Zaza," *Journal of Arabic, Islamic and Middle Eastern Studies*, 2 (2), 1995.

Leaflets

Hizb ut-Tahrir, "Bayan Min Hizb Ut-Tahrir Al-Muqaddam Li-L-Hukuma Al-'Ordaniyya 1/6/1953," 1953.

———, "Bayan Fi Majlis Al-Nawwab," 1955.

———, "Bayan Min Hizb Ut-Tahrir," 1962.

———, "Hukm Al-Amal Ma'a Al-Hayia Al-Tahrir Al-Felistiniyya," 1964.

———, "Kitab Maftuh Min Hizb Ut-Tahrir Ila Ra'is Al-Wuzara' Sulaiman Demeeril," 1967/a.

———, "Bayan Suqut Al-Aqsa," 1967/b.

———, "Kitab Maftuh Min Hizb Ut-Tahrir Ila-L-Malik Hussein," 1969.

———, "Jawab Su'al 9–3–1970," 1970/a.

———, "Jawab Su'al 21–1–1970," 1970/b.

———, "Jawab Su'al 1970," 1970/c.

———, "Khitab Mawajah Min Hizb Ut-Tahrir 3–6–1971," 1971.

———, "Al-Siyasa Wal-Siyasa Al-Dowliyya," 1974.

———, "Ziyara Anwar Al-Sadat 13–5–1975," 1975.

———, "Muthakira Min Hizb Ut Tahrir Muqadamma Illa-L-Aqeed Al-Ghad-dafi," 1978/a.

———, "Kitab Maftuh Min Hizb Ut Tahrir 1978," 1978/b.

———, "Nas Naqd Al-Dustur Al-Mashro' Al-Irani," 1979.

———, "Bayan Min Hizb Ut-Tahrir," 1982.

———, "Afkar Siyasiyya," 1994.

———, "Al-Dawla Al-Islamiyya," 1995.

———, "A Message from the Amir of Hizb Ut-Tahrir," 2008.

Hizb ut-Tahrir Britain, "The Global Financial Crisis—The Self Destruction of Global Capitalism and an Introduction to the Alternative Islamic Economic Model," 2009.

Hizb ut-Tahrir Denmark, "The Environmental Problem—Its Causes and Islam's Solution," 2009.

Hizb ut-Tahrir Egypt, "Al-Khilafah Al-Islamiyya Hamiya Bilad Al-Muslimeen," 2000.

Hizb ut-Tahrir Indonesia, "Bi Iqamat Al-Khilafah Nunqith Anfusina Wa Nun-qith Al-'Alam," 2004.

Jama'ah-tul-Muslimeen, "Allah Did Not Give Us Permission to Be Leaderless and Divided at Any Time," undated.

———, "A Challenge to the Muslim Groups, Parties, Scholars and Students Concerning the Illegitimacy of the Division of the Muslim Ummah," undated.

———, "The Continuation of Imaarah in the Case of a Captive Imaam," undated.

———, "Does the Baya'ah of Obedience to the Imaam Change the Life of a Muslim?" undated.

———, "Not Understanding the Shari'h Method of Unity Is the Key to Failure and Misery," undated.

———, "Possessing Large Numbers, Agreement with the Majority and Consent of the Masses Is Not the Scale to Judge the Truth," undated.

Yousaf, Abu Abdullah ibn, "The World without the Shahada," undated.

Magazine and Newspaper Articles

al-Mustaqbal, "I'tiqal Al-Islami Al-Urdani "Abu Humam" Fi Britaniyya," February 16, 2006.

BIBLIOGRAPHY

Alderman, Geoffrey, "Can Israeli Actions in Gaza Be Justified on the Basis of Jewish Scripture?" *The Guardian*, January 12, 2009.

Anthony, Andrew, "Richard Dannatt: 'If the Tories Win, I Will Not Be a Defence Minister'," *The Guardian*, December 20, 2009.

Amara, Tarek, "Tunisia Islamist Causes Outcry with 'Caliphate' Talk," *Reuters*, November 15, 2011.

Atwan, Abdel Bari, "Interview with Bin Laden—Explosions in Riyadh," *Al-Quds Al-Arabi*, November 16, 1996.

Bakewell, Joan, "The Believers Who Despise Our Ways," *New Statesman*, May 29, 2000.

BBC Monitoring Service, "Text of Report by Iranian Students News Agency (Isna) Website," November 13, 2006.

Bin Laden, Osama, "New Powder Keg in the Middle East," *Nida ul Islam*, November 1996.

Brown, Nathan J., "The Irrelevance of the International Muslim Brotherhood," *Foreign Policy*, September 20, 2010.

Dodd, Vikram, "Anti-Terror Code 'Would Alienate Most Muslims'," *The Guardian*, February 17, 2009.

el-Errian, Essam, "What the Muslim Brotherhood Wants," *The New York Times*, February 9, 2011.

Fisk, Robert, "Anti-Soviet Warrior Puts His Army on the Road to Peace," *The Independent*, December 6, 1993.

———, "Why We Reject the West," *The Independent*, July 10, 1996.

Guardia, Anton La, "Fanatics Around the World Dream of the Caliph's Return," *Daily Telegraph*, August 8, 2005.

Henderson, Barney, "Radical Muslim Leader Has Past in Swinging London," *Daily Telegraph*, February 20, 2010.

Kaiser, Robert G., and David Ottoway, "Oil for Security Fueled Close Ties," *Washington Post*, February 11, 2002.

Miller, Lisa, and Matthew Phillips, "Caliwho?" *Newsweek*, October 12, 2006.

Staff Writer, "The Muslim Brothers; Appease or Oppose?" *The Economist*, October 8, 2009.

Staff Writer, "Israel to Come under Sharia Law, Says Israeli Arab Cleric," *Israel Today*, October 21, 2007.

Walsh, Declan, "Pakistan Army Officer Held over Suspected Hizb Ut-Tahrir Links," *The Guardian,* June 21, 2011.

World Islamic Front, "Text of the Announcement of the World Islamic Front," *Al-Quds Al-Arabi*, February 23, 1998.

Yusufzai, Rahimullah, "Conversation with Terror," *Time Magazine*, November 1, 1999.

BIBLIOGRAPHY

Reports

BBC *World Service*, "Wide Dissatisfaction with Capitalism—Twenty Years after Fall of Berlin Wall," PIPA, 2009.

FBIS, "Compilation of Usama Bin Ladin Statements 1994—January 2004," 2004.

International Crisis Group, "Radical Islam in Central Asia: Responding to Hizb Ut-Tahrir," in *Asia Report*, Brussels: International Crisis Group, 2003.

Mogahed, Dalia, "Special Report: Muslim World—Islam and Democracy," Washington D.C.: The Gallup Center for Muslim Studies, 2006.

Pew Forum on Religion and Public Life, "Tolerance and Tension: Islam and Christianity in Sub-Saharan Africa," Washington, 2010.

WorldPublicOpinion.org, "Muslim Public Opinion on Us Policy, Attacks on Civilians and Al-Qaeda," Maryland: The Center for International and Security Studies at Maryland, 2007.

———, "Defamation of Religion," Maryland: The Center for International and Security Studies at Maryland, 2009.

Research and Conference Papers

Theses

Ahmad, Shagufta, "Dr.Israr Ahmad's Political Thought and Activities," Masters, Mc Gill University, 1993.

Ali, Souad Tagelsir, "'Ali 'Abd Al-Raziq's 'Al-Islam Wa Usul Al-Hukm': A Modern, Liberal Development of Muslim Thought," PhD, The University of Utah, 2004.

Gazzini, Claudia Anna, "Jihad in Exile: Ahmad Al-Sharif Al-Sanusi 1918–1933," PhD, Princeton University, 2004.

Haddad, Mahmoud Osman, "Rashid Rida and the Theory of the Caliphate: Medieval Themes and Modern Concerns," PhD, Columbia University, 1989.

Hassan, Mona F., "Loss of caliphate: The Trauma and Aftermath of 1258 and 1924," PhD, Princeton University, 2009.

Wegner, Mark Jonathan, "Islamic Government: The Medieval Sunni Islamic Theory of the caliphate and the Debate over the Revival of the Caliphate in Egypt, 1924—1926," PhD, The University of Chicago, 2001.

Zollner, Barbara, "Hasan Isma'il Al-Hudaybi's Role in the Muslim Brotherhood: A Contextual Analysis of 'Preachers Not Judges'," PhD, University of London, 2004.

Web Pages and Resources

Ahmad, Israr, "Dr Israr's View on Hizb Ut Tahrir (an Effort to Unite Hizb Ut Tahrir and Tanzeem E Islami)." http://www.youtube.com/watch?v=OzTkX-Bjhbg&feature=player_embedded. (Accessed: March, 2011).

BIBLIOGRAPHY

al-Arabiyya, "Muslims Shun "Worthless" Paper Money." http://www.alarabiya. net/articles/2010/02/20/100913.html. (Accessed: March, 2011).

al-Nadwi, Abul Hasan, *Matha Khasara Al-'Alam Binhitat Al-Muslimin.* http:// www.saaid.net. (Accessed: March, 2011).

al-Zawahiri, Aymen, "Knights under the Prophets Banner." http://www.aaa3. net/vb/showthread.php?t=1191. (Accessed: May, 2007).

———, "Speech Marking 4 Year Anniversary of Iraq War 5/7/2007." http:// www.switch3.castup.net/cunet/gm.asp?chipmediaID=822400&ak=null. (Accessed: May, 2007).

Alouni, Tayseer, "Interview with Osama Bin Laden, October 2001." http:// archives.cnn.com/2002/WORLD/asiapcf/south/02/05/binladen.transcript. (Accessed: March, 2011).

al-Nabahani, Ibrahim, "Interview with Ibrahim al-Nabahani." khilafah.dk/ audiodate/20091124_ibrahim_sheikh_taqqiuddinnabahani.asx. (Accessed: March, 2011).

al-Sabaateen, Yusuf, "Muthakaraat Yusuf Al-Sabateen." http://www.alokab. com/forums/index.php?showtopic=23784&st=20. (Accessed: March, 2011).

as-Sufi, AbdalQadir, "Democracy: The Terrible Truth." http://www.shaykhab-dalqadir.com/content/articles/Art025_20112004.html. (Accessed: March, 2011).

———, "The Dumb and the Blind." http://www.shaykhabdalqadir.com/ content/articles/Art094_07062009.html. (Accessed: March, 2011).

———, "The Last Phase of Arab Shame." http://www.shaykhabdalqadir.com/ content/articles/Art087_01012009.html. (Accessed: March, 2011).

———, "Launch of the Islamic World Currency." http://www.shaykhabdalqa-dir.com/tv/NewWorldIslamicCurrency.html. (Accessed: March, 2011).

———, "The Political Class in Crisis." http://www.shaykhabdalqadir.com/ content/articles/Art110_31072010.html. (Accessed: March, 2011).

———, "The Role of the Muslims of Britain." http://www.shaykhabdalqadir. com/content/articles/Art056_20022006.html. (Accessed: March, 2011).

Azzam, Abdullah, "Defence of Muslim Lands." http://www.religioscope.com/ info/doc/jihad/azzam_defence_1_table.htm. (Accessed: March, 2011).

BBC, "Second Terror Suspect Wins Bail.". http://news.bbc.co.uk/1/hi/ uk/7392879.stm. (Accessed: March, 2011).

Bell, Duncan S.A., "The Cambridge School and World Politics." http://www. theglobalsite.ac.uk/press/103bell.htm. (Accessed: March, 2011).

Bewley, Abdalhaqq, "The Recovery of True Islamic Fiqh." http://web.archive. org/web/20080119022323/http://ourworld.compuserve.com/homepages/ ABewley/saq.html. (Accessed: March, 2011).

Bin Laden, Osama, "Address on 2/7/2006.". http://www.memri.org. (Accessed: March, 2011).

———, "Declaration of Jihad against the American Occupying the Land of the Two Holy Places." http://www.pbs.org/newshour/terrorism/internatio-nal/fatwa_1996.html. (Accessed: March, 2011).

———, "Fax 'to Our Brothers in Pakistan' 24/9/2001.". http://www.jihaduns-pun.com. (Accessed: March, 2011).

———, "Nucleus of the caliphate.". http://www.memri.org. (Accessed: March, 2011).

———, "Open Letter to King Fahd on the Occasion of the Recent Cabinet Reshuffle—July 1995" http://www.answers.com/topic/open-letter-to-king-fahd-from-bin-laden. (Accessed: March, 2011).

———, "Speech on the Festival of Sacrifice 4/2/2003—Document 476.". http://www.memri.org. (Accessed: March, 2011).

Bush, George, "Address to Joint Session of Congress—20/9/2001." http://www.whitehouse.gov/news/releases/2001/09/20010920–8.html. (Accessed June, 2007).

———, "Remembering 9/11–9/9/2006." http://www.whitehouse.gov/news/releases/2006/09/20060909.html (Accessed June, 2007).

Castineira, AbdalHasid, "Statement on the Shariah Currency and Legal Ten-der." http://www.muslimsofnorwich.org.uk/?p=901. (Accessed: March, 2011).

Cheney, Dick, "Interview with Tim Russert—10/9/2006." http://www.white-house.gov/news/releases/2006/09/20060910.html (Accessed June, 2007).

Clarke, Charles, "Lecture at the Heritage Foundation—Published October 21, 2005." http://www.heritage.org/Research/Lecture/Contesting-the-Threat-of-Terrorism. (Accessed: March, 2011).

Fedynsky, Peter, "Rumsfeld Says Military Effort Alone Will Not Bring Success in Iraq—11/12/2006," *Voice of America*. http://www.voanews.com. (Accessed: March, 2011).

Goodenough, Patrick, "OIC Fulfills Function of Caliphate, Embodies 'Islamic Solidarity,' Says OIC Chief Monday, May 10, 2010.". http://www.cnsnews.com/news/article/65537. (Accessed: March, 2011).

Haddad, Gibril F., "Have You Eyes, Murabitun Brethren?". http://www.livin-gislam.org/o/hyem_e.html. (Accessed: March, 2011).

Hammond, Andrew, "Islamic Caliphate a Dream, Not Reality—13/12/2006," *Reuters*. http://www.alertnet.org/thenews/newsdesk/L04275477.htm. (Acces-sed: March, 2011).

Hizb ut-Tahrir Pakistan, "Declaration to the People of Power.". http://www.hizb-pakistan.com/home/prs/press-note-american-agent-rulers-failed-to-stop-hizb-ut-tahrir. (Accessed: March, 2011).

Ismael, Jamal, "Interview with Bin Laden Aired on Al-Jazeera—10/6/1999," *al-Jazeera*. http://www.robertfisk.com/osama_interview_qatari_press_arabic.htm. (Accessed: March, 2011).

BIBLIOGRAPHY

Jamaat-ul-Muslimeen, "Baiyah of an Ameer without Any Government." http://www.aljamaat.org/books/jamaatpamphlets/english/baiyah%20of%20an%20Ameer%20without%20a%20Government/index.html. (Accessed: March, 2011).

———, "The Distinctive Features of Jamaat-Ul-Muslimeen.". http://www.aljamaat.org/jamaat-ul-muslimeen/features.htm. (Accessed: March, 2011).

———, "The Invitation to Haq.". http://www.aljamaat.org/jamaat-ul-muslimeen/invitationtohaq/index.html. (Accessed: March, 2011).

Luongo, Robert, "Radical Muslim Leader Has Bohemian Past." http://robertluongo.blogspot.com/2010/06/radical-muslim-leader-has-bohemian-past.html. (Accessed: March, 2011).

Millar, John, "Interview with Bin Laden May 1998," PBS. http://www.pbs.org/wgbh/pages/frontline/shows/binladen/who/interview.html. (Accessed: March, 2011).

Mustansir, Zayd, "The Only Legitimate Political System in Islam Is Shari'ah under One Leader." http://www.unifiedumma.com/sections/articles/data/TheOnlyLegitimatePoliticalSystem.html. (Accessed: March, 2011).

———, "Unveiling of the British Establishment's Hatred of Islam." http://www.unifiedumma.com/sections/articles/data/Unveiling.html. (Accessed: March, 2011).

Prusher, Ilene R., "Palestinian Group Sounds Like Al Qaeda but Forgoes Violence," The Christian Science Monitor. http://www.csmonitor.com/World/Middle-East/2008/0122/p01s03-wome.html. (Accessed: March, 2011).

Geoffrey Robertson, "Why It's Absurd to Claim That Justice Has Been Done." http://www.independent.co.uk/opinion/commentators/geoffrey-robertson-why-its-absurd-to-claim-that-justice-has-been-done-2278041.html. (Accessed: March, 2011).

Sr., George Bush, "Toward a New World Order—9/11/1990." http://www.sweetliberty.org/issues/war/bushsr.htm. (Accessed: March, 2011).

Tanzeem e Islami, "Tanzeem E Islami.". http://www.tanzeem.org. (Accessed: March, 2011).

The Murabit Blog, "Biography of the Shaykh." http://murabitblog.wordpress.com/2010/02/13/biography-of-the-shaykh/. (Accessed: March, 2011).

Unifiedumma.com, "About Us.". http://www.unifiedummaUmma.com/aboutus.htm. (Accessed: March, 2011).

———, "A Call to Unify the Muslims Upon the Islamic Method." http://www.unifiedumma.com/sections/articles/data/ACallToUnifyTheMuslimUmma.htm. (Accessed: March, 2011).

Williamson, Lucy, "Stadium Crowd Pushed for Islamist Dream," BBC News Website, August 12, 2007. http://news.bbc.co.uk/1/hi/world/south_asia/6943070.stm (Accessed: March, 2011).

INDEX